Dateline
Havana

Dateline Havana

The Real Story of U.S. Policy and the Future of Cuba

REESE ERLICH

To Rich,
For peace & justice.

Reese Erlich

Foreword by Stephen Kinzer

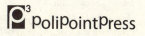
PoliPointPress

Dateline Havana: The Real Story of U.S. Policy and
the Future of Cuba

Copyright © 2009 by Reese Erlich

14 13 12 11 10 09   1 2 3 4 5

Portions of this book appeared in a different form in "Meanwhile
Back in Havana," *The East Bay Monthly* magazine, November 1999,
and in "Crack in Cuban Embargo Is Wide Enough for Pianos,"
Christian Science Monitor, January 9, 1996.

Production management: BookMatters
Book design: BookMatters
Cover design: Debra Naylor
Author photo on jacket flap © Janyce Erlich-Moss

LIBRARY OF CONGRESS CATALOGING-IN-PUBLICATION DATA

Erlich, Reese.
   Dateline Havana : the real story of U.S. policy and the future of
Cuba / Reese Erlich.
     p. cm.
   Includes bibliographical references.
   ISBN 978-0-9815769-7-8 (alk. paper)
   1. Cuba— History— 1990– 2. United States—Relations—
Cuba. 3. Cuba—Relations—United States.   I. Title.
F1788.E69 2009
972.91064--dc22   2008041312

Published by:
PoliPointPress, LLC
P.O. Box 3008
Sausalito, CA 94966-3008
(415) 339-4100
www.p3books.com
Distributed by Ingram Publisher Services
Printed in the United States of America

Contents

To all those Americans and Cubans
who would like to visit each others' countries someday.

Foreword

Stephen Kinzer

Set in an azure sea almost within sight of the United States, Cuba has always beckoned Americans. It is a tantalizing presence, mysterious and romantic but also a vivid symbol of history's tormented path. Tyranny, anticolonial rebellion, betrayal, gangster rule, debauchery of every sort, revolution, fiery anti-Americanism, and even a brief fling as a global strategic power—all of these have shaped Cuba's turbulent history.

Today Cuba is at a moment of historic transition. The long rule of Fidel Castro is over, and a new era is beginning. No one can be sure what it will bring. Every scenario from stable democracy to civil war is imaginable.

This uncertainty alone, in a country that has for generations fascinated the United States and the wider world, makes the story of today's Cuba important. It is also important for at least two other reasons. First, the course of events in Cuba, for better or worse, will inevitably have security implications for the United States, perhaps serious ones. Second, the success or failure of Cuba in the years to come will help shape the way future generations assess Fidel Castro's presidency. If Cuba makes a peaceful transition, many will argue that Castro's policies were successful. If political or even military upheaval leads Cuba toward the abyss of instability, Castro will be compared with Yugoslavia's Marshall Tito, his legacy stained by his failure to create a political system that could outlive him.

As this drama begins to unfold, outsiders who want to understand today's Cuba need a guide. *Dateline Havana* is an especially useful one. It is a portrait of Cuban society as it enters a period of great uncertainty. For those of us who can't visit Cuba personally, it is a chance to penetrate the curtain of demonization with which successive American presidents have sought to shroud Cuba. Because Cuba is such a vibrant place, overflowing with a vigor that expresses itself from the kitchen to the music hall to the baseball field, this is a wonderful trip.

American interest in Cuba is at least as old as the Republic. Presidents since Thomas Jefferson have dreamed of bringing Cuba under U.S. rule. They, like many ordinary Americans, considered it a natural part of the United States, and have assumed that the Stars and Stripes would one day fly over Morro Castle in Havana. Some nineteenth-century demagogues even came up with a geological rationale to support this cause; the island of Cuba, they said, must have been formed from sand and rock that had washed away from Florida, so it should logically belong to the United States.

Cubans, not surprisingly, saw their condition otherwise. In the late nineteenth century, they organized large-scale rebellions against Spanish rule that were directed in part from Florida and New York—another example of the close bond between the two countries. As Cuban rebels were approaching victory, the United States offered to send help. The rebels gratefully accepted, but only after the U.S. Congress passed a law—the Teller Amendment— pledging to make Cuba "free and independent" and disclaiming "any disposition or intention to exercise sovereignty, jurisdiction, or control over said island."

American and Cuban troops finished off the dying Spanish force in short order during the summer of 1898 in what the American statesman John Hay called "a splendid little war." That set the stage for one of the great diplomatic betrayals in Western Hemisphere history. With the Spanish defeated, Cuban patriots set off toward the independence the United States had pledged to accept. They were stunned when Congress and President William McKinley announced that they had decided not to observe the Teller Amendment. Instead of allowing Cuba to become independent, the United States turned it into a protectorate. Cuba became the first Caribbean victim of American— what shall we call it?—expansionism, imperialism, colonialism, or simply, as Senator Henry Cabot Lodge named it more than a century ago, "the large policy."

For more than half a century after the Spanish-American War, the United States remained the dominant power in Cuba. Americans ruled the island directly for a time, through military governors, and then through a series of pliant dictators. The economy was dominated by wealthy Americans and their Cuban partners, first in the sugar industry and then in tourism, gambling, and prostitution, often in cooperation with organized crime barons from *el norte*. The majority of Cubans lived in poverty.

The explosion came with Castro's revolutionary victory in 1959. In his first speech as victorious leader, he pledged that this time "it will not be like 1898, when the Americans came and made themselves masters of the country." It was a vivid example of how a nation's collective resentment of intervention, occupation, and exploitation can fester over decades and then explode in unexpected ways.

"Here is a country that you would believe, on the basis of our history, would be one of our real friends," a perplexed President Dwight Eisenhower mused after Castro's takeover. "I don't know what the problem is."

Washington and Havana soon became bitter enemies. The Central Intelligence Agency (CIA) sponsored various attempts to assassinate Castro or overthrow his regime, most memorably the failed Bay of Pigs invasion in 1961. Then, for the next half century, the United States enforced a trade embargo, making it illegal for Americans to do business with Cuba. This allowed Castro to claim quite plausibly that Washington was engaged in yet another round of its age-old imperial campaign against Cuba. That argument drew many patriotic Cubans to his side.

Washington's policy of isolation and economic embargo not only made the United States the only country in the world where Cuban cigars may not legally be sold but the only one where Cuban musicians and artists may not travel freely. It also strengthened the government it was intended to undermine. Even a Cuban dissident quoted in this book admits that in a free election, the ruling Communists would win.

The long hostility between Washington and Havana, however, has done remarkably little to weaken the ties that bind Americans to Cubans. Proximity, a long period of close relations before 1959, the presence of a large Cuban community in the United States, and the fascination the two peoples have for each others' cultures combine to create a unique and multifaceted relationship. Americans and Cubans have come to rely on each other. At times their governments have been friends. At other times they have served each other's purposes by playing the role of dangerous enemy. As the post-Castro era dawns, their relationship is poised to enter a new stage. *Dateline Havana* is a timely, insightful guide to a nation and a people that Americans are about to rediscover.

STEPHEN KINZER is a former *New York Times* correspondent in Latin America and coauthor of *Bitter Fruit: The Story of the American Coup in Guatemala.*

1

A Very Personal Journey

WE ZOOMED DOWN THE STREET IN HAVANA AS WAVES crashed against the famous Malecón seawall, inundating the four-lane road. I quickly rolled up the taxi's windows, but it was too late, and we took a short bath from the sea water. It was March 2008. "A cold front has hit Havana," explained the taxi driver, making a shivering motion with his shoulders for extra emphasis. The waves were high, the sky was filled with dark clouds, and rain threatened. People on the streets wore jackets. The temperature had dropped to the low 70s. Welcome to Havana's version of a frigid winter.

I'd traveled this road for many years. As we approached the turnoff for Old Havana, the same grand houses stood along the Malecón, with their cracked marble facades, crumbling cement pillars, and peeling paint. During my first trip to Cuba in 1968, I marveled at how those old buildings had survived the waves and salt air. Forty years later, some looked like they hadn't been repaired since my first journey. I then remembered seeing a photo of these same houses in the 1920s. Even back then they looked weathered and in need of a coat of paint.

But in 2008 some of the houses along the Malecón were being remodeled and repainted. Foreign-owned businesses were setting up shop on the ground floors of some buildings; residents were repairing others. I saw similar activity all over Havana, a sign of the relative economic improvements since my last trip five years earlier.

The wet drive down the Malecón showed that appearances could be deceiving. American journalists come to Cuba for a short trip. They see the crumbling infrastructure and report about Cuba's massive economic problems and lack of democracy. If they did more research or stayed longer, they might learn that most Cubans, particularly those in rural areas, live better today than they did in 1959.[1] Leftist supporters of the Revolution, on the other hand, visit the island for a short time and praise the country's free hospitals and schools. They learn about the bad conditions before 1959 but often don't acknowledge the country's very real problems today. Young Cubans in particular complain angrily about the lack of food, consumer goods, and affordable access to the Internet.

Cuba has become an icon for both sides in a bitter battle. For 50 years the U.S. government has called Cuba a strategic threat. For conservative Cubans in Miami, the island is a totalitarian dictatorship denying the most basic human rights to its people. For supporters of the Cuban Revolution, the government has resisted U.S. domination and built a shining, socialist society. In reality, Cuba is neither the totalitarian hell depicted in the United States nor the socialist paradise claimed by some admirers.[2]

I began freelance reporting from Cuba in 1968 and have been back a total of 11 times, covering developments for National Public Radio, the *San Francisco Chronicle*, and the *Christian Science Monitor*, among others. I also reported from hotspots around the world where the United States accused Cuba of aggression: Grenada right after the 1983 U.S. invasion, El Salvador, Nicaragua under the Sandinistas, and Angola.

I visited Washington DC to understand why the United States had established normal diplomatic and trade relations with China and Vietnam, but not with Cuba. In Miami I met with conservative and ultraconservative Cubans, some of whom had funded terrorist attacks against civilians on the island. They spoke openly about their views and the power of the Cuba Lobby, even though they denied any ties to terrorism.

One sector of Miami Cubans, Republican leaders, and major Democratic politicians in Washington support the U.S. embargo against Cuba, a policy backed by no other country in the world. The embargo has proved so ineffective that even some of the Miami stalwarts admit its flaws. Joe García, a former leader of the Cuban American National Foundation (CANF) and 2008 candidate for Congress from Miami, compared the embargo to belief in Christianity. "There is an ideology and credo. We all recite it. There is a history of miracles but we've never seen them. It's been in existence for 50 years, but we don't see results. But we are strongly committed to the credo. As a guy who still works that church, you don't argue with the saints." Understanding those saints—along with the money and power of the rightists in Florida—is key to understanding the future of U.S.-Cuban relations.

In 2008 I reencountered people I had interviewed years earlier. Their lives reflect the rapid changes in Cuba today. Most of the people had stayed on the island and continued to support the Revolution. Two had immigrated to New York (I later flew up to Buffalo to find out why). I talked with Cubans about controversial issues such as racism, homophobia, economic reforms, the Internet, and democratic political control. Everyone on and off the island spoke openly and intelligently. Only a few people asked that their names be withheld.

Many books have been written about Cuba. *Dateline Havana* seeks to combine analysis with firsthand reporting. Cuba has undergone major changes over the past 40 years, and so have I.

≡

In 1968 I traveled to Cuba for the first time as a staff reporter for *Ramparts* magazine.[3] I also went as part of a group of 40 members of

Students for a Democratic Society (SDS), the largest radical student group in the country.[4] Neither I nor my editors saw any contradiction in the fact that I was both a member of SDS and reporting on the trip. In fact, it gave me more access and insight. I was writing in the spirit of gonzo journalists like Hunter S. Thompson—but possessing less talent and fewer hallucinogenic substances. However, I did develop a lifelong admiration for a well-made *mojito*.[5]

By the time of that trip I had accumulated a bit of a resume. I had helped organize Stop the Draft Week in October 1967, when 10,000 people blocked the streets of downtown Oakland to protest the Vietnam War and the draft. The University of California, Berkeley, kicked me out of school because we used the campus as a launching pad for the protest. Then, Alameda County indicted several of the leaders on conspiracy charges, and we became known as the Oakland 7. I had gotten a job at *Ramparts* despite having no journalism experience, but sympathetic editors trained me on the job. And just a month before my Cuba trip, I turned 21.

Not surprisingly, I opposed U.S. policy on Cuba. The Kennedy and Johnson administrations had sponsored terrorist attacks on Cuba by Miami exiles.[6] They prohibited Cuban trade with the United States, and did everything possible to stop Cuban economic activity with Latin America and Europe. Many of Cuba's problems in those years flowed directly from the U.S. embargo.[7]

I was enthusiastic about the Cuban Revolution. Bearded, long-haired revolutionaries overthrew a hated dictatorship and were thumbing their noses at U.S. presidents. The romanticism of the Revolution appealed to me as well. Ernesto "Che" Guevara emphasized the need for moral incentives, not just higher wages, to increase production. Cuba was going to harvest a record 10 million tons of sugar cane by mobilizing volunteer labor. The Isle of Pines, renamed the Isle of Youth, would become the world's first communist island, where everyone worked according to their ability and took according to their need (see chapter 7).

There was only one problem. Those policies didn't succeed. Che's moral incentives didn't put food on the table and, in fact, the work ethic declined after the early enthusiasm of the 1960s. People on the Isle of Youth faced extreme food shortages, and the notion of building communism on one island was abandoned. Che Guevara was murdered in Bolivia in 1967 by the CIA. His guerrilla "foco" theory had failed to attract support among Bolivians.[8]

Some years later, I figured out that Cuban leaders had put their own revolutionary enthusiasm ahead of reality. And I was doing the same thing as a student radical. I wanted revolution; everyone I knew in SDS wanted revolution; therefore, it was only a matter of time before the working class joined us. When American student radicals acted on these ideas, nobody came out to our demonstrations. When Cuban leaders did it, the consequences affected the lives of millions.

This is not one of those "I was a socialist before 30, but now I've come to my senses" stories. The ideals that we fought for in SDS in the 1960s are still valid: opposition to interventionist wars; political empowerment for people of color; and support for gay, women's, and workers' rights. The ideals of the Cuban Revolution remain valid: land reform, ending racism, ending U.S. domination, economic equality, and self-sufficiency, among others.

But the Cuban Revolution has made serious mistakes and hasn't progressed nearly far enough. To understand why, we'll have to go back to that first trip in 1968. And, as with any voyage of discovery, getting there was half the fun.

≡

I found my old diary from the 1968 trip and was immediately struck by one thing: I had incredibly neat penmanship. I've been able to reconstruct the trip from those original notes and interviews with some of my former trip mates.

President Kennedy imposed the embargo against Cuba in 1962, which severely restricted travel to the island. SDS recruited people nationwide to take trips starting in 1967. Our trip lasted part of August and September 1968. We represented a range of political views from the bubbling cauldron of America's New Left. The trip members included Ted Gold, who died several years later in a New York townhouse where Weathermen were making bombs.[9]

It wasn't easy getting to Cuba. You had to fly from Mexico or take a freighter from Montreal. Just weeks before our departure, Mexican authorities detained and deported a group from the National Lawyers Guild and another from the Black Panther Party. Acting at the behest of U.S. officials, Mexican police threw them in jail and, in the case of the Panthers, stole their money and luggage. So, those of us on the SDS trip were worried.

We converged in Dallas from all over the country and stayed at the house of the *Dallas Notes*, the local underground newspaper. Conditions weren't great. There were no showers, not enough toilets, and we mostly slept on the floor. Three of us flew ahead to Mexico City because we had official State Department clearance to visit Cuba as journalists. Those were perilous times in Mexico. Students were preparing for massive demonstrations at the Olympics in October. A few months after our visit, Mexican police murdered hundreds of students at the Plaza Tlatelolco.[10]

As soon as we arrived at the Mexico City airport, we rushed to the taxi stand and jumped into the second cab in line. We had seen enough James Bond movies to know that the first cab is always driven by the American spy. Unfortunately, none of us spoke Spanish. In my best Marlon Brando-cum-Emiliano Zapata accent, I mumbled, "Embajada de Cuba (Cuban Embassy), muy rápido." Unfortunately, the cab driver had absolutely no idea where the Cuban Embassy was. We got out of the cab. I spent 15 minutes checking the phone book. We found another cab. When we finally did arrive at the embassy, our contact person wasn't there.

We carefully planned how to avoid being kidnapped by the Mexican police. The other 37 passengers would arrive from Dallas and never leave the airport. We were prepared to offer nonviolent resistance by sitting down in the airport and refusing to drink anything but Corona beer. That never became necessary. We flew to Havana without incident and were welcomed at the airport with frozen daiquiris.

As veterans of battles against the Vietnam War and university administrations, we were full of self-importance. But we also had serious questions about Cuban society. We wanted to find out about democracy. Was there still sexism and racism in Cuba, and if so, what was the government doing to combat it? For the next three weeks, we were feted like visiting dignitaries. We stayed in the finest hotels and ate elaborate meals washed down with rum and beer. We lived better in Cuba than we did at home. And, of course, we lived far better than the average Cuban. We resented it. One SDS member told me, "They're treating us more like a delegation from the American Hotel Manager's Association than a group of radicals."

As we explored on our own and met ordinary Cubans, however, we began to understand more about the society. The most interesting adventures involved going off the beaten path, literally. One day, we were hiking in the Sierra Maestra foothills east of Santiago. Most of the residents still lived in *bohios*, the traditional thatched-roof houses. Some of us developed stomach problems. In the small town of Chivirico, seemingly in the middle of nowhere, we found a modern medical clinic. We met a young doctor who had studied in Havana. He told us the clinic provided free medical care, including dentistry and ophthalmology. The doctor explained that such medical care was rare before 1959 in rural areas.[11]

The government provided top-notch medical education for free; in return, doctors agreed to serve in poor urban or remote rural areas for two years. The young doctor was full of revolutionary enthusiasm, but he clearly missed urban life. He invited us to stay for lunch and much-needed conversation, but we had to get back to the group.

Back in Havana, I met with lots of enthusiastic communist leaders eager to win us over ideologically. Julio Palamino, first secretary of the Young Communist League at the University of Havana, argued that Cuba was different from the USSR. He admitted that the Soviet Union had developed a "technical elite," which had lost touch with the masses. Cuba's leadership was responsive to the people, he assured me. Yet he defended the Soviet invasion of Czechoslovakia as a blow against the restoration of capitalism.[12]

Orlando Aloma, managing editor of the *Casa de las Américas* magazine, offered a different viewpoint. Casa de las Américas was a government cultural organization known for promoting nonconformist views. Aloma told me most intellectuals had opposed the Soviet invasion and were disappointed when Fidel Castro supported it in a famous speech.[13] Aloma was upset by one particular line in the speech, almost to the point of tears. "Fidel said our Revolution is not idealistic and romantic," said Aloma. "Those used to be the epithets that foreign communist parties hurled at us. Now, Fidel uses them."[14]

Within a few years, Aloma had left Cuba to live in the United States.

I wandered into grocery stores where the shelves were mostly empty. In March 1968, the government had closed small restaurants, groceries, bars, and other privately owned businesses. As a result, there were long lines in front of state-owned restaurants.

Raúl Roa Kouri, son of Cuba's foreign minister, and himself then an official with the Food Ministry (Ministerio de Alimentación), admitted that Cuba was going through a major food crisis.[15] In a conversation that lasted long into the night, he blamed the crisis on the U.S. trade embargo. The embargo clearly hurt, but the Cuban government was making mistakes as well. Closing all the small businesses in order to concentrate production in large state enterprises actually reduced food production. Those policies were eventually reversed in the early 1990s.

Cubans received subsidized food through government stores, where they presented a *libreta* (ration book). According to my 1968 notes, here was the food available for each individual: ¾ lb. meat/person/week; 1 quart milk/day for children under seven; four eggs/week; 3 lbs. rice/month. The *libreta* system still exists today, and Cubans receive about the same quantity of food. Cubans have more access to food these days, however, because of the large number of farmers' markets and urban gardens. But it's still disappointing to me that 50 years after the Revolution, Cubans must still get their basic food through the rationing system.

Despite those very real problems, there was something different about the Cuban Revolution. Fidel Castro enjoyed genuine popularity, and people remained enthusiastic. One night Palamino invited me to the university. He wouldn't tell me what we would be doing except to say that now "you'll see why the Cuban government could never deteriorate" as happened in Czechoslovakia.

We went to a local sports stadium to watch basketball. The two competing teams were second rate, so I certainly didn't learn any political lessons from them. Then two other teams came out. *Los Caneros* (the cane cutters) consisted of members of the Cuban Communist Party Central Committee, led by captain Fidel Castro. I couldn't imagine a team made up of President Johnson, Dean Rusk, and Robert McNamara playing any sport, let alone in front of an audience. Yet, here was Fidel in front of 10,000 people, all cheering every time he went in for a lay-up.

Fidel had been a first-string basketball player in his University of Havana days. At age 42, however, he had slowed down. He specialized in bulling his way past defenders and charging in for a jump shot close to the basket. He committed more than one foul and got into arguments with the referee. At one point, the two men were shouting at each other at the top of their voices. Finally the ref took a step backward, pointed a finger, and yelled authoritatively, "One more word out of you, Fidel, and you're out of the game." Fidel Castro shut up.[16]

I left Cuba near the end of September. Although I had official State Department permission to travel, the Mexican authorities refused to give me a reentry visa, which was required of Cuba travelers in those days. I later found out that others returning from Cuba were similarly harassed, part of a U.S.-inspired effort to discourage travel to Cuba. So I ended up flying from Havana to Madrid to New York to San Francisco.

It cost me $107.50 in air fares to get to Cuba and three times that to get home. On the other hand, I stayed in Madrid for three nights for less than $15.

In 1968, I really learned how to be a journalist. Looking back at my old diaries and notes, I see a knack for a good description and the ability to recognize a punchy quote. But I didn't know how to write a coherent article. The editors at *Ramparts* trained me the old-fashioned way: by yelling, screaming, and then rewriting my convoluted prose. I went out with experienced reporters such as Gene Marine, watched how he conducted interviews, and then collaborated on the writing.

By early 1969, I emerged with solid journalistic skills that I put to use in some nontraditional ways. In the spring of 1969, the Oakland 7 went on trial for over three months. We had been charged with conspiracy to commit three misdemeanors, which is a felony. For some reason, disturbing the peace is a misdemeanor, but when antiwar activists got together to plan the disruption, it was a felony. We held lots of demonstrations and press conferences at the courthouse. Public opinion was shifting against the Vietnam War, and a jury of ordinary citizens was very receptive to our arguments against the war and the draft. The jury acquitted us on all counts.

So what is a newly freed radical journalist to do with his life? I returned to UC Berkeley and enrolled in my last quarter, needing only one unit to graduate. Then President Nixon and Henry Kissinger widened the Vietnam War by invading Cambodia, setting off protests around the United States and the world. I helped organize a campus-wide student and worker strike at UC, and was kicked out of school yet again. Faced with a lawsuit, however, the university gave me my degree that summer.

I had constructed an individual major called "Political and Social Change," but I always referred to my major as "Revolution." So I graduated from Berkeley with a degree in Revolution and a diploma signed by Governor Ronald Reagan.

Of all the 1970 graduates, I was one of the few to get a job in my major. I went to work in East Bay factories to organize. I later became a Maoist and a leader of the League of Revolutionary Struggle, a Marxist-Leninist organization when it began in 1978, which evolved into a social democratic group by the time of its demise in 1990. I edited the LRS newspaper *Unity* for a time and always kept up my freelancing.

I became more and more critical of Cuba from a Maoist perspective, which in retrospect was clearly wrong. The USSR, Cuba, and China all had serious problems. The Chinese Communist Party in the 1970s was ultraleft with its Cultural Revolution and rigid controls on society. China was certainly wrong for invading Vietnam in 1979.[17] And the Soviet Union was wrong to invade Czechoslovakia and Afghanistan. Cuba was wrong to support those Soviet occupations. Over the years, I've come to believe that unilaterally sending troops into other countries is wrong, period—whether in the name of American democracy or revolutionary socialism.

But the world had changed by the early '90s, when I resumed my reporting trips to Cuba. The Soviet Union had collapsed, Cuba was reevaluating its policies in the midst a horrific economic crisis, and I no longer had a Maoist ax to grind. But I did have many of the same questions as during my 1968 trip. How can Cuba feed itself? How can ordinary people affect decisions at the top? How can people committed to the Revolution raise objections without losing their jobs or facing ostracism?

I tracked down old friends and people I had interviewed in the past to find some answers.

≡

I can't use his real name for reasons that will become apparent in a moment. Let's just call him Rudolfo. He is a mid-level government official and a former diplomat whom I met in the early '90s. A few years later, I went to his house for a visit and found a shattered man.

He had been fired from his government job for reasons he wouldn't explain. He had been unemployed for over a year. Finally, he got a job working construction but had lost over 60 pounds, he said, due to the stress and lack of food. He sat at home most days reading a Spanish language edition of *The Hobbit*. I got really depressed after meeting with Rudolfo, a man I knew to be a supporter of the Revolution. If a man like this could lose a responsible job, what lay ahead for ordinary Cubans?

In 2008, I went back to find Rudolfo. Frankly, I wasn't sure if he would still be in the country or even alive. The good news about Cuba, however, is that once you get someone's home phone and address, you can almost certainly contact people years later. There's an extreme housing shortage, and even in the unlikely event that they have moved, the neighbors will probably know where they've gone. I phoned Rudolfo, and he answered the phone. We arranged to meet right away.

The taxi took me to a somewhat seedy section of Havana. Rudolfo greeted me with the big hug of long-lost friends. He was 63, retired, and looking fit and trim. His weight loss had been due to an ulcer and esophagus problem. Once diagnosed and treated, his weight stabilized. He continued to smoke copiously, however, and the low gravelly tone in his voice didn't bode well for the future.

We took off to a local café and ordered many small cups of strong Cuban coffee known as *cafecitos*. We talked for a long time. Rudolfo speaks with a clipped, very rapid Cuban accent. His form of discourse is also very Cuban. He takes wild excursions away from the topic to ruminate on other issues. I had to bring him back to my original question many times. His story eventually emerged.

Rudolfo grew up quickly during the tumultuous years before the Revolution. His father was a businessman with ties to gangster Meyer Lansky. Rudolfo would visit Lansky with his father and swim in the gangster's pool. A captain in dictator Fulgencio Batista's police force was threatening Rudolfo's father, asking for bigger bribes. One day Rudolfo, then age 14, went to Lansky and said he needed a favor. He needed a pistol to kill a cop. "It's purely personal, not business," he assured Lansky.

It sounded like a scene out of *The Godfather*, and I wondered how much Rudolfo had enhanced the story over the years. At this point I asked Rudolfo if Lanksy spoke Spanish. "Sure," he said, "not like a member of the Spanish Council on Art and Literature, but you could understand." Lansky gave Rudolfo a pistol, which he used to kill the police captain. Rudolfo spread some phony revolutionary leaflets around the crime scene so the police would suspect the July 26 Movement led by Fidel Castro. He never got caught. Within a few years Rudolfo became a member of the Communist Party's youth section and, while still a teenager, he was an aide to top army officers in the revolutionary army.

I was fascinated by my old friend's history. But what I really wanted to know was why he, a lifelong revolutionary, had been fired from his job. He finally got around to telling me. On July 13, 1994, some Cubans hijacked a 1902 tugboat with the intention of taking it to Florida. A fireboat collided with the hijacked tug, killing 32 people, according to official accounts.[18] The Cuban government initially said the ramming was accidental. Very early on Rudolfo had information that angry port workers used a water cannon to attack the hijackers and intentionally rammed the tug. The Cuban Coast Guard intervened, made the fireboat back off and rescued the remaining people.[19] The port workers, he emphasized, were violating Cuban regulations on how to handle such incidents.

The deaths made headlines around the world and became a cause célèbre in Miami. Rudolfo had gone to a high authority with information about what really happened but incurred the wrath of at least one important leader. That leader was demoted, and the details eventually came out. But when he came back to power some time later, he went looking for the guy who had spilled the beans. That's when Rudolfo was forced to resign.

His life had been tough in the mid-'90s, as it was for most Cubans. He worked construction with a friend. But things eventually improved. By 2008, he was collecting a government pension of over 800 pesos ($33), quite generous by Cuban standards, and shared the house with his mother and other relatives. With their combined incomes, they lived well. Cubans pay no rent and have no medical costs. Water, natural gas, and phone services are very cheap.

I asked why the system doesn't provide institutional help for those who are willing to speak truth to power. He paused for a long moment and said, "That's a very perceptive question." He told me that the cover-up scandal would have gone much higher if he had fought his dismissal. He decided to fall on his own sword rather than endanger the credibility of the Communist Party. He considered himself a true revolutionary.

Was it the right decision? Only Rudolfo knows for sure.

Most Cubans aren't willing to fall on their swords, however. I talked to some former supporters of the Revolution in a most unlikely spot: Buffalo, New York.

≡

I first met Urbano Canizares in 1992 in Old Havana. He taught English to students at Havana's only dental college. Once I spoke to his class and saw that he clearly had the respect of his students. He and his wife, Gilda Zerquera, always described themselves as supporters of the Revolution. They wanted to see reforms, such as more farmers' markets, but they supported socialism. One of Urbano's brothers was a Communist Party militant who had run for the local legislature. He and I spent a lot of time walking the serpentine streets of Old Havana to interview ordinary Cubans throughout the '90s.

When I telephoned them in 2003, their line wasn't working. I finally took a taxi to their house only to find out they were gone. Neighbors told me they had moved to Buffalo, New York. In 2008, I tracked them down and visited them in Buffalo. Here's their story.

Zerquera had received one of the approximately 20,000 visas issued by the United States each year. When they formally notified the Cuban government of their intention to emigrate, Canizares lost his job at the university. The Cuban government reasons that people emigrating to the United States who have benefited from free education and other services should no longer be employed by the state. Because most Cubans are employed by the state, the policy seeks to discourage others from emigrating.

"We had a lot of problems," Canizares told me. "I didn't have an income. I had to teach privately, trying to eke out a living. I got a little money from my brother here in the United States. That's how we managed to survive."[20] I asked what had turned him from a supporter of the Revolution into someone who emigrated. Certainly, the harsh economic conditions were a major factor. Even though the economy had improved since its low point in 1993, getting enough food and basic consumer goods remained a daily struggle. But they had also become disillusioned politically. "At first we were believers in the system. Then we realized that the socialist ideal was not what they told us it would be. We lost hope. There were many people like me."

I asked what surprised him the most about the United States. They arrived in Buffalo during the dead of winter. "It was quite a change coming from a tropical country to an arctic region," he told me, and "the opulence, so much food, the creature comforts. A lot of stuff is not even necessary, like having so many televisions and the latest gadgets."

Like all Cuban immigrants, they received subsidies from the U.S. government. Starting in 2001, each month they received about $400 in cash, $400 in food stamps, and some other low-income assistance. Unlike any other immigrant group, Cubans also immediately get work permits and become permanent residents within one year.

Canizares worked hard. Although he had an advanced education and years of teaching at the university, initially he could only find work cleaning restaurants after hours. He worked for a time teaching Spanish at a private school. Later he got a blue-collar factory job. He continued to work there even after he landed a part-time job teaching English as a Second Language to adults. The two of them couldn't afford to buy a car, and they lived frugally in a one-bedroom wood-frame apartment in the Latino barrio of Buffalo.

The Canizares family really worried about the cost of medical and dental care. His teaching job provided minimum coverage. "We're saving some money so that when we have to use the medical services, we can pay. If there is a serious accident, we would have to go into debt." Canizares said, somewhat wistfully. "In Cuba you don't have to worry about that. You go to the doctor and get your medicines. There might not be enough medicine, but you know what you have. Here you're on your own."

On balance, Canizares and Zerquera prefer life in the United States. He had become a U.S. citizen, and she was about to complete the process as well. They hoped to visit family and friends in Cuba some day. And they'd take care of one other matter while there. "We will get some dental work done and even see a doctor," Zerquera told me.

Many Cubans, both on and off the island, share similar misgivings. Life in Cuba is hard, but the United States doesn't offer much of an alternative model. To better understand that complicated reality, we must look at some history.

2

A Short History
of U.S.-Cuban Relations

AMERICANS AND CUBANS STUDY RADICALLY DIFFERENT
versions of history. Americans learn that we liberated Cuba from
Spanish colonialism in 1898. Cubans learn that one form of domination replaced another. According to the American version, the United
States defeated Spain and helped establish democracy in Cuba. It then
occupied Cuba for only four years, during which time it helped write
a democratic constitution and fought disease. The United States gave
full independence to the island, had none of the colonial aspirations of
Europe, and wanted to establish relations of equality.

That myth began back in the 1890s as the United States prepared to
invade Cuba, promising to liberate it from Spain but not meddle in its
affairs. At that point, the U.S. Senate passed the Teller Amendment,
which prohibited the occupation of Cuba and mandated that U.S.
troops remain only long enough to pacify the country, then "leave the
government control of the island to its people."[1] The United States had
convinced Máximo Gómez, one of Cuba's top independence leaders,
that it would conduct a humanitarian intervention. Gómez wrote,
"Spain has done badly here, and the United States is carrying out for
Cuba a duty of humanity and civilization."[2] But Gómez and other
Cubans soon learned not to take U.S. leaders at their word.

During three years of war, from 1895 to 1898, Cuban independence fighters had battled Spanish colonialism to a standstill. That's when the United States declared war on Spain. After fighting for only three months, the United States defeated the weakened Spanish forces. After the war, however, the United States ignored the guerrillas and the local independence leaders. A U.S. military governor became dictator of the island until 1902. The United States carried out similar actions after it conquered Puerto Rico, Guam, and the Philippines, as part of the same Spanish-American War. The U.S. war to subdue Filipino resistance formally ended in 1902, but fighting continued until 1913.

U.S. actions were controversial at the time. The 1898 Treaty of Paris between the United States and Spain excluded the participation of the local peoples. Mark Twain wrote, "I have read carefully the Treaty of Paris, and I have seen that we do not intend to free, but to subjugate the people of the Philippines. We have gone there to conquer, not to redeem."[3] He was not alone. President Grover Cleveland (1884–88, 1892–96) and William Jennings Bryan, the unsuccessful Democratic Party candidate for president in 1896, spoke out against the Spanish-American War.

But other powerful interests supported it. Theodore Roosevelt, Henry Cabot Lodge, President William McKinley, and William Randolph Hearst favored unvarnished imperialism. The United States had already expanded from coast to coast, killing or subduing the Native American population. By the 1890s, key U.S. business and political leaders sought to expand the United States beyond its continental borders. They saw Cuba and the other Spanish colonies as the first steps toward greater economic and military power.

U.S. troops stayed in Cuba from 1898 to 1902, during which time the United States laid plans to maintain long-term control of the island, despite promises to the contrary. It didn't want Cuba to establish its own army; instead, it created an armed Rural Guard and immediately introduced racial segregation. Officers were white Cubans, whereas most enlisted men were black.

The United States gave ministerial-level jobs to trusted Cuban exiles, hoping to maintain power by working through those trusted exiles, landlords, and businessmen. But when local elections were finally held in 1900, pro-independence parties won a surprise victory.

That's when the United States changed tactics. Sen. Orville Platt introduced his infamous amendment to the U.S. Senate in the spring of 1901. It guaranteed U.S. control of Cuba's public finances; gave the United States the right to establish permanent military bases; and, most importantly, allowed unilateral U.S. military intervention. The Platt Amendment, which became the basis for taking control of the Guantánamo Naval Base, was presented to the Cuban Constituent Assembly—in the process of writing the country's constitution—in June 1901. If the Cuban leaders didn't accept it, they faced continued U.S. occupation. Even so, the onerous amendment passed by a slim 16–11 vote.

Even though most Americans know little or nothing about the Platt Amendment, it has remained a potent symbol for Cubans. After the formal granting of independence, the United States actually invaded Cuba three more times: 1906–09, 1912, and 1917–23. The Guantánamo Naval Base treaty allows the United States to keep armed forces at the base "in perpetuity." And although the Platt Amendment was formally revoked in 1934, for many Cubans, U.S. policy never really changed.

Many Miami Cubans and dissidents in Havana with whom I spoke refer to the years 1902–58 as a period of Cuban "democracy." [4] Cuba held periodic elections, and the governments usually maintained close relations with the United States, which seems to be the working definition of democracy these days. In reality, Cuba had a series of elections, coups, and uprisings, always with the United States as the dominant economic and political power.

The career of Fulgencio Batista reflects the real history of those years. In what became known as the Sergeant's Coup, Batista seized power in 1933. After Batista met with U.S. Ambassador Sumner Wells, who took a liking to the new military dictator, the United States threw its support behind him. Batista later gave up formal power but ruled from behind the scenes during the 1930s.

In 1940 Batista was elected president, then lost the 1948 election and planned to run again in 1952. With opinion polls showing him dead last, however, he engineered a second coup just months before the election. The United States quickly recognized the new military government.

Batista had long cultivated ties with U.S. gangsters. After his 1952 coup, he offered subsidies to Meyer Lansky and other mob leaders to build hotels and casinos. In turn, he regularly accepted bribes from the gangsters. Havana became a major port for the illegal heroin trade. The film *Godfather Part II* has a great scene in which the Corleone family and a character similar to Meyer Lansky meet with other U.S. businessmen to pledge their support for Batista just prior to the 1959 Revolution. The scene accurately reflects the influence of the mob in Cuba, which Batista and his U.S. allies viewed as just another financial interest group.

Meanwhile, the Cuban people were getting increasingly angry with U.S.-style "democracy" in Cuba. The July 26 Movement guerrillas, led by Fidel Castro, were gaining support in the mountains. Union and student groups were organizing in the cities. Initially, U.S. authorities didn't know what to make of the July 26 Movement. Castro was not a member of the pro-Moscow Communist Party.

While Cubans were celebrating New Year's Eve 1959, Batista fled the country, taking suitcases stuffed with tens of millions of dollars in ill-gotten gains. The July 26 Movement had already seized control of several major cities in eastern Cuba, and within days the guerrillas marched into Havana. January 1 became the anniversary of the Revolution.

Since then, a common story line has emerged in U.S. political discourse: Castro lied to the Cuban and American people about his plans for the Revolution. He had always planned to impose a communist dictatorship on the island and had used deceptive rhetoric to fool people in the early years. A closer look at Castro's ideological development shows that there was nothing inevitable about how events unfolded. He was an independent Marxist, opposed to U.S. imperialism and favoring socialism for Cuba. But he had strong differences with the pro-Moscow Cuban Communist Party.[5]

The United States could have coexisted with an independent, socialist Cuba that had relations with the USSR. Through geographic proximity and historic ties, the U.S. government could have remained a significant influence on Cuba. But the United States never even considered such an option. It had already overthrown neutralist and moderate leftist leaders such as Jacobo Árbenz in Guatemala and Mohammad Mossadegh in Iran.[6] U.S. authorities were certainly not prepared to tolerate a socialist Cuba.[7]

Within two months of the January 1, 1959, revolution, President Eisenhower's National Security Council was discussing ways to "bring another government to power in Cuba.[8] The first major U.S.-Cuban schism came not over socialism or ties with the USSR but over land reform. On May 17, 1959, the revolutionary government implemented the Agrarian Reform Law, distributing large, mostly foreign-owned estates to farmer co-ops. The law authorized compensation to foreign corporations, which had owned 75 percent of Cuba's arable land. The compensation was based on the assessed tax value, which infuriated U.S. companies because they had massively underpaid their taxes.

The Eisenhower administration strongly objected to the land reform and threatened to stop buying Cuban sugar. It was seeking to protect U.S. corporate profits and maintain the traditional U.S. domination of the island. Anticommunism was the excuse, not the cause, of U.S. antagonism. And that antagonism quickly turned violent.

═══

Both the Eisenhower and Kennedy administrations hatched plots to assassinate Castro and restore pro-U.S. leaders to power. According to the 1975 report prepared by a U.S. Senate committee headed by

Senator Frank Church, from 1960 to 1963 the CIA engaged in at least eight plans to assault or murder Fidel Castro.[9] Castro said that's only a partial count. He claimed there had been more than 600 assassination attempts from 1960 to 2005.[10]

Some of the plots detailed in the Church Report seem ludicrous. Several were aimed at publicly embarrassing the leader. Prior to a radio appearance, the CIA planned to spray the studio with an LSD-like substance that would cause Castro to become incoherent. Another plot involved poisoned cigars that, if smoked, would disorient him before an important public speech.

My personal favorite was the CIA plot to put a depilatory powder in Castro's shoes to cause his beard to fall out. The beardless leader would thus, presumably, be discredited in the eyes of the world. People on the CIA payroll would administer the powder when Castro left his shoes to be shined outside his hotel room during a foreign trip. He never made the trip.

The CIA also engaged in very serious murder attempts. In 1960, the CIA asked former FBI agent Robert Maheu to contact Las Vegas mobster John Rosselli. By using Maheu, the CIA could deny any role in the murder—a practice U.S. intelligence agencies use to this day. The CIA, taking advantage of capitalist solidarity, knew that the mob had lost vast holdings in Cuba and wanted revenge. According to the Church Report, the CIA agreed that "Maheu would approach Rosselli as the representative of businessmen with interests in Cuba who saw the elimination of Castro as the first essential step to the recovery of their investments."[11]

That fiction didn't last long, and Rosselli quickly figured out he was working for the CIA. To execute the plan, he hired Momo Salvatore (Sam) Giancana, an infamous Chicago gangster, and Santos Trafficante, formerly a top mafia leader in Tampa and Havana. The gangsters tried twice to have accomplices poison Castro by dropping capsules of botulism into his drinks.

Castro admitted that one plot came very close to success. The CIA asset was supposed to drop an ampoule of botulism into his milkshake at the Havana Libre hotel coffee shop. The plot failed when the ampoule got stuck in the restaurant freezer where it had been stored.[12] On another occasion in 1961, a U.S. diplomat presented Castro with a wetsuit dosed with deadly botulism. Castro said he suspected that the diplomat didn't know he was part of the assassination attempt.[13]

The plots continued, sometimes directly instigated by the U.S. government, others freelanced by Cuban American terrorists with tacit U.S. support. By the mid-1970s Cuban Americans trained by the United States had started working for governments such as the Pinochet dictatorship in Chile. They helped carry out the assassination of former Chilean Defense Minister Orlando Letelier and his colleague Ronni Moffitt in Washington DC in 1976.[14]

But probably the most significant assassination attempt—and one that could have changed history—was planned to coincide with the Bay of Pigs invasion.

≡

Before the Vietnam War, and long before the disasters in Afghanistan and Iraq, there was the Bay of Pigs. Starting in late 1960, the Eisenhower administration drew up plans for what today would be called "regime change" in Cuba. The CIA based its plan on the successful U.S.-backed military coup against the democratically elected Guatemalan government of Jacobo Árbenz in 1954.[15]

Here was the plan: A U.S. economic embargo would weaken the Castro regime. The CIA would train several thousand armed Cuban exiles and provide them with airplanes and ships. Mafia hit men would assassinate Castro on the eve of the invasion, leaving the government leaderless. The United States would deliver the exile invasion force onto Cuban soil. This "provisional government" would ask for U.S. assistance, and the people of Cuba would rise up to overthrow Castro's regime. The United States would recognize the exiles as a legitimate government and fly in handpicked leaders from Miami.

The plan went wrong almost from the start. On April 15, 1961, CIA-trained pilots flew eight sorties from Nicaragua over Cuba but failed to destroy the small Cuban Air Force. Two days later, at the beginning of the ground invasion, a pilot flew from Nicaragua to Miami, claiming to be a defector from the Cuban Air Force. That same day 1,400 Cuban exiles landed at Playa Girón, located in the Bay of Pigs, in eastern Cuba. The Mafia murder plot failed, and Castro and other revolutionary leaders immediately swung into action. Castro personally commanded a tank battalion against the invaders. Cuba's small air force successfully attacked the CIA-trained force and sank two ships. The revolutionary government rounded up 35,000 Havana residents suspected of collaboration with the United States. There was no popular uprising. In fact, the country united against the foreign invader.

The CIA ordered U.S. pilots in three planes to bomb Cuba with napalm and high explosives. Four of the six pilots were shot down and killed. As the failure of the operation became obvious on the morning of April 17, Kennedy refused to order a second U.S. air strike. Within three days, the battle was over. The United States suffered a humiliating defeat: 114 dead exiles and the remaining men captured.

As part of its propaganda campaign, the United States claimed that it wanted to preserve the positive developments of the Revolution and only remove the dictatorial Castro from power. But it clearly sought to restore the former elite. Castro's forces interviewed each of the prisoners and determined that the invasion force included significant numbers of former landowners and factory owners or their sons; 194 were former Batista militia and police.[16]

In 1961, U.S. leaders weren't used to losing wars or even battles. Failures like the Bay of Pigs weren't supposed to happen, particularly in the Western Hemisphere. So the losers created myths to explain the failure. Liberals of that era claimed that President John Kennedy only reluctantly implemented plans already made by President Eisenhower. Left to his own devices, these historical revisionists argued, he wouldn't have carried out the invasion.

Kennedy adviser and renowned liberal Arthur Schlesinger, in his book *A Thousand Days: John F. Kennedy in the White House*, maintained that Kennedy had opposed the invasion from the beginning. He wrote that Kennedy had no choice but to carry out the plan inherited from Eisenhower just 77 days before. Just days before the invasion, Schlesinger gave an interview to French journalist K. S. Carol in which he took a militant stand against Cuba's revolutionaries and claimed that 90 percent of Cubans opposed Castro. Schlesinger himself had authored a State Department white paper justifying U.S. action against Cuba.[17]

In reality, Kennedy knew about the assassination plots against Castro even during the 1960 presidential campaign. And when one anti-Castro Cuban exile warned his administration about the inevitable failure of the invasion, he was threatened with possible deportation.[18]

Kennedy may indeed have had tactical doubts about the invasion, but they weren't strong enough to cancel it. His subsequent actions showed he supported the strategy of overthrowing Castro. Five days after the failed invasion, Kennedy issued a stern warning of possible future interventions, using the excuse of fighting communism and the Soviet threat. "We shall not allow men whose hands are covered with blood from the streets of Budapest to teach us a lesson in noninterference. Communism in this hemisphere is not negotiable."[19]

Kennedy also took hits from the right wing. Cuban exiles were furious that he had called off the second U.S. air strike. To this day, some Miami hard-liners blame Kennedy for the fact that they are not back in power. In reality, air strikes would have caused casualties but could not have swung popular opinion toward the invasion force. Both Miami conservatives and Kennedy liberals had badly misjudged Castro's popularity.

After the Bay of Pigs invasion, the United States pursued a policy of covert military attacks combined with stepped-up economic pressure. In February 1962, President Kennedy declared a U.S. economic embargo banning virtually all Cuban exports and imports, but not before he had press secretary Pierre Salinger buy 1,200 Petite Hupmann Cuban cigars for Kennedy's private humidor.[20] The following year, Kennedy imposed the travel ban and prohibited Americans from spending money in Cuba. Officially, the United States favored only peaceful means to pressure Cuba. In reality, U.S. leaders also used violent, terrorist tactics. And heading up that effort in the early years was none other than Bobby Kennedy.

Operation Mongoose began in November 1961 with Attorney General Robert Kennedy at the helm. It included a variety of economic, propaganda, and sabotage activities aimed at Castro. U.S. operatives attacked civilian targets, including sugar refineries, saw mills, and molasses storage tanks. Some 400 CIA officers worked on the project in Washington and Miami.

A declassified CIA document noted that Robert Kennedy began a meeting of CIA and military leaders with a complaint. He said, "More priority should be given to sabotage operations," as long as the "massive activity would appear to have come from within" Cuba. The meeting's minutes include discussion of recent incidents in which U.S. divers had been caught landing in Cuba and the bad publicity resulting from Cuban exiles shooting up a civilian apartment complex on the island. Kennedy, CIA Director John McCone, and others discussed the possibility of mining Cuban waters, under the condition that the action couldn't be traced back to the United States.[21]

According to another declassified CIA document, Robert Kennedy thought the United States hadn't done enough to encourage Cuban exiles to attack Cuba. It should "release the frustrated energy of these refugees in freeing their homeland and creating a favorable political climate in Latin America for the liberation of Cuba."[22] It also sponsored what it hoped would be an armed uprising in the Escambray Mountains of eastern Cuba but found little popular support. I interviewed Eloy Gutiérrez Menoyo, a founder of Alpha 66, one of the terrorist groups that operated in the Escambray. In 1964, he came ashore in Cuba with other Alpha 66 members. "I landed in Cuba with arms, with a uniform, and went to the Escambray. We were taken prisoner. We were only there a little over a month."[23]

Operation Mongoose and various other terrorist operations caused property damage and injured and killed Cubans. But they failed to achieve their goal of regime change.

Considering the stated goals of Operation Mongoose, Cuban leaders had good reason to fear another U.S. invasion. In 1962, the Soviet Union asked Cuba to allow medium-range Soviet missiles to be installed on the island. The United States had set up nuclear missiles in Italy and Turkey, and under international law the Soviet Union had the right to place similar missiles in Cuba. Soviet Premier Nikita Khrushchev described the missiles as defensive: the Soviet Union didn't intend to launch an offensive attack on the United States.

But that was a very dangerous assumption. U.S. leaders looked at the placement of medium-range missiles capable of hitting Washington as an offensive act. At least 134 nuclear warheads had been shipped to Cuba, although U.S. officials didn't know this at the time.[24] Khrushchev assured Castro that the presence of the missiles would be kept secret, yet he refused to allow the Cubans to shoot down U.S. spy planes flying over Cuban territory, fearing a wider confrontation. When the United States soon discovered the missile launching sites, the CIA and the Pentagon wanted to bomb them and invade Cuba, finishing off what they had begun with the Bay of Pigs. But the Kennedys were wary.

On October 22, 1962, Kennedy announced a naval blockade of Cuba and insisted on inspecting Soviet ships headed for the island. Kennedy had cleverly set some traps for Soviet diplomats, who didn't know the United States had photographic proof of the missile sites. In a famous United Nations confrontation on October 25, UN Ambassador Adlai Stevenson accused the USSR of installing the missiles while a sputtering Soviet Ambassador Valerian Zorin flatly denied it.

The United States went to its highest military alert, preparing for all-out nuclear war should there be a confrontation at sea. Interestingly enough, the Soviet Union did not follow suit and readied none of its forces for possible nuclear war. But Kennedy officials withheld that information from the public.[25] Ultimately, the Soviet ships turned around without trying to reach Cuba. The United States and the Soviet Union held secret negotiations without consulting the Cuban government. In public, Kennedy said the Soviets had agreed to remove the missiles, and the United States had made no concessions. Thus Kennedy had redeemed U.S. honor lost at the Bay of Pigs, and Khrushchev was humbled before the world.

In secret, however, Kennedy had promised not to invade Cuba and to withdraw U.S. Jupiter missiles from Turkey, which was done in April 1963. Nevertheless, Castro's sense of revolutionary justice and national pride was damaged. Castro thought his ally was defending the island from attack. But big power politics trumped any concern for Cuba. Castro later said Cuba would have agreed to withdraw the missiles but wanted the United States to stop its sabotage campaign, end the economic embargo, and exit from the Guantánamo Bay Naval Base.[26]

Throughout the Cold War, the United States argued than an aggressive Soviet Union wanted to militarily attack and even invade the United States. In reality, the USSR wasn't planning an offensive military strike or a war it would have lost. The USSR certainly competed economically with the United States, and it sought political and military influence around the world. But such activities wouldn't get the American public angry enough to fight the reds and justify huge military expenditures. So the U.S. intentionally exaggerated the Soviet military threat. For example, Khrushchev's famous phrase "we will bury you," was intentionally distorted. He had meant that the USSR would bury the U.S. economically."[27]

Wayne Smith, former head of the U.S. Interests Section in Havana, said Khrushchev seriously misjudged the situation leading up to the Cuban Missile Crisis. Khrushchev wanted to increase Soviet international leverage but didn't realize the risk. "The basic Soviet objective was a greater balance with the United States. That's not necessarily aggressive or offensive in nature."[28]

From Khrushchev's perspective, the missiles would be a relatively cheap way to check U.S. power. "Khrushchev was trying to keep costs down," said Smith. "It wasn't really aggressive. But we did perceive it as aggression and as a threat to us." Khrushchev gambled and lost, and he didn't even bother consulting the other player whose chips he was betting.

Even though the United States kept its promise not to invade Cuba, it tried a variety of other means to effect regime change in Cuba. In 1971, during the Nixon administration, U.S. agents introduced swine fever virus into Cuba. Cuba had to slaughter over 500,000 infected hogs. The virus originated in Africa and had been unknown in Cuba before the outbreak. *Newsday* revealed that a CIA-trained Cuban exile had been given the swine virus at Ft. Gulick in the U.S.-controlled Panama Canal Zone. U.S. operatives gave him instructions to deliver the virus to Cuba. Even though the CIA denied involvement, the article showed a clear link to U.S. clandestine efforts.[29] In 1977, the *Washington Post* confirmed, "The CIA had a program aimed at Cuban agriculture, and since 1962 Pentagon specialists had been manufacturing biological agents to be used for this purpose."[30]

In 1981, during the Reagan administration, some 350,000 Cubans were infected with type II dengue virus, which produces potentially deadly fevers. According to Cuban sources, 158 people died, 101 of whom were children. The virus had not been known anywhere in the world and had been created in a laboratory.[31] In 1984, a leader of Omega 7, a terrorist exile group based in Miami, admitted in court to spreading the dengue virus.[32]

In 1996, during the Clinton administration, a U.S. plane sprayed a substance over Matanzas Province. It contained an Asian insect, previously unknown in Cuba, which destroyed crops and was nearly impossible to kill with pesticides. U.S. officials denied involvement.[33] The United States carried out such covert activities with the justification that Cuba constituted a strategic threat. But is that really true?

3

Is Cuba a Strategic Threat?

EVERY U.S. ADMINISTRATION SINCE THE CUBAN MISSILE crisis has argued that Cuba was a strategic threat. It's true that the USSR continued to maintain troops on the island and had set up a sophisticated base to monitor U.S. communications. It's also true that Cuba had chosen to operate outside the U.S. orbit and developed a very close alliance with the USSR. But none of this meant that either country planned to launch a military attack or invasion of the United States.

Col. Lawrence Wilkerson was the top aide to Colin Powell, both when he was chairman of the Joint Chiefs of Staff and later as secretary of state under George Bush, Jr. He frequently met with officers in charge of military planning for Cuba. In a rather revealing interview, he told me that after "October 1962, southern commanders—that is, those people who had Cuba in their responsibility in the military— didn't think Cuba was a threat."[1]

Wilkerson participated in war games designed to plan the United States response to various Cuban crises. The military's nightmare scenario consisted of political instability in Cuba leading to a large-scale assault by Cuban Americans on the island. Wilkerson said, "What really struck me about the Cuban contingencies when we exercised and gamed was that it didn't turn into any kind of U.S. force presence in Cuba. It turned into a cordoning off of Florida to keep Cuban Americans with various small arms . . . from invading Cuba."

Whereas Democratic and Republican administrations continually declared that Cuba remained a "strategic threat," the U.S. military saw the strategic threat coming from the CIA-trained paramilitaries. During the past 50 years, exactly one U.S. president acknowledged that Cuba wasn't a major threat and made serious efforts to normalize relations. That was President Jimmy Carter, and the effort didn't last long.

Fed up with the Vietnam War and Watergate scandals, Americans hoped for a new start in foreign policy. And at least for the first two years of his administration, Carter delivered some significant changes regarding Cuba. He lifted the Trading with the Enemy Act currency controls in 1977. He upgraded diplomatic relations and allowed Americans to freely travel there for the first time since 1962. Many thousands of Americans, including business executives and entertainers, visited Cuba. Cuban musicians and artists were allowed to perform in the United States.

The Cuban American ultraright was furious and carried out a series of terrorist attacks aimed at disrupting relations. In 1978, paramilitaries bombed the New York Cuban Mission to the UN twice and the Soviet Mission once. U.S. authorities made no arrests. Omega 7 bombed the Cuban consulate in Montreal.

The United States government faced some serious setbacks during the later part of Carter's administration. In 1979, leftist revolutionaries took power in Nicaragua and on the Caribbean island of Grenada. Then in December 1979, the USSR invaded and occupied Afghanistan. In response, the Carter administration reversed course and launched a renewed effort to win the Cold War. It began backtracking on Cuba as well.[2] That became clear during the infamous Mariel boatlift.

On April 1, 1980, 12 Cubans drove a van through the gates of the Peruvian Embassy in Havana and demanded asylum. Despite the fact that one Cuban guard was killed, Peruvian diplomats granted the Cubans asylum. In an escalating crisis, Peru invited any Cuban seeking asylum to come to the embassy. Within a matter of days, thousands had crowded in. On April 19, Fidel Castro led a march of over one million Cubans past the Peruvian Embassy, protesting U.S. and Peruvian policies and showing support for his government.

In response to the Peruvian Embassy crisis, President Carter said in a speech, "We'll continue to offer an open heart and open arms to refugees seeking freedom from Communist domination and from economic deprivation, brought about primarily by Fidel Castro and his government."[3]

Castro proved to be far more adept at managing international crises than Carter. Castro took Carter up on his offer and invited any Cuban who wished to emigrate to assemble at the small port of Mariel. Hundreds of boats left Florida for Mariel, picked up the Cubans, and returned to the United States in defiance of Carter's policies. Carter had attempted to prohibit the Miami Cubans from taking their boats to Cuba, but failed. The Cuban government put prison inmates and mental patients onto the boats as well. Eventually, 125,000 people left Cuba. Chaos ensued in Florida and nearby states that were forced to care for the immigrants.

Cubans would have immigrated to any country, mainly because of difficult economic conditions on the island. By opening the spigot only to the United States, Castro cleverly made Yankee imperialism the enemy once again. The Mariel crisis returned U.S.-Cuban relations to the pre-détente stage. The Carter administration demanded that Cuban troops leave Africa before full diplomatic relations could be established. Cuba refused.

President Ronald Reagan continued the hard-line policy toward Cuba and reimposed the currency controls in 1982. Opponents of the embargo took a case to federal court. In 1984, the Supreme Court upheld the currency controls by a 5–4 vote, ruling that presidential foreign policy concerns outweighed individual citizens' rights.

The court decision stated that the embargo was legal under the 1917 Trading with the Enemy Act, which allowed currency restrictions during time of war or national emergency. And although in the 1980s the United States was neither at war nor in a national emergency, the Reagan administration argued that the declaration of emergency that began the Korean War in 1950 was still in effect.[4]

In 1984, the Reagan administration added Cuba to the State Department's list of terrorist states, those the United States considers to be major sponsors of terrorism around the world. For years, the United States argued that Cuba gave sanctuary to American radicals wanted for violent crimes. Eldridge Cleaver and Huey Newton took refuge there in the 1970s. A number of other black radicals formerly associated with the Black Panther Party live in Cuba today. Cuba also shelters members of the Spanish-based ETA (Basque Homeland and Freedom) and FARC (Revolutionary Armed Forces of Colombia).

Wayne Smith called charges that Cuba supports terrorism "utterly absurd." He told me that some of the Latin American revolutionaries now living in Cuba arrived there as part of political deals arranged by their home governments. Most of the U.S. fugitives were black power advocates who sought asylum in Cuba in the 1970s. "There is no evidence that any of those people living in Cuba are engaged in terrorist acts," Smith said.[5]

More recently, the United States has claimed that Cuba isn't doing enough to combat fundamentalist terrorist groups such as Al Qaeda. In the 2007 *Country Reports on Terrorism*, the State Department wrote, "The Government of Cuba remained opposed to U.S. counterterrorism policy, and actively and publicly condemned many associated

U.S. policies and actions. To U.S. knowledge, the Cuban government did not attempt to track, block, or seize terrorist assets . . ."[6]

In fact, Cuba has roundly condemned terrorism such as the 9/11 Al Qaeda attacks.[7] Cuba's leadership stands ideologically and politically opposed to fundamentalist Muslim groups, whose first priority, after all, is to kill communists. Yes, Cuba criticized U.S. torture of accused terrorists and the U.S. invasions of Iraq and Afghanistan. But that hardly makes them supporters of terrorism.

Fidel Castro and other Cuban leaders have always opposed terrorist tactics. "No war is ever won through terrorism," said Castro. "It's that simple. Because [if you employ terrorism], you earn the opposition, hatred and rejection of those whom you need in order to win the war."[8]

The United States clearly uses the State Department terrorism list for political purposes. All the countries on the list are considered hostile to the United States, whether or not they actually support terrorism: Syria, Iran, Libya, Sudan, North Korea, and Cuba. Some countries whose rulers do sponsor terrorist groups have never been listed: Saudi Arabia and Pakistan, among others.[9]

In the spring of 2008, President Bush scheduled the removal of North Korea from the terrorism list as part of a negotiated agreement regarding that country's nuclear program. North Korea had made no changes whatsoever in its policies toward terrorism. By the fall, the administration was backtracking on the agreement due to disagreements on nuclear policy, not terrorism.

≡

The United States accused Cuba of sponsoring terrorism and spying inside the United States in a case that became known as the Cuban Five. In September 1998, Miami residents woke up to headlines that a nefarious group of Cuban spies, nicknamed "The Wasp Network," had been arrested in the United States. The U.S. attorney ultimately charged five individuals, René González and four others, of being unregistered agents of a foreign power. Ramón Labañino, Fernando González, and Antonio Guerrero were accused of conspiracy to commit espionage for spying on a U.S. naval air station. Gerardo Hernández was charged with the most serious crime: conspiracy to commit murder in conjunction with the Cuban Air Force downing of two planes piloted by the Miami-based group Brothers to the Rescue in 1996.

U.S. attorneys admitted that the Cuban Five, known as *Los Cinco* in Cuba, had not engaged in espionage and that the government had found no classified documents or similar incriminating evidence. A news account in the *Miami Herald* noted, "None of the agents is charged with espionage because prosecutors agree they never obtained any U.S. secrets. To win conviction on espionage conspiracy charges, prosecutors must prove only that the defendants agreed to break the law, not that they succeeded."[10]

All five defendants admitted they worked for the Cuban government but said they had infiltrated ultraright-wing groups in Miami with the intention of combating terrorism. They argued that the U.S. government had refused to stop numerous terrorist attacks by Miami exile groups, such as the 1997 bombings of Havana hotels, even after the Cuban government had given U.S. diplomats and FBI agents evidence about these terrorist activities (see chapter 4 for more details).[11]

Attorneys for the Cuban Five asked for a change of venue to avoid the rightist atmosphere prevailing in Miami, but the request was denied. In 2001, the Five went on trial in Miami. On June 9, they were convicted and received heavy sentences. Guerrero, F. González, and Hernández received life. Labañino got 19 years and González, 15 years.

In 2005, a three-judge panel in the Federal Court of Appeals threw out the verdicts on the grounds that they should have received a change of venue. But the full appeals court overturned that decision in 2006. In June 2008, a New Orleans appeals court let the verdict stand but criticized the harshness of the sentences against three of the five, then sent those cases back to the trial court for resentencing. The court upheld Hernández's life sentence.

The government never provided a direct link between Hernández and the decision to shoot down the two Brothers to the Rescue airplanes. Many times in the early 1990s, right-wingers had flown small planes from Miami to Havana to drop leaflets. They broke international law and U.S. law by filing false flight plans. None had ever been arrested. In 1996, the Cuban government warned the FAA several times to stop the illegal flights.

"The Cubans have been very patient in trying to get U.S. authorities to do something about these flights, which violated their airspace," said Colonel Wilkerson. "The Cubans were left with the alternatives of allowing this to continue or taking some action that would be draconian in protection of their national interests."

I asked what the United States would have done if Cuban pilots had dropped leaflets over Miami? If they refused to turn around, Colonel Wilkerson said, we would "fire a missile across their nose. Then if they didn't turn around, shoot them down."

The Cuban Five is clearly no ordinary criminal case. The Justice Department went to extraordinary lengths to ensure a conviction by keeping the trial in Miami and relying on conspiracy counts rather than proving the underlying crime. The evidence was flimsy at best. As Colonel Wilkerson told me, they "were doing no more . . . than trying to keep that group of Floridians . . . from invading their country. They weren't terrorists. They weren't spies. And we've got them in jail."[12]

If the United States finally gets around to normalizing relations with Cuba, the release of the Cuban Five will certainly be part of the negotiations. In the meantime, the Cuban Five conviction reflects the continuing power of what some call the "Miami Mafia," others call the "Miami Freedom Fighters," but we'll just call the "Cuba Lobby."

4

The Origins of
the Cuba Lobby

MIAMI IS A VAST SUBURB WITH NO HEART. THERE ARE historic sections of the city, but it seems like all the working people live in nondescript tract homes that stretch on for miles. The rich live in seaside mansions with huge yachts and water taxis.

Calle Ocho, the famous heart of Little Havana, falls in the middle of that spectrum. It looks nothing like Cuba. It could be suburban Los Angeles with its stucco storefronts, apartment buildings, and mini-malls. At one end of Calle Ocho sits the Versailles Restaurant, whose clientele includes businessmen, politicians, and terrorists. Over the years, it has become the symbolic center of Little Havana. During various Cuban crises, CNN and other media camp outside the Versailles to hear the views of the Cuban American community.

I went to the Versailles for dinner one night with friends. The restaurant served Cuban food right out of the 1950s. Chandeliers hung from the ceiling, but the tables had Formica tops. Etched glass windows featured faux French design. The décor led me to several descriptive phrases, none of them in Spanish. Kitsch. Faux French chi-chi. Bad taste.

The action started about 11 in the evening when women in pre-1959 fox furs and diamonds the size of Santiago strutted in. Men with gelled hair looked like they just got off the DC-10 from Havana. The night we were there, a prominent Cuban exile businessman was meeting with a famous attorney.

The elite who meet and greet at the Versailles constitute an important sector of the powerful Cuba Lobby, a constellation of businessmen, right-wing activists, paramilitaries, and politicians advocating a strident hard line against Cuba. Some analysts argue that the Cuba Lobby really controls U.S. policy because U.S. presidents are held hostage by the need for votes from Cuban Americans in Florida. I had my doubts about that theory but decided to visit Washington DC to find out more.

≡

One winter afternoon, I stopped by George Washington University to interview a consummate insider whom we met earlier. Col. Lawrence Wilkerson is a former army officer and aide to Colin Powell since 1989. He's got enough baubles and bangles hanging from his dress uniform to convince anyone of his bravery and his conservative credentials. After leaving the Bush administration, Wilkerson was teaching at several Washington area universities.

I walked to a part of the campus that is really a series of former houses converted into classroom buildings. After his seminar was over, Wilkerson welcomed me into a basement conference room. He wore professorial tweed, not army green. He looked like a graying college professor. Since leaving the government, Wilkerson had become a prominent critic of Bush foreign policy.

Wilkerson explained that a relatively tiny number of people in Washington even pay attention to Cuba policy. That gives an inordinate amount of influence to the Cuba Lobby, which is allied with diehard anticommunist cold warriors in the State Department, national security agencies, and members of Congress who are concerned with

Cuba. This powerful Washington elite, in turn, helps fund the Cuba Lobby through government programs.

"I believe it is mutual cooperation," said Colonel Wilkerson. "I call it incestuous. The administration and key members of Congress will vote millions of dollars to go to southern Florida to run things like [U.S.-propaganda stations] Radio Martí and TV Martí. This is a jobs program for Cuban Americans in southern Florida because it has absolutely no impact on Cuba. It's like the Iraqi National Congress and Ahmed Chalabi: our inspector general at the State Department said they were spending our money on Mercedes, taxis, London hotels, and so on. They weren't spending it on Iraq."[1]

The analogy with the Iraqi National Congress is revealing. Chalabi, who supposedly represented the Iraqi people, actively lobbied and planted phony media stories in order to promote a U.S. invasion of Iraq. But he could not have succeeded without the agreement and commitment of the administration in power. And so it is with the Cuba Lobby: it strongly influences a lot of U.S. policy toward Cuba day-to-day, but it doesn't necessarily prevail when wider issues of national security are at stake.

The policies of the Cuba Lobby run directly counter to the opinion of the majority of the American people. A USA Today/Gallup opinion poll showed that 61 percent of Americans favor establishing full diplomatic relations with Cuba.[2] Even a majority of Cuban Americans oppose some of the Cuba Lobby's most important positions. Polls show that 57 percent of Cuban Americans living in Florida want the United States to establish diplomatic relations, and a majority favor modifying the embargo.[3]

Wilkerson told me that he and Colin Powell had opposed the embargo when they served in the Bush administration. Wilkerson was even quoted in a magazine article as calling the policy "stupid." So I asked a rather obvious question: why didn't you change the policy? To understand the answer, we need to first look back at some recent history.

≡

Conservative Cubans in Florida have created a myth about their coming to America: They were a poor but heroic people who fled the communist tyranny of Cuba. Through diligence and hard work, they built up their economic and political power in Florida.

Of course, some Cubans, particularly those who arrived in later years, were poor. However, key wealthy individuals arrived with their entire families and bank accounts intact. These early 1960s immigrants included officials of the Batista dictatorship, professionals, and millionaire businessmen, such as the owners of Bacardi rum. Settling in Puerto Rico, Miami, Los Angeles, and New Jersey, they quickly established businesses and political contacts. They started operating as they had in Cuba: mixing business, politics, and corruption.

For example, Rafael Díaz-Balart ran the dreaded Ministry of Interior as deputy minister under Batista. His sons Lincoln and Mario went on to become key players in the Cuba Lobby and eventually won election to the U.S. House of Representatives. Former Havana police officials migrated to Miami and quickly set up the same rackets they had run back home. Ann Louise Bardach, in her book *Cuba Confidential*, quotes one veteran FBI agent: "To some extent, the *gangsterismo* of Havana was transported to Miami by a handful of early *batistiano* (Batista) arrivals.... [T]hey set up shop here just like they did in Havana—running protection rackets and illegal gambling."[4]

Yet, even with all their wealth and political connections, Cubans might have become just one more anticommunist ethnic group, like the Hungarians or the Russians. But the U.S. government had other plans. Through the Army, CIA, and other agencies, the United States trained key founders of the Cuba Lobby to lead armed assaults on Cuba—with all the intrigue, human rights violations, and corruption that entailed. That's how Jorge Mas Canosa, future cofounder of the Cuban American National Foundation (CANF), met Luis Posada

Carriles. They were both trained by the CIA as part of an assault force that never landed during the aborted Bay of Pigs invasion. They later worked together during their service in the U.S. Army.

When the Bay of Pigs invasion failed, the United States continued to train the exiles to carry out sabotage and other terrorist tactics against Cuban civilians in an effort to wear down Castro's government, according to U.S. government reports and declassified CIA documents. Posada and Mas Canosa plotted in 1965 to blow up a Cuban or Soviet ship anchored in Vera Cruz, Mexico. The attack never took place.[5]

The CIA couldn't always control the Cuban American paramilitaries they had trained. In 1968, Orlando Bosch Ávila fired a bazooka round from the Miami causeway at a Polish freighter docked in the port of Miami. He was later convicted in a federal court for that crime and for sending death threats to the leaders of Spain, Italy, and France. He served two years of a ten-year sentence. Rather than be questioned about the murder of a fellow exile leader in Miami in 1974, however, Bosch violated parole and fled to South America.

Bosch then hooked up with his old friend Posada in what Cuban and Venezuelan authorities said was a conspiracy to blow up a Cubana Airlines plane flying from Caracas to Havana in 1976. Seventy-three people, including the Cuban fencing team, were murdered in that bombing. According to declassified FBI documents, a leader of Bosch's organization admitted the group's involvement in that bombing.[6]

Posada was also charged and was awaiting trial in a civilian court. Mas Canosa financed Posada's escape from Venezuela in 1985. Posada flew to El Salvador where he began working on the illegal U.S. efforts to arm the Nicaraguan Contras. He worked with the White House and the CIA in what later became known as the Iran-Contra scandal.[7] During this period, some Cuban paramilitary exile groups launched attacks in the United States against civilians whom they accused of supporting Castro. They also fought viciously among themselves.[8]

In 1976, WQBA-AM news editor Emilio Milian publicly criticized Cuban exile violence. A bomb went off in his car, blowing off his legs, but he survived. The Spanish-language magazine *Replica* also dared to criticize the exiles and had its offices bombed numerous times. Exiles bombed the Nicaraguan, Mexican, and Venezuelan consulates during the 1980s. Exile groups such as Omega 7 worked with drug dealers to finance their operations. A 1983 *Miami Herald* investigation showed, "Growing evidence has linked many reputed anti-Castro terrorists to Mafia-like criminal groups that deal in drugs, extortion and murder."[9]

Posada, Bosch, and other exile leaders didn't carry out these military actions on their own; they had the ongoing assistance of key members of the Cuba Lobby such as Mas Canosa. And the Cuba Lobby promoted them as heroes. The City of Miami declared March 25, 1983, Orlando Bosch Day. Former Miami Mayor Maurice Ferrer defended a $10,000 city grant to the terrorist group Alpha 66 by saying it hadn't carried out terrorism inside U.S. borders.[10] The U.S. government has never prosecuted Posada or scores of other ultrarightists for terrorist acts, nor has it allowed Venezuela or Cuba to extradite the accused.[11]

By the early 1980s, the Reagan administration wanted to formalize the relationship between Washington and conservative Miami Cubans. Reagan's National Security Advisor Richard Allen was instrumental in forming CANF in 1981, when he met with three Cuban American millionaires, including Mas Canosa.[12] They modeled CANF on the American Israel Public Affairs Committee (AIPAC), the highly successful pro-Israel lobbying group. CANF never reached AIPAC's pinnacle of influence, but Mas Canosa did assemble a coterie of Congressional supporters.

From the beginning, CANF curried favor with both Republicans and Democrats. Sen. Joe Lieberman (D-CT) was an early and strong backer.[13] Eventually, CANF and other ultraconservative Cuban American groups helped elect supporters to the House and Senate:

Rep. Ileana Ros-Lehtinen (R-FL), elected in 1989; Rep. Lincoln Diaz-Balart (R-FL), elected in 1992; and his brother Rep. Mario Diaz-Balart (R-FL), elected in 2002. Other Cuba Lobby stalwarts included Sen. Mel Martinez (R-FL) and Sen. Robert Menendez (D-NJ).

From the beginning the Cuba Lobby had both a political wing and a covert military wing. Mas Canosa functioned as the political face, but he always maintained close ties to Posada. Posada told the *New York Times* that he received over $200,000 from Mas Canosa and CANF for a decade beginning in the 1980s.[14] CANF leaders provided the boat and arms for a commando team sent to assassinate Fidel Castro in Venezuela in 1997.[15] In 2000, Posada and a CANF activist were arrested in Panama for once again plotting to assassinate Fidel Castro. Posada was caught with 200 pounds of explosives. He spent four years in prison, but the outgoing Panamanian president pardoned him in the closing days of her administration. The pardon was later ruled illegal by Panama's highest court, but by then Posada was safely in the United States.

The U.S. government went along with the fiction that groups such as CANF represented a nonviolent movement and continued to dole out largesse to keep the Lobby strong. President Ronald Reagan created the Commission on Broadcasting to Cuba, which led to formation of Radio Martí in 1983 and TV Martí in 1985. Commission members included such well-known conservative businessmen as Richard Mellon Scaife (Mellon family heir), Joseph Coors (Coors Beer), and Herbert Schmertz (Mobil Oil). Those propaganda stations hired right-wing polemicists and broadcast personalities in Miami, thus further helping fund the Cuba Lobby.

Right-wing Cubans in Miami used their political contacts to increase their wealth and in turn buy still more political support. Mas Canosa had formed a construction company called Iglesias y Torres, later renamed the more American sounding Church and Tower. The company made him a multimillionaire. Unfortunately, he also faced criminal charges for falsely billing Miami Dade County for $58 million. The DA investigated another $17 million in fraudulent billing, but criminal charges weren't filed against Mas Canosa. He was too well protected politically.[16]

Mas Canosa ran Miami like a personal fiefdom. When a *Miami Herald* editorial in 1992 opposed the Torricelli bill, which severely tightened the U.S. embargo against Cuba, CANF launched an intimidation campaign. Editors and owners received death threats. Employees received bomb threats at the *Herald* offices and faced numerous other acts of harassment.[17] Mas Canosa and CANF denied any responsibility for the violence but did advocate a boycott of the paper. After that campaign, the *Herald* and *Nuevo Herald* lurched to the right in their coverage of Cuba and Cuban Americans.

Mas Canosa saw himself as the next president of Cuba, a kind of Miami-based *caudillo* (populist strongman). In one infamous interview with Spain's *El País* newspaper, Mas Canosa derided the possibility of the United States directly taking over Cuba. "They haven't even been able to take over Miami. If we have kicked them out of here, how could they possibly take over our own country [Cuba]?"[18]

Human Rights Watch issued reports in 1992 and 1994 condemning the lawlessness in Miami. They described the kinds of human rights violations normally associated with Latin American dictatorships. Human Rights Watch Americas wrote in 1994 that in Miami, "The atmosphere for unpopular political speech remained marked by fear and danger . . . Human Rights Watch stepped up its calls on state, local and federal officials to take affirmative action to protect those who exercised their First Amendment rights to freedom of opinion and expression."[19]

≡

Francisco Aruca knows firsthand about the Cuba Lobby. He hosted a daily radio show in Miami from 1991 to 2008 and also owned Marazul, a charter company that provided legal travel to Cuba. In 1992, two Cuban exiles came into the radio station where Aruca broadcasted, vandalized his office, and beat up some innocent employees.

Aruca told me that before 1959, Cuban politicians used what they called the *botella* (bottle) system. Government jobs were handed out to party loyalists like bottles to be filled with cash. In Miami, right-wing Radio Mambi transmitted Radio Martí at night. "Radio Mambi is a strong supporter of Bush's policies," Aruca told me. "Radio and TV Martí provide direct remuneration for the conservatives. Many employees got jobs through the three Congress people. It's the old *botella* system."[20]

Throughout the '80s and most of the '90s, CANF advocated hard-line policies aimed at bringing Cuban American leaders to power in Cuba. Mas Canosa felt free to throw his weight around Washington as well.

Jay Taylor was a career diplomat who had become friends with conservative foreign policy State Department official Elliott Abrams. At Abrams's initiative, Taylor was appointed chief of the U.S. Interests Section in Havana, a position that would have been titled ambassador if the two countries had full diplomatic relations. Taylor served in Cuba from 1987 to 1990.

At that time, hard-line American conservatives didn't want to include Cuba in peace negotiations with the United States, South Africa, and Angola, where Cuba had sent troops. Taylor cabled Washington to recommend that Cuba be included in the talks, a position that the Bush Sr. administration eventually adopted. During one Washington visit, Taylor stopped by the CANF offices to meet with Mas Canosa. That was already unusual for a diplomat of ambassadorial standing to meet with a lobbyist. But Taylor was surprised to find out that Mas Canosa knew about his secret cable sent to the State Department.

CANF had a source high in the National Security Council, Taylor told me. "He knew Jay Taylor had sent a cable supporting the idea of Castro taking part [in the Angola talks]. It reflects the power of that sector of the Cuban community."[21] Taylor met with Mas Canosa because that reflected the wishes of his boss Elliott Abrams. It would seem that a few key decision makers in the State Department shared the anticommunist views of the Cuba Lobby.

Philip Peters, as director of press and public affairs for the Latin American bureau of the State Department, also helped promote such views. He had served in the State Department from 1986 to 1988 and then from 1989 to 1993, spanning three different administrations. I sat down with him at the Lexington Institute, a Washington think tank with conservative-libertarian leanings.

"U.S. policy toward Cuba during the Cold War was perfectly justified," Peters told me. "In a way it's a perfectly good policy."[22] By 1991, Cuba was in the middle of a major economic crisis, so many in Washington thought the Castro regime was terminally ill. "If you went to the State Department, they would say, 'Cuba is on its last legs.' This is not time to give oxygen to the dictatorship." Peters noted that U.S. officials had badly miscalculated. Cuba survived and proved to be quite adaptable. But that wasn't immediately obvious in the spring of 1992.

≡

Robert Torricelli, a liberal Democratic Congressman from New Jersey, visited Cuba in November 1988. He spent four hours talking with Fidel Castro and later publicly praised social progress in Cuba. Interests Section Chief Taylor had dinner with the congressman during his trip. Torricelli "went into this glowing report about what the Revolution had achieved in Cuba," Taylor told me. "It was just astounding."[23]

Within a few years, however, Torricelli went through a political born-again experience and emerged a strident anticommunist opponent of Cuba. Many Cuban Americans live in New Jersey, and CANF began funneling money into Torricelli's campaigns. By the early '90s, Torricelli issued a famous edict to his staff, "Whatever the foundation wants, the foundation gets."[24] That edict was about to pay off for the Cuba Lobby.

In a congressional hearing in July 1991, Mas Canosa proposed a law called the Cuba Democracy Act (CDA), later to become known as the Torricelli Act. It would tighten the embargo against Cuba by, among other things, prohibiting investments by subsidiaries of U.S. companies operating abroad and punishing third countries that traded with Cuba. In January 1992, Representative Torricelli introduced the bill in the House, and Sen. Robert Graham (D-FL) introduced the Senate version.

The CDA pushed the embargo further than any previous administration had dared to do. Many business leaders and politicians opposed it, particularly because it forced foreign subsidiaries of U.S. companies to abide by the U.S. embargo. Cuban officials argue that the U.S. embargo is really a blockade because it seeks to force other countries to abide by the U.S. policy. The CDA codified this concept. President George Bush Sr. opposed the bill because of its violations of international law.

Washington attorney and lobbyist Robert Muse told me that by then CANF had honed its pressure tactics. It gave generously to the campaigns of congressional committee chairs. Mas Canosa also "threatened Sen. Claiborne Pell (D-RI) that if Pell opposed a particular measure, he would flood his district during his reelection campaign with money for his opponent."[25] Then Bill Clinton entered the fray. Clinton, who was running for president in 1992, saw an opportunity to rally support among Cuban Americans and burnish his anticommunist credentials. Clinton flew to Miami to speak at fundraisers, then endorsed the Torricelli bill.

Muse told me Clinton "showed up in Miami in April of 1992 and told Jorge Mas Canosa that he could support this bill and bring the hammer down on Fidel Castro. Meanwhile, George Bush Sr. had threatened to veto the bill in principled opposition. Once Bill Clinton chimed in, poppy Bush had no alternative. He endorsed the bill, signed it, and lost anyway in November."

Cuba Lobby money later helped elect Torricelli to the U.S. Senate in 1996. But he withdrew his 2002 reelection bid at the last minute because of corruption allegations.

≡

Philip Peters stayed on as State Department spokesperson through the beginning of Clinton's first term. He recalled events in October 1992. "I remember one day in the State Department ... There had been a boat that approached the Cuban resort of Varadero and sprayed [a] hotel with machine gun fire. And then to my astonishment, I saw a press release that a group in Miami put out called Commandos L, claiming that they had done it."

The Commandos L had indeed fired shots at the Hotel Melia in Varadero on October 7, endangering the lives of foreign tourists and hotel staff. U.S. authorities had been investigating the group. Peters assured me that the United States did not sponsor the attack. But neither did it arrest any of the participants.

"The Cuban perception is that the United States has a 'boys-will-be-boys attitude,' and that we don't crack down on people who live here and undertake operations in Cuba," Peters told me. "I think part of it is true. If someone with a terrorist record from any other place in the world came into the United States, they would not be walking free."

Once again, the Cuba Lobby was operating with both political and military tactics. It hoped the Torricelli Act, combined with the terror campaign to discourage tourism, would lead to the collapse of the Castro regime. But those plans didn't work. In fact, the Cuban economy began to improve after bottoming out in 1993. So the Lobby and the Clinton administration concluded that the embargo needed tightening again. Peters told me that State Department officials agreed that U.S. pressure in the early '90s had been a good idea. "In theory we're right," officials said at the time. "The problem is all these foreign investors have rescued Cuba politically." That logic led a few years later to the infamous Cuban Liberty and Solidarity Act, better known as Helms-Burton.

In February 1995, Sen. Jesse Helms (R-NC) significantly upped the ante.[26] Among other provisions, his bill allowed Cubans who emigrated to the United States after 1959 to sue in U.S. courts to recover property confiscated in Cuba. It also authorized lawsuits in U.S. courts against foreign companies using buildings or land once owned by those émigrés. It forbade U.S. diplomatic recognition of Cuba so long as Fidel or Raúl Castro was in power.

Rep. Dan Burton (R-IN) introduced a similar version in the House, and Helms-Burton immediately caused a furor. It was almost impossible to know what buildings or real estate had once been owned by Cuban Americans and would thus be subject to a lawsuit. Foreign companies were outraged that they might get sued in U.S. courts for carrying out normal business activities in Cuba. Even some Cuban Americans and some U.S. companies opposed the bill because it violated international law and created a whole new class of people trying to get their hands on Cuban assets frozen in the United States since the early 1960s.

Attorney Robert Muse was a registered lobbyist against Helms-Burton, representing some of those companies. His clients were already seeking compensation because they had had properties expropriated by the Cuban government. If Cuban émigrés who arrived after 1959 suddenly became entitled to sue as well, there might be less money available for his clients in any eventual settlement. He told me, "These companies were alarmed at the Helms-Burton law because it extended retroactive benefits of U.S. citizenship to Cuban

Americans. International law was uniformly against that concept." But that provision of Helms-Burton certainly benefited one major company, Bacardi, whose owners were Cuban citizens in 1959 and therefore not entitled to sue under existing U.S. law. "Bacardi was one of the chief proponents of the act," said Muse. "It was laughingly called a Bacardi rum protection act." The bill was cowritten for Senator Helms by Ignacio Sanchez, a trustee of CANF and outside attorney for Bacardi rum.[27]

Helms-Burton was so bad that even the State Department opposed it. State Department officials testified that the bill violated international norms by opening up inappropriate lawsuits in U.S. courts. Helms-Burton also invited retaliatory laws by other countries against the United States. But that widespread opposition disappeared in February 1996.

Brothers to the Rescue, a Miami-based group, had a history of violating Cuban airspace by flying over Havana to drop antigovernment leaflets. On February 26, 1996, Cuban MiG fighters shot down two Brothers to the Rescue Cessnas, killing four pilots. U.S. government officials joined with ultraconservatives in Miami to condemn the downing of the plane and the totalitarian dictator Fidel Castro. Helms-Burton sailed through both houses, and President Bill Clinton signed it into law on March 12, 1996. Bill Clinton later claimed that he opposed Helms-Burton until the February 26 incident.

According to Muse, however, Clinton never came out in opposition to Helms-Burton. "There's a bit of revisionism going on. We repeatedly asked the White House for a veto statement from President Clinton. He was never going to veto that law." Francisco "Pepe" Hernandez confirmed Muse's view. He is president of CANF and lobbied in favor of Helms-Burton. "We probably would've had the necessary votes to overcome a veto," he told me. "I think he eventually would have [signed the bill]. We were closing in on elections that he would not have won otherwise."[28]

Helms-Burton included a crucial provision giving Congress control over the embargo, something that had always been a presidential prerogative. In this way, the Clinton administration added another major stumbling block to future Cuba relations and handcuffed future administrations as well.

So what does this experience tell us about the relationship of American political leaders to the Cuba Lobby? Clearly, the Cuba Lobby pulled out all the stops to pass Helms-Burton, drawing on its strong congressional and corporate backing. But Clinton's willingness to sign the act even before the Brothers to the Rescue incident is revealing.

Former Interests Section Chief Taylor told me, "Clinton was clearly measuring it [Helms-Burton]. What does he have to gain politically and what does he have to gain internationally by relaxing the embargo? He came down the side that he wouldn't gain that much" by opposing it. The Cuba Lobby prevailed because the administration in power fundamentally agreed with its policies. But when an administration disagreed strongly enough, the results were different.

Mas Canosa died in 1997, and his son Jorge Mas Santos couldn't fill his dad's shoes. Then two years later, the Cuba Lobby faced a major setback in a confrontation with the Clinton administration. And it came from a most unexpected source: a five-year-old boy.

≡

In November 1999, a group of people left Cuba for the United States on a makeshift boat. Nine of the twelve people on board perished at sea. Five-year-old Elián González survived. CANF immediately took up the case and said young Elián should not return to Cuba to live with his father. They demanded that he stay with distant relatives in Miami that he had never met. Growing up without a mother or father, they reasoned, was better than growing up under communism.

All of Miami's Cuban American elite united around the case.

The mayor and Cuban American congress members strongly advocated that Elián not be returned to his father. Entertainers such as Andy Garcia, Gloria Estefan, and Arturo Sandoval all got on board. Attorney General Janet Reno, herself a former Miami district attorney, correctly pointed out that both U.S. and international law called for reuniting the boy with his father.

Then the case got downright weird, revealing the strong religious mysticism among some Miami Cubans. They believed that Elián had been surrounded by dolphins when he was discovered by fishermen, a reference to Cuba's patron saint, who is supposed to rescue fishermen. (Elián wasn't found by fishermen, nor was he surrounded by dolphins.) One columnist even wrote that young Elián was Cuba's Moses destined to lead his people out of slavery.[29]

After a series of court cases and negotiations with Elián's family in Cuba, Attorney General Janet Reno made the decision to uphold the law. On April 22, 2000, armed immigration agents took Elián from a house in Miami where he had been staying with distant relatives. Elián was reunited with his father, and they both returned to Cuba in June.

Ultimately, the Elián case backfired for the Cuba Lobby. Most Americans just couldn't understand why the Cuban American leaders wanted to prevent a boy from reuniting with his father. The Cuba Lobby suffered its worst political defeat to date. Public opinion polls showed only 28 percent of Americans thought Elián should remain in the United States. And 84 percent thought the Elián case had hurt the image of Cuban Americans.[30]

CANF President Hernandez told me, "We couldn't understand why the rest of the nation had a completely different view of what had to be done. The closer you got to our community here in South Florida, the worse it was." CANF went through a reevaluation of its political positions and moderated its views to a certain degree. It remained stridently anticommunist but called for changing the embargo to allow Cuban American families unrestricted visits and remittances.

Even those mild changes were too much for CANF hard-liners. CANF fractured, and the ultrarightists formed their own organization called the Cuban Liberty Council (Consejo de Libertad Cubano, CLC). The Elián case left the entire Cuba Lobby considerably weaker. Ninoska Pérez Castellón, a CLC leader and Radio Mambi talk show host, told me that CANF clearly doesn't have the same political clout it once had.[31]

Both wings of the exile movement hoped to recoup that influence by electing George Bush Jr. as president in 2000. And they used any means necessary to accomplish their goal.

5

The Cuba Lobby:
Bush and Beyond

THE CUBA LOBBY WAS WEAKENED BY THE ELIÁN González case, but it was far from defeated. Ultraconservative Cuban Americans threw money and political organization behind George Bush in the 2000 election. When the Florida election results came into question, right-wing Cubans acted as a shock force for the Republican Party.

In late November, Miami officials discovered they had 10,750 *uncounted* presidential ballots. At that point the election was extremely close, with Bush leading in Florida by less than 1,000 votes. The Miami ballots were not being *recounted*; they had never been counted in the first place.

Fearing a defeat, the Republican Party mobilized supporters to physically attack the Miami electoral commission, which was in charge of counting votes. Cuban Americans played a prominent role in shouting, pounding on doors, shoving electoral commission members, and generally causing a mini-riot in the vote-counting room. Ultimately the commissioners canceled the vote count.[1] Such tactics would be shocking in a third world country. Their success in Miami showed how illegal and undemocratic practices used for years in the campaign against Cuba had now come home to roost in U.S. presidential politics.

Once Bush assumed power, he quickly installed right-wing ideologues in key positions affecting Cuba policy. Otto Reich was Assistant Secretary of State for Western Hemisphere Affairs from 2001 to 2002. Reich had become notorious as head of the Reagan administration's Office of Public Diplomacy in the mid-1980s, when he planted phony stories aimed at discrediting the Sandinista government in Nicaragua. The Comptroller General wrote that Reich had engaged in "prohibited, covert propaganda activities."[2] Reich was so controversial that he failed to secure Senate approval and ultimately left his State Department post. In 2008, Reich became a foreign policy advisor for Sen. John McCain's presidential campaign.

Bush appointed Elliott Abrams to several National Security Council positions that lasted from 2001 to 2008. Abrams was a leading neoconservative who was discredited for his participation in the Iran-Contra scandal.[3] Abrams was convicted on two counts of withholding information from Congress. The Bush administration resurrected Abrams, and he remained a hard-line advocate of the U.S. embargo.

Abrams, Reich, and other administration officials backed the military coup against the elected government of Venezuela's President Hugo Chávez in 2002. Reich had met with coup plotters for months prior, and on the day of the coup, he gathered Latin American ambassadors into his office to praise the coup and denounce Chávez. The coup failed, and Chávez was restored to power within two days.[4]

John Bolton, another major neoconservative, served as Bush's Undersecretary of State for Arms Control and International Security (2001–2005) and U.S. Ambassador to the UN (2005). Bolton falsely claimed that Cuba had developed a biological weapons program, an assertion so off base that even the State Department never endorsed it.[5] The U.S. Senate refused to confirm Bolton, and he resigned his UN post in 2006.

Col. Lawrence Wilkerson told me that the Bush administration vetted Cuba policy with Karl Rove, the Rasputin of domestic strategy. "Karl Rove and others in the White House were making sure payback was made to Cuban Americans. That payback was in the form of tightening the travel restrictions and tightening the embargo in general."[6]

In 2004, the Bush administration changed long-standing policy and restricted family visits by Cuban Americans to once every three years. It had been once a year. The administration capped annual remittances to Cuba at $1,200 per person. Those were positions long advocated by the most conservative elements of the Cuba Lobby, such as the CLC.

I asked Colonel Wilkerson if President Bush and Vice President Cheney actually supported the embargo. After all, as president of Halliburton, Cheney had opposed unilateral embargoes as ineffective and harmful to U.S. business interests.[7]

"I hesitate to say whether President Bush or Vice President Cheney thought the policies were sound. I'm sure they were aware they were doing political payback. Were they able to rationalize it by saying this is the best policy, too, because Fidel Castro really is a threat . . . ? I find that hard to believe . . . This is *realpolitik*."

At the end of the day, however, it doesn't matter *why* the Bush administration tightened the embargo. It cooperated with the Cuba Lobby to adopt a highly restrictive Cuba policy. Joe García, former CANF leader and 2008 Democratic candidate for Congress, told me that even though he disagreed with that particular tightening, in general the Cuba Lobby played by the rules.

He acknowledged that Cuban Americans have disproportionate influence because so few Washington insiders care about the Cuba issue. "That's a fact. That's the way Washington works. Most Americans believe in gun control, but the NRA wins every vote in Congress. This is a country that works with special interests. And that's a good thing. People in Iowa or Montana or Washington aren't vested in Cuba policy."[8]

That's a telling commentary on the undemocratic nature of American politics. But the Cuba Lobby's activities go well beyond standard pressure-group tactics. Theirs is a history of chicanery and corruption. The federal government spent $74 million from 1996 to 2005 to funnel "humanitarian aid" to people in Cuba. The program, administered by USAID (U.S. Agency for International Development), was supposed to provide support to Cubans seeking freedom against the Castro regime.

But a November 2006 Government Accountability Office (GAO) report showed that the government awarded 92 percent of the grants to Cuban American groups without competitive bidding and found examples of highly questionable spending on such items as a chain saw, cashmere sweaters, and Godiva chocolates. The GAO couldn't determine how much aid actually got to Cuba.[9] In its own report, CANF admitted that four of the largest recipients of the grants used only 17 percent for direct aid to Cuba. The rest was eaten up in salaries and expenses in the United States.[10]

In a 2006 news article, the *Washington Post* wrote, "Rep. Jeff Flake (R-Ariz.), . . . [and] Rep. William D. Delahunt (D-Mass.), said the lack of oversight and the failure to follow government rules led to creation of a money trough that existed largely to provide jobs and operating funds to Miami-based activists who oppose Cuba's communist government."[11]

In March 2008, Felipe Sixto, a special assistant to President Bush, resigned after a FBI investigation. He admitted misusing funds while chief of staff at the Center for a Free Cuba, a recipient of the USAID largess, and a key organization of the Cuba Lobby.[12]

In years past, congressional critics condemned the "bridge to nowhere" backed by Alaska Senator Ted Stevens.[13] In a far worse example, the U.S. Congress and successive presidents have been sponsoring a TV station to nowhere since 1986. The U.S. government spends millions annually for reporters, staff, studios, and broadcast equipment for the U.S. propaganda station TV Martí. But the Cuban government has jammed the station from day one, and almost no one in Cuba has actually ever seen a broadcast.[14]

Radio Martí, similar to Radio Free Europe, is so one-sided and filled with right-wing invective that few Cubans listen. The U.S. government gives contracts to the most extremist of the Miami Cubans to prepare programming for Radio Martí. All in all, the U.S. government spends $37 million annually to fund TV and Radio Martí. By comparison, the propaganda network Radio Free Europe broadcasts to 19 countries in 28 languages and costs $75 million.[15]

Who are these ultrarightists who benefit from their Washington ties?

≡

Late one afternoon, I drove across the city limit from affluent Coral Gables into Little Havana. The modern Univision radio station building appears on the right. With its green awnings and modern architecture, it could be anywhere USA. Instead, it houses several Spanish-language radio stations, including Radio Mambi. I walked straight down the corridor and then hung a sharp left. Mambi occupies only about four studios and production booths. Large posters in Spanish say "Free Cuba; No to succession" (a dig at Raúl Castro), and another favorably displays a photo of accused terrorist Luis Posada Carriles.

I was ushered into the studio where Ninoska Pérez Castellón hosted her Spanish-language call-in show. Pérez is the doyenne of the Cuban ultraright. She is a former spokesperson for CANF and now helps lead the CLC, the right-wing group that split off from CANF in the wake of the Elián González case. During commercial breaks, I asked Pérez about her unusual first name. "I got that name because my mother liked Russian literature, before the Russians came to Cuba," she explained, obviously not for the first time.[16]

On that particular day, Cardinal Tarcisio Bertone, the Vatican's secretary of state, had just left Havana after calling for greater cooperation between the Vatican and the Cuban government. It was standard diplo-speak, but it enraged Miami's ultrarightists. Ninoska fiercely denounced Bertone on air for "praising Raúl and Fidel." One listener read a long and boring open letter to the Vatican slamming Bertone and the Vatican. Even Pérez's eyes glazed over as the denunciation continued for endless minutes.

Every caller during the time I was in studio was elderly and Cuban. How could I tell? They spoke so slowly even I could understand their thick, Cuban accents. The issue of Cuba and the Vatican revealed some interesting details about the ultraright. Pérez explained why her listeners were indignant. "Here is this cardinal who has gone to Havana and is ready to accept Raúl Castro as the president of Cuba. He makes a point that his visit is not political, but he blasts the embargo. Why is not repression addressed?"

I pointed out that the Vatican has criticized human rights violations in Cuba many times. "Not really," she asserted. "I have not seen one statement saying anything." In reality, the cardinal, upon his departure for Cuba a few days earlier, had raised the issue of the country's "political prisoners and their families."[17]

But that's typical of the ultraright mindset. The Vatican and others are dubbed pro-Castro if they criticize the U.S. embargo. Pérez's listeners began to lambaste not only the Vatican but the Catholic religion. They praised their own brand of evangelical Christianity. That was too much for Pérez, who cut off the callers with a curt comment against attacking Catholicism. The interchanges did reveal, however, the splits among the ultraright, which is fractured both by religion and politics.

Pérez remains a power in Miami because she can mobilize hundreds of stalwarts for violent actions. For example, Radio Mambi called people into the street to oppose the peace group Code Pink and in support of Luis Posada Carriles in January 2008 (see the description of the Code Pink demonstration later in this chapter). But Pérez and other ultrarightists are faced with a demographic time bomb as the older generation dies off and younger, less strident Cuban Americans come of age.

≡

Cubans in south Florida fall into two broad categories: those who arrived before the 1980 Mariel boatlift and those who came after. The 1960s and '70s émigrés were relatively wealthy, often emigrated with their entire nuclear family, and were virtually all white. Many of the 125,000 *marielitos,* those who came during the Mariel boatlift of 1980, were of humbler origin. Many of them were black Cubans, and they still have close relatives living on the island. That's also true of the estimated 250,000 Cubans who have legally emigrated since 1994. When children born in the United States were included, the pre-Mariel Cubans made up only 10 percent of the 800,000 Florida residents of Cuban descent in 2008.[18]

The political attitudes of people born in the United States and post-Mariel emigrants differ markedly from those of the older generation.

For example, a 2006 poll showed that 57 percent of Cubans who immigrated after 1980 favored allowing Americans to visit Cuba. Only 33 percent of the older generation agreed with that view.[19]

Professor Andy Gomez is a senior fellow at the Institute for Cuban and Cuban American Studies at the University of Miami. He told me that many Cuban Americans now think the State Department needs "to look at Cuba from the national interest of the U.S. rather than that there is a powerful Cuban American Lobby. That constantly gets us in trouble, not just on Cuba but on other issues."[20]

The Florida International University has conducted regular polls and seen attitudes soften toward Cuba over the past 10 years. In 2007, approximately 64 percent of Cubans wanted to see Bush's policies on travel and remittances rescinded. About 58 percent admitted sending remittances to Cuba, probably in violation of U.S. restrictions. Only 24 percent said the U.S. embargo is working well. The percentage of people supporting the embargo declined from 66 percent in 2004 to 58 percent in 2007.[21]

Cuban American attitudes are shifting away from supporting the ultraright wing. But anticommunism and conservative sentiments remain strong. Many remember their experiences on the island and stay in regular contact with relatives suffering economically in Cuba. They realize that even though the embargo isn't impacting Cuban government policy, they *want* to find a way that will.

Cuban American attitudes are similar to those of Americans who oppose the Iraq war because so many American soldiers are dying. They would support the war if it appeared the United States were winning. The majority of Cuban Americans want to see the downfall of the Cuban system; they just aren't sure current methods are working.

Cuban Americans express those opinions at the ballot box. One poll showed 91 percent of Cuban Americans are registered to vote, much higher than among other Latino groups or Americans in general.[22] The United States grants immigrant Cubans legal status immediately upon arrival, gives them green cards one year later, and allows them to apply for citizenship five years after arrival. Other Latinos who immigrate without documents may never become citizens. Even those who arrive legally may take years to apply for citizenship.

Significantly, an estimated 72 percent of Cubans are registered Republican. So even though attitudes are changing, conservative Cubans argue, with some legitimacy, that opinion polls don't mean much in the real world. Pérez told me, "When they talk about polls and how the community has changed, to me the final poll is the election." And to date, Cubans vote as a solidly conservative bloc. During every presidential election since the 1990s, the media and liberal advocates have predicted that the changing demographics of Miami will finally weaken the power of the hard-liners. And in every election to date, the hard-liners have won. The ultraconservatives have more money and are better organized politically, even if their views are out of sync with their constituents.

For example, the ultraright maintains significant influence in the Florida state government. In 2006, Florida prohibited any funds from state academic institutions from being used for research inside Cuba. The ban—which included, state, federal, and even private grants—has led some professors to leave the state and seek professorships in more hospitable climates.[23] And then in 2008, the Florida legislature, at the behest of conservative Cuban American legislators, voted to require travel agents legally arranging Cuba travel to post a bond of up to $250,000 in order to stay in business. The travel agencies challenged the law in federal court. The law would drive up the cost of Cuba travel and make it more difficult for Cuban Americans to legally visit the island. That doesn't seem to bother family-friendly Florida State Representative David Rivera, who told the *Miami Herald*, "If somebody has asked for political asylum in the United States, they have no business returning to the country which they were supposedly fleeing."[24]

≡

Miami leaders argue that, whatever the community's faults, at least the paramilitaries are no longer active. In 2008, I met with Joe García, former executive director of CANF and the 2008 Democratic candidate opposing Rep. Mario Diaz-Balart. The garrulous García burst into a Cuban coffee shop one morning in Miami Beach where we had scheduled a meeting. Raúl Castro had officially become Cuba's new president the previous day, and García was swamped with media calls. He gave a TV reporter a few sound bites, and then we sat down for a long interview as we sipped demitasse cups full of strong Cuban espresso.

He told me that Jorge Mas Canosa and CANF had changed the politics of his community. "It was his ability to put political success into the hands of Cuban Americans that got rid of the military movement here and the military action theorists."[25] That's the official story. In reality, Mas Canosa continued to secretly support and fund military actions. He was intimately involved in providing personnel to the Contras fighting the elected Sandinista government in Nicaragua. He was involved in the Iran-Contra scandal, at one point giving Col. Oliver North $50,000 to pass along to the Contras.[26]

But this is not just ancient history. In August 2007, Robert Ferro of southern California was sentenced to five years in federal prison and fined $75,000 for possessing more than 1,500 weapons, including machine guns, silencers, and a rocket launcher. His excuse was that he didn't intend to hurt anyone in the United States; the arms were intended to overthrow Castro. Ferro told the *Inland Valley Daily Bulletin* that he believed he had the government's blessing to have the guns because authorities seized them in 1991 while investigating another explosives case, and then gave them back. "Maybe it was wrong," he said. "I don't know. They didn't charge me in 1991, so I thought it was OK to keep them until we went to Cuba."[27]

In another incident, prominent exile leader and Miami developer Santiago Álvarez Fernández-Magriñá was arrested in 2006 with a cache of machine guns, hand grenades, and C-4 explosives. Álvarez pleaded guilty just before trial. His supporters then turned over an even larger armory, including "200 pounds of dynamite, 14 pounds of C-4 explosives and 30 assault weapons."[28] Álvarez is also suspected of aiding the illegal entry of Luis Posada Carriles into the United States in 2005. In early 2008, Alvarez was serving a 10-month jail sentence for refusing to testify in Posada's immigration case.

Cuban American ultrarightists have developed a new source of illegal income: immigrant smuggling. In June 2008, four Cubans with ties to Miami were implicated in an immigrant smuggling ring operating out of Cancún, Mexico. One of the leaders was murdered in an internal dispute, according to Mexican police, and others may have had ties to conservative Miami political groups.[29] From 2003 to 2008, the number of Cubans detained in Mexico shot up by 500 percent, according to a member of the Mexican parliament. In June 2008,

Miami-based Cubans hijacked a Mexican immigration bus carrying detained Cubans, who were later delivered to the U.S. border. Lt. Matt J. Moorlag, public affairs officer for the Seventh Coast Guard District in Miami, told the *Los Angeles Times*, "These are criminal enterprises, and they're really reckless. They have little to no regard for their cargo."[30]

Even though the ultraright wing remained armed, it was not using those arms in Miami as it had in years past. Progressive radio host Francisco Aruca told me Miami was "still repressive, but it has improved. In the late '70s, Miami was a terror capital. There were political assassinations and bombings of dissidents. The social pressure was also worse."[31]

He argued that the repression of dissent through intimidation and pressure continued. "My radio show was successful from the beginning. But no advertisers lasted more than one week. They get threats. In one case, they got a rock through a window. People to this day are afraid of such activities."

Aruca and others argued that the U.S. Constitution still doesn't apply in Miami. In 2001, when Cuban pianist Chucho Valdés was scheduled to perform at the Latin Grammy ceremony in Miami, threats of violence led organizers to move the event to Los Angeles.

In late January 2008, the women's peace group Code Pink decided to hold a small demonstration in front of the Versailles Restaurant to demand the arrest and trial of Posada for terrorism. Right-wingers on Radio Mambi and other media called for a protest against Code Pink. Code Pink leader Medea Benjamin told me that when they arrived and tried to get out of their car, "We saw this huge crowd of 400–500 people. They ran out into the street to attack us. We were ambushed. They were tearing apart our float, running out into the street. We were surrounded. There were police, but they were not doing anything."[32]

Unlike years past, however, the attack sparked criticism among Miami's moderates, with numerous media and academic figures condemning the violence. Code Pink returned February 9 and held a peaceful demonstration, this time with full police protection. Benjamin told me the political atmosphere in Miami is "changing, but way too slowly. Miami hasn't caught up with the Constitution. Little Havana is a no-free-speech zone. You've got to go through tremendous contortions to get police protection."

≡

On the surface, the Cuba Lobby's support among Cuban Americans and their power over mainstream politicians seems solid. But countervailing currents may yet see those alliances break apart. The Lobby hasn't achieved all its goals. For example, it has long opposed the U.S. immigration policy called "wet foot/dry foot": If Cubans set foot on U.S. soil (dry foot), they automatically become legal immigrants and quickly get a green card. But if they are stopped at sea (wet foot), they are returned to Cuba. Miami Cubans advocate that any Cuban found at sea should receive asylum. Successive administrations have rejected that option, fearing an uncontrolled influx of Cuban migrants hitting U.S. shores.

The ultraconservatives also express anger that Helms-Burton has never been fully implemented. Both Clinton and Bush have signed waivers prohibiting U.S. lawsuits against foreign companies that are using property once owned by Cuban Americans (Helms-Burton, Title III). Only a handful of foreign companies have been penalized for investing in Cuba under another section, known as Title IV. Foreign companies and U.S.-allied governments have strongly objected to these provisions. The United States doesn't want to further anger its allies or risk an adverse decision in the international court.

That sets an interesting paradigm for the future. In both cases, U.S. national interests won out because political leaders in Washington perceived U.S. national interest overriding the narrow concerns of the Cuba Lobby.

And official Washington perceives the well-being of U.S. companies as an important part of the country's national interests. The normalization of diplomatic and trade relations with China and Vietnam certainly benefited U.S. companies. They became a strong pressure group advocating normalized relations, despite disagreements over the systems of government in those countries.

In 2000, pressure from the farm lobby forced a change to the U.S. embargo to allow food shipments to Cuba. Within a few years, the United States became the single largest exporter of food to the island. Cuba gets most of its soy, wheat, rice, and chicken from U.S. agribusiness. The Cuban government encouraged this trade, hoping to create a business lobby against the embargo. Cuba has an estimated 4.6 billion barrels of offshore oil deposits. U.S. oil companies are certainly interested in developing them. They could become a powerful lobbying group as well.

But so far no business lobby has been able to lift the embargo. Cuba has only 11 million people. Wayne Smith, a former head of the U.S. Interests Section in Havana, told me, "as one of the people in the Clinton administration put it, if Cuba had a population of 100 million people, there wouldn't be an embargo and wouldn't have been an embargo for all these years. . . . It's just not a big enough market to bring things to critical mass."[33]

Colonel Wilkerson told me Cuba remains unimportant to most Washington decision makers. "Cuba was not on the stove let alone the front burner." Wilkerson said that prior to joining the Bush administration, he and Colin Powell agreed that that the U.S. embargo made no sense. "I remember him vividly saying the policy is stupid, it's moronic. If we opened up to Cuba, we flood Cuba with everything from our entertainment industry to agriculture, and over time, people would change."

When I asked Wilkerson why he and Powell never changed Cuba policy (see beginning of chapter 4), he told me they never even discussed it. "Colin Powell had much more serious issues to fight for . . . so he wasn't going to waste his time on Cuba. There were forces marshaled in the Republican Party and the Bush administration to fight to the death over Cuba. In essence, he [Powell] gave into those forces . . . He let that happen because he knew he would have to expend far too much political capital, blood, to change it, and he had more serious things to spend that capital and blood on."

That's not much of an excuse, really. Millions of Cubans suffer because of the embargo, and the American right to travel and free association is violated. The United States stands completely isolated internationally because Washington has other, bigger issues to debate.

And to really understand the extent of that isolation, we need only look at the specifics of the U.S. embargo of Cuba.

6

The U.S. Embargo

THE U.S. GOVERNMENT MAINTAINS THE ECONOMIC embargo of Cuba ostensibly to promote democracy on the island and to protect U.S. national security. The embargo appears straightforward. Most trade is banned, and Americans can't visit the island. Violations can result in big fines and possible imprisonment. That's what keeps lots of folks above Tijuana and below Toronto from traveling to Cuba.

At one time the embargo legally banned travel to Cuba. However, back in 1967 the Supreme Court ruled that such provisions violated a U.S. citizen's freedom to travel. According to the court, however, it's okay for the government to prohibit the spending of money under the 1917 Trading with the Enemy Act. So, contrary to popular understanding, it is legal for Americans to *travel* to Cuba; it's illegal for Americans to *spend money* there.[1]

It gets weirder.

It's okay for American agribusiness to sell chicken wings to Cuba, but Cubans can't sell sugar to the United States. In 2008, President Bush Jr. announced plans to make an exception to the embargo and allow cell phones to be sent to Cuba; however, when activated in the United States, they won't work on the island.[2]

The U.S. embargo—far from being a well-crafted, thoughtful effort to put pressure on an unfriendly government—is a mishmash of ad hoc measures thrown together over the course of almost 50 years. It's the most stringent embargo imposed by the United States on any country in the world. U.S. citizens are free to travel to Iran, Syria, Vietnam, China, and even North Korea—but not Cuba.

No other country observes the embargo. Every year since 1992, the UN General Assembly votes by overwhelming majority to condemn it. In 2007, the vote was 184–4 against the United States. The only countries voting with the United States were Israel, Palau, and the Marshall Islands.[3] Despite its UN vote, Israel ignores the U.S. embargo and actively trades with Cuba.

Even many free-market conservatives in the United States oppose it. I interviewed iconic conservative economist Milton Friedman in 1994. He told me, "In general, economic embargoes don't work. In Cuba there never has been a justification for the embargo except on strategic goods that might be used for military purposes. I see no justification for an embargo on food or clothing."[4]

The U.S. embargo incorporates the worst of two worlds: it has no impact on Cuba's decision making but allows the Cuban government to blame the island's problems on the embargo. So why has every presidential administration since Dwight D. Eisenhower continued to maintain economic sanctions against Cuba? Wayne Smith, former chief of the U.S. Interests Section in Havana, told me that American policy makers never got over losing control of the island. And that makes the embargo different from sanctions against any other country. The embargo "has a psychological dimension that North Korea would never have," said Smith. "American leaders, from Jefferson and John Quincy Adams forward, fully expected that Cuba would become part of the union. That was the rightful order of things. Well, it didn't. The Cubans didn't want it.[5]

Over the years, the United States used a variety of arguments to justify the embargo: Cuba nationalized U.S. property, it was arming Latin American guerillas, had troops in Africa, and was a tool for Soviet foreign policy. But by the 1990s, none of those arguments made any sense. So what happened? The United States tightened the embargo even more, passing the Cuban Democracy Act (Torricelli Act) in 1992 and the Cuban Liberty and Democracy Solidarity Act (Helms-Burton) in 1996.

The justification for the embargo had shifted once again. In 1994, as part of a story for National Public Radio, I interviewed Michael Skol, then the principal deputy assistant secretary of state for Inter-American Affairs. He acknowledged that Cuba no longer had troops in Africa, wasn't trying to spread revolution in Latin America, and obviously wasn't allied with the USSR. But, he told me, the embargo was now an effective pressure for democracy. "If the embargo were lifted, there would be a change in the amount of capital entering Cuba. That would help Castro survive without having to change. Lifting the embargo would be a slap in the face, not just to Cubans who would like to see democracy return, but to people all over the hemisphere."[6]

I pointed out that people all over the hemisphere, including pro-U.S. dissidents in Cuba, opposed the embargo. I questioned him about why the United States had ended trade embargoes against China and Vietnam, but not against Cuba. He really had no answer. U.S. government officials can never explain why no one else in the world observes the embargo. Foreign tourists enjoy the Cuban beaches; European, Asian, and Latin American firms invest in Cuba; Venezuela ships oil to Cuba and helped refurbish a major oil refinery; Brazil has become a major investor and trade partner.

Even worse, from the standpoint of U.S. officials, they can't even stop Americans from traveling to the island. An estimated 150,000 Americans visited Cuba illegally in 2007, in addition to over 60,000 legal travelers.[7] Cuban Americans are prohibited from sending more than $1,200 per year to relatives in Cuba, but many simply wire additional money through Mexico or Canada. U.S. remittances remain one of the largest sources of hard currency for Cuba. So even at the most elemental economic level, the embargo is failing.

≡

The embargo does have a negative impact, however, on both Cubans and Americans. For instance, all U.S. presidents since 1961 have restricted Cuban musicians and actors from performing in the United States. Successive administrations have argued that because artists receive salaries from government-sponsored associations, their earnings help bolster the Castro regime.

It's rather ludicrous to argue that the 600–700 pesos per month ($24–28) that top-notch Cuban musicians receive in salary would have any impact on the Cuban government. When Cuban musicians perform abroad, they keep most of their earnings, giving a normal agents fee to government booking agencies and paying income taxes (see chapter 9 for details). So, allowing them to perform in the United States wouldn't bolster the Castro brothers. In reality, the United States limits travel as part of the political offensive against Cuba. If it allowed too many cultural interchanges, officials fear, the Castro government would perceive it as a concession. Such performances might also lead to popular American pressure against the embargo.

U.S. officials denied it, of course. State Department official Skol told me that cultural performances were limited because Cuba had failed to meet U.S. demands to democratize. "Why should Cuba be rewarded for having made no progress?"[8]

For a few years under Jimmy Carter and during the second term of Bill Clinton, Cuban musicians and artists were allowed to perform in the United States. They couldn't officially earn money, mind you. U.S. policy allowed only reimbursement of travel expenses and a small per diem.[9] Nevertheless, from about 1996 to 2001 Cuban musicians flooded into the United States, performing in clubs, at music festivals, and at college campuses.

American jazz trumpeter Roy Hargrove, who has visited Cuba and performed with many of the island's top musicians, praised the quality of their playing. "There's a lot of virtuosity going on, from a depth of cats, not just a few. My mouth was wide open the whole time. It gave me a lot of insights into playing rhythmically."[10] I asked him what would happen if the U.S. embargo were lifted and Cubans could tour freely in the United States. "There would be a lot less gigs for American musicians," he told me with a laugh.

No chance of that happening under the Bush Jr. administration, which tightened the embargo on musicians to the point of strangulation. By 2002, the administration had virtually stopped musicians from entering the United States by slowing the visa process while never admitting its intention to stop cultural exchanges. Finally, in October 2004, the Bush administration gave up all pretense of fairly processing Cuban artist visas and prohibited virtually all performances. It was part of a general tightening of the embargo ostensibly aimed at promoting freedom on the island.

The embargo affects Cubans in other ways. I've visited hospitals lacking critical high-tech equipment that is manufactured in the United States or controlled by U.S. companies. Similarly, certain pharmaceuticals and medical supplies are hard to obtain. The Cubans have become adept at working around the embargo, but obtaining such items drives costs up by 30 percent or more. The United States constitutes a natural market for Cuban sugar, nickel, and oil. American tourists would spend a lot of money visiting Cuba if the embargo were lifted.

The Cuban government estimated that the embargo cost the island $89 billion from 1961 to 2007.[11] That includes extra expenses for transportation as well as lost revenues from trade and tourism. It's impossible to independently verify the accuracy of those figures, and the

Cuban government tends to blame every problem on the embargo. But the embargo does hurt the Cuban people economically, while completely failing to impact Cuban government policy. And there is growing awareness about the issue inside the United States.

═══

For many years, a number of American groups have engaged in civil disobedience to oppose the embargo. The Venceremos Brigade organizes Americans to tour and work in Cuba. It has violated Treasury Department's Office of Foreign Assets Control (OFAC) rules by sending more than 8,000 people to Cuba since 1969. Beginning in 1992, the group Pastors for Peace has taken food and medical supplies to Cuba.[12] But perhaps the most unusual protest came from a New York piano tuner.

Ben Treuhaft is the son of leftist attorney Bob Treuhaft and muckraking journalist Jessica Mitford.[13] In 1995, he launched a campaign to get Americans to donate pianos to Cuba, dubbed "Senda Piana to Havana." His campaign highlighted the absurdity of the embargo by rigorously testing its provisions. He's been causing grief to government authorities ever since by combining the best of Mahatma Gandhi and Groucho Marx.

His plan was simple. The embargo has an exception for humanitarian assistance. He applied to the Department of Commerce to ship pianos to Cuba on humanitarian grounds. For some still unexplained bureaucratic reason, his application was forwarded to the department's Office of Nuclear and Missile Technology Controls. Within a month, he had official permission to ship pianos. "Had I asked to ship TOW missiles to Iraq," Treuhaft told me cheerily, "they probably would have approved it right away. But pianos took a few extra weeks."[14]

He also had to promise not to use the pianos for torture or human rights abuse. How could pianos abuse human rights? Treuhaft quotes a journalist who wrote of his case, "None of the pianos will be painted white, have candelabras placed on them, or be played by anyone wearing a sequined jacket."

At one point, Treuhaft had considered working with his disabled friend Danny McMullan to find orthopedists to send prosthetic devices to Cuba. Treuhaft said he would put it "under our Commerce license and call it 'Arms for Cuba.'" However, the idea never had any legs.

Treuhaft noted that although the Commerce Department had approved shipping pianos, the OFAC never gave him permission to go to Cuba to deliver them. So how could he make sure his pianos were not being used for human rights abuse? Treuhaft visited Cuba anyway and carefully collected receipts from cheap *pensiones* and the Burgui fast-food stand, where he enjoyed an occasional chicken wing. He put the receipts in an envelope and mailed them to Senator Jesse Helms, of Helms-Burton fame. On April 24, 1996, the Treasury Department told Treuhaft that he faced a $10,000 fine.

There it was. Treuhaft stood accused of felonious travel in pursuance of piano tuning. His mother, Jessica Mitford, was horrified. In her posh English accent—unsullied after a half century in Oakland—she moaned, "Oh Bengie, how *could* you turn yourself in to the Treasury Department *just* when all those pianos were getting to Cuba?" She soon changed her tune when she saw all the positive press that ensued.

Technically speaking, Treuhaft wasn't being charged with a criminal offense but rather a civil violation, which most other illegal travelers to Cuba also face. But $10,000 was a lot of money, whatever you want to call it. Treuhaft told me at the time that he couldn't afford a $10,000 fine, but suggested the government could seize some of his assets. He estimated his 1967 Pontiac Catalina was worth about $1,500 "because it's a convertible."[15]

Treuhaft demanded an appeal hearing. He also organized a grassroots campaign against OFAC. His attorney, Tom Miller, wrote to the *San Francisco Chronicle*: "Our leaders in Washington now believe they can bring the Cuban people to their knees by forcing them to listen to out-of-tune pianos. This theory, no doubt from the same department that played loud rock music to make Panama dictator Noriega surrender, is bound to fail. The Cuban people have had to listen to loud music broadcast over poor sound systems for years and have survived."[16] The Bay Area press covered the story in news articles and political cartoons. Outraged pianists wrote and phoned OFAC. Politicians such as Rep. Ron Dellums (D-CA) supported the piano-tuning cause.

The Department of Treasury was fighting this battle minus one crucial weapon. It always offered hearings to accused embargo violators. But the government had no provisions for actually conducting an agency hearing, no hearing officers, no secretaries, no computers, and no plastic floor mats with little spikes that are so essential to keeping government carpets clean. Nevertheless, on July 5, 1996, OFAC director Richard Newcomb raised the ante by increasing the potential penalties to $1.3 million and 10 years imprisonment should Treuhaft engage in more unlicensed travel to Cuba.

The media wars continued. Senator Robert Torricelli (D-NJ) told CBS, "Those pianos prop up Fidel Castro's regime."[17] Senda Piana to Havana's fundraising was improving exponentially with all this coverage. Then Treuhaft told OFAC officials that he planned another trip to Cuba in order to start a joint venture with the Cuban government called the Helms-Treuhaft Piano Bass String Company. The company would manufacture piano bass strings and would be known colloquially as Ben and Jesse's.

On Halloween Eve 1996, Treuhaft boarded a plane bound for Cuba disguised as a 1935 studio upright piano. An Associated Press photo showed Treuhaft's head sticking out of the cloth and Velcro lid, sitting there like a bust of Brahms. The front panel read "Havana Piana Co., San Francisco USA" with real sheet music on the desk and Treuhaft's hands emerging from two holes underneath, resting on 88 paper keys. The bottom was open for his legs.

All the bad publicity led the Treasury Department to offer a compromise. It was ready to settle for $3,500. Treuhaft wrote to attorney Miller, "Congratulations on your fine work, my boy. Tell Treasury we accept. Ask when we can expect a check." Miller relayed this response to OFAC officials, who stopped speaking to Treuhaft. In fact, he didn't hear from them again for years. In 2004, OFAC finally got around to setting up the agency hearings. The Bush administration loaned Treasury some administrative judges borrowed from Homeland Security. OFAC sent out a lot more threatening letters to Americans traveling to Cuba, and some were forced to pay fines. The atmosphere for Cuba travel definitely cooled, and people who might have risked a trip in the 1990s didn't go during the Bush era.

But Treuhaft's case was by then quite old. Miller suspected that government officials would have a hard time proving Treuhaft was afforded due process even if they did grant him a hearing. Over a period of 13 years, Treuhaft shipped 242 pianos, which were distributed to schools throughout Cuba. Somehow, U.S. national security has not suffered.

Formally, Treuhaft's case was still pending in 2008.

Meanwhile, much more serious forces were taking a critical look at the embargo.

In November 2007, the GAO investigated the impact of the embargo on overall U.S. security. The report revealed how wasteful enforcing the embargo had became under George Bush, Jr. In 2007, at the Miami airport, according to the GAO report, Customs and Border Protection (CBP) spent 20 percent of its secondary inspections on arrivals from Cuba compared with an average of 3 percent for other international arrivals. "Secondary inspections of Cuba arrivals at the airport may strain CBP's ability to carry out its mission of keeping terrorists, criminals, and other inadmissible aliens from entering the country."[18]

Border authorities in other cities similarly paid much more attention to embargo enforcement than to other security issues. "After 2001 OFAC opened more investigations and imposed more penalties for embargo violations, such as buying Cuban cigars, than for violations of other sanctions, such as those on Iran." In other words, looking for Cuban rum and cigars hurt the government's ability to find real criminals.

The GAO report noted the U.S. isolation on the embargo issue made enforcement very difficult. "Some governments have actively opposed the U.S. embargo by refusing to identify U.S. travelers making unauthorized visits to Cuba via third countries, complicating agencies' enforcement activities, or have declined to limit their trade, financial, and travel relations with Cuba, further undermining the embargo's stated purpose."

Opposition to the embargo inside the United States has also been a headache for the authorities, according to the report. It has led to "widespread, small-scale violations of restrictions on family travel and remittances . . . In addition, human rights, religious, and other groups have criticized the increased restrictions on family travel and remittances; and several of these groups have engaged in acts of civil disobedience, such as traveling to Cuba without a license."

≡

A relatively small number of people in Florida benefit from the embargo: Florida citrus, sugar, and tobacco growers, as well as tourism operators, don't have to compete with Cuba; some journalists and academics receive U.S. government funds to create justifications for the embargo. Those forces argue that new investment and tourism would prop up the Castro regime and thus weaken the chance for democratic change. Embargo opponents say flooding the country with freedom-loving Americans would bring democratic ideas and American capitalist values to the island, thus helping make change.

Wayne Smith told me, "American citizens traveling abroad are the best way to spread the message of American democracy. It would add pressure for change in Cuba: the greater the interchange, the greater the benefit for the cause of openness in Cuba."[19]

But the situation is far more complicated. After all, millions of Spaniards, Italians, Canadians, and others have visited Cuba. Corporations from those countries are free to invest and trade. That interaction has not caused any major political changes in Cuba. That's because political and economic change depends mainly on internal developments, not outside contact.

The Cuban government has so far not chosen to follow a Chinese model of widespread foreign investment and greater emphasis on market forces. Cuba wants foreigners to invest in key industries such as tourism, energy, and oil and mineral extraction. But McDonald's and Starbuck franchises would not likely open anytime soon. The Cuban government was even leery about too much tourism. Attorney and Washington lobbyist Robert Muse told me, "Cuba has always been ambivalent about tourism. It provides a lot of low-skill jobs. Cubans deserve a better life than delivering cocktails to tourists."[20]

"The idea that Cubans will allow one million Americans to arrive on the day the embargo is lifted is fanciful," said Muse. "They have something like 40,000 hotel rooms that would meet U.S. standards. They have long-term relations with Canadian visitors and holidaymakers. Why would they want to automatically replace a French Canadian with an American from Detroit? They are certainly not going to allow a Cancún spring break atmosphere. It will be controlled by visas."

In any case, ending the embargo doesn't mean U.S. companies would rush to invest. They would be happy to export more to Cuba but would likely complain about bureaucratic rules and inefficiencies in the Cuban system when it comes to investing. Philip Peters, a free-market conservative at the Lexington Institute, told me that some Canadian and European corporate investors are unhappy with the business climate in socialist Cuba. "American companies would have the same reaction," he told me. "I bet 19 of 20 would say what a beautiful place, I would love to do business here. They would also say, what a bureaucracy, what a cockamamie system! How many meetings am I supposed to sit through before I can get a simple decision?"[21]

Some former U.S. policy makers, such as Colonel Wilkerson, advocate a gradual lifting of the embargo. "I think it should be carefully done, in accordance with the government in Havana. I would start with her agricultural products. I would lift the embargo for oil exploration... Over a period of three to five years, I would effect a complete rapprochement with Cuba."

Experts such as Wayne Smith and Philip Peters, on the other hand, advocate an immediate lifting of the embargo. "We should end the restrictions on Americans' contacts with Cubans," Peters told me. "That's the most important thing. Some day the American business community will decide it's important, and they will lobby for it." Ending the embargo, argued Peters, would also eliminate a major excuse for the failings in the Cuban system. "That would create a very interesting dynamic in Cuba because the embargo is gone. That would create ... pressure toward an opening."

Virtually every Cuban I have ever met, from the highest government officials to the most strident dissident, agrees the embargo should end. Would that expose the failures of Cuba's system? I asked Rafael Padilla, my former government press center guide in Havana. "I don't think so," he said with a smile, "But that's a chance we're happy to take."

7

Cuba's Controversial Domestic and Foreign Policies

EVEN BACK IN 1968, I WAS STRUCK BY HOW MUCH CUBAN revolutionaries emphasized their independence while increasingly relying on the Soviet Union. This applied to both domestic and foreign policy. By the time I arrived in Havana, the Soviet Union and China had split, with China undergoing its disastrous Cultural Revolution. Communist Party leaders in Czechoslovakia experimented with decentralization of the economy and political liberalization known as the Prague Spring. But their reforms ran afoul of the Soviet leadership. On August 21, 1968, Soviet tanks rolled into Prague.

Much of the independent left around the world, along with the Chinese Communist Party, denounced the invasion as unnecessary and hegemonic. Fidel Castro didn't immediately announce Cuba's views on the invasion, and the Cuban government allowed Czech demonstrators living in Cuba to hold pickets and rallies against it. Many progressives hoped that Fidel would criticize it as well.

On August 23, Castro gave a speech laying out the position of the Cuban leadership. They supported the invasion and called Czech leaders "counterrevolutionaries." Castro may have dinged Soviet leaders by asking rhetorically if they would also send troops to preserve socialism in Vietnam, but at its core, Cuba supported the invasion. Castro thought the market experiments in Prague were leading to a restoration of capitalism, the same thinking he had applied to small businesspeople in Cuba when he closed all their shops in 1968.

Castro was unapologetic for Cuba's stand even years later. "We were opposed to all the liberal economic reforms that were taking place there and in other places in the Socialist camp, a series of measures that tended increasingly to accentuate mercantile relationships within the heart of the Socialist society: profits, earnings, enrichment, material stimuli, all those factors that stimulate individuals and egos. That was why we accepted the bitter necessity to send forces into Czechoslovakia . . ."[1]

Given subsequent changes in China, Vietnam, and even Cuba, the Prague Spring hardly seems antisocialist today, let alone counterrevolutionary. But Cuba's leaders considered themselves staunch revolutionaries and upholders of orthodox Marxism. Those attitudes would have tragic results in other areas of Cuban foreign policy.

From the very beginning, Cuba's leaders sought to spread revolution in Latin America. In the 1960s, they gave political, economic, and military support to revolutionary movements in Bolivia, Venezuela, and elsewhere. Cuban leaders said they were acting out of revolutionary solidarity and often made decisions without first consulting Soviet leaders. That's how the Cuban military got involved in Angola in 1975.

By that time, the United States had been seriously weakened by the defeat in Vietnam and the Watergate crisis.[2] On April 25, 1974, leftist military officers overthrew the pro-U.S. dictatorship in Portugal, and those officers actively supported the independence of the former colonies of Angola, Guinea-Bissau, and Mozambique in Africa and East Timor in Asia. The United States was initially caught off guard but quickly mobilized its allies in the region. It then decided to take a stand in oil-rich Angola.

There had been three liberation movements in Angola: the pro-

Soviet Popular Movement for the Liberation of Angola (MPLA) led by Agostinho Neto; the CIA-backed National Liberation Front of Angola (FNLA) led by Holden Roberto; and the U.S.- and South African–backed Union for Total Independence of Angola (UNITA) headed by Jonas Savimbi. The three groups had negotiated an agreement to share power after independence scheduled for November 1975. But South Africa hoped to preempt the process by installing UNITA in power.

On October 2, 1975, South Africa invaded Angola from the south while Holden Roberto attacked from the north, having received backing from Zaire's dictator Mobutu Seso Seko and the CIA. Cuba backed the MPLA as the only legitimate revolutionary movement. When the MPLA asked for Cuban military assistance, Cuba sent in a planeload of commandos without consulting the USSR.[3] However, seeing an opportunity to expand its sphere of influence, the USSR quickly backed both the MPLA and Cuba with financial support, arms, and military advisors. Their combined efforts beat back both the FNLA and the UNITA/South African forces. South Africa was forced to withdraw but continued backing UNITA. The war quickly became a complicated and drawn-out civil war.

Cuba also sent thousands of troops to Ethiopia. In 1974, a popular rebellion led by military officers overthrew pro-U.S. dictator Haile Selassie. In 1977, Col. Mengistu Haile Mariam seized power, and Cuba hailed him as a revolutionary ally. But Mengistu's regime brutally suppressed the opposition, and he continued to attack Eritreans fighting for national liberation. (Eritrea had been a separate Italian colony, but Haile Selassie incorporated it into Ethiopia in 1952.) Ironically, Cuba had earlier supported Eritrean liberation; but in a Cold War switcharoo, changed sides with Mengistu's rise to power.

In 1977, neighboring Somalia invaded and occupied the Ogaden region of Ethiopia. Cuba sent troops, again with Soviet support. Officially, Cuba said it was defending Ethiopian sovereignty, but the intervention freed up Ethiopian troops to repress the Eritrean minority. Cuba kept troops in Ethiopia until 1989. A rebellion overthrew Mengistu in 1991 and, in a national referendum, Eritreans voted overwhelmingly for independence in 1993. So Cuba's participation in a major Cold War battle turned sour in the light of actual events.

U.S. officials also blamed Cuba for meddling in Grenada, a small island in the eastern Caribbean, but the circumstances there were quite different from Africa.

On the morning of October 25, 1983, a friend phoned to tell me the United States had invaded Grenada, a small island in the eastern Caribbean. This invasion signaled a major shift in U.S. policy because it was the first since the end of the Vietnam War. The Reagan administration claimed that the Soviet Union was planning to land MIG fighters on Grenada, and Cuba was storing weapons for shipment to Central American revolutionaries. Thus, once again, Cuba was accused of constituting a strategic threat to the United States. Unlike Angola and Ethiopia, however, Cuba had not sent combat troops.

I decided to go to Grenada to see for myself. *Mother Jones* magazine gave me credentials, and I flew on commercial jets to the island of Barbados. After transferring to a U.S. military plane, I arrived in the capital of St. George's just 11 days after the invasion. I was already suspicious about the U.S. version of events, but I was much less clear on the Cuban role. But first, some background.

In 1979, the New Jewel Movement (NJM) came to power in a peaceful coup against a pro-U.S. strongman, making the charismatic Maurice Bishop prime minister of the former British colony. Grenada made some impressive improvements in health, education, and social welfare. Literacy rose from 85 to 98 percent. Unemployment dropped from 49 to 14 percent. The leftist government established free health care and expanded free secondary education.[4]

Even after the invasion, I saw evidence of the popular gains at the sites of numerous child care centers and health clinics in poor neighborhoods. A journalist colleague and I traversed the entire island in a beat-up old car belonging to some new-found Grenadian friends. The NJM was not a pro-Soviet communist party, but an independent Marxist movement that developed close relations with Cuba. In interviews we learned that the Cubans had provided doctors, teachers, and construction workers to the island. Although Cuba had also sent a few dozen military trainers, the Cuban presence on the island was mainly civilian. Nobody I met in Grenada believed the U.S. propaganda that their island somehow posed a threat to the United States.

The Reagan administration had justified the invasion with a number of falsehoods. U.S. medical students studying on the island were supposedly in mortal danger, when, in fact, they were safe. The Grenadian government was expanding an airport runway supposedly to accommodate Soviet MIG fighters. In fact, Grenada, under contract with a British construction company, had been expanding its airport so tourist jets could land. The United States had been planning the invasion for some time, even carrying out war games on the Puerto Rican island of Vieques, which simulated later events in Grenada. Then, developments on the island gave the U.S. an excuse to attack.

Just weeks prior to the U.S. invasion, an ultraleft faction of the NJM captured and executed Maurice Bishop and a number of other leaders, claiming they were counterrevolutionaries. Fidel Castro said he had urged the NJM leaders not to kill Bishop, but to no avail. The Grenadian people were so shocked by the murder of a popular leader that they turned against the NJM hard-liners, and few offered resistance to the U.S. invasion. Cuban construction workers, some of whom were army and militia veterans, fought for several days. But the United States had overwhelming force.

The United States then installed a compliant government and kept 250 occupation troops on the island until 1985.[5] The free health care system and other social services were dismantled. But the U.S. occupying forces did have one priority project. They expanded the airport runway to accommodate jumbo jets for tourism.

Though forced out of Grenada, Cuba continued its military support for governments in Africa, with controversial results.

≡

After years of civil war in which outside powers had lined up behind Angola's two remaining political groups, South Africa sought a decisive victory. In March 1988, South African and UNITA forces surrounded a beleaguered MPLA-led force in the city of Cuito Cuanavale. In a series of battles, Cuban and MPLA troops beat back the attack. Within months, a peace agreement was signed calling for withdrawal of all foreign troops. Cuban officials argued that the battle contributed significantly to the ultimate withdrawal of South African troops from occupied Namibia and to the downfall of apartheid itself.

But other factors were at work as well. By the end of the 1980s, Soviet support for Angola was diminishing as the USSR spiraled downward economically. International sanctions and internal revolt were weakening the all-white government of South Africa. In 1990, Namibia became independent. But after the final Cuban troops withdrew in 1991, Angola's civil war continued. In 1994, South African apartheid ended when the black majority triumphed in free elections. In 2002, the MPLA killed UNITA leader Savimbi in battle. That led to an eventual political reconciliation between the MPLA and UNITA. Today, both groups participate in parliament with the MPLA holding the majority of seats.

Over a period of 16 years, Cuba sent 300,000 combat troops and 50,000 civilians to Angola, according to Fidel Castro.[6] Sending an army to fight on foreign soil is fraught with problems. Cuba's stated mission to protect Angola from outside invasion quickly morphed into support of one faction in a very long civil war, just as it did in Ethiopia.

Ultimately, the people of South Africa would have overthrown apartheid. Without foreign interference, the Angolan factions would have eventually reached the political reconciliation they finally achieved.

Castro supporters staunchly defend Cuba's actions in Africa. Many of these same folks are willing to rethink the Soviet impact on Cuba's economy. I would simply note that a country's domestic and international policies are always tied together. Support for an aggressive Soviet policy abroad was inextricably linked to a pro-Soviet economic policy at home.

===

In the 1960s, Cuba was full of revolutionary enthusiasm to transform the economy. In 1968, I traveled to the Isle of Youth, where Fidel Castro and other revolutionaries had been imprisoned. By then it was undergoing a major transformation. Orlando Bosch Salado, not to be confused with the terrorist of a similar name, was an 18-year-old university student when he volunteered to go to the Isle of Youth. He and other students lived communally, planted orange tree seedlings in the morning, and taught peasant farmers at night.

"I have incredible memories of those years," he told me years later.[7] "There was a lot of sacrifice and hard work. The food was awful. We earned 30 pesos per month and could only buy bread and omelets." At the official exchange rate, the peso was worth one U.S. dollar, but they received housing and other essentials for free. Bosch was enthusiastic about his year there. "I was a fanatic. I wanted to stay. We were young and very revolutionary."

I interviewed a leading Cuban Communist Party (PCC) official on the island. He said young people originally came to do hurricane relief, but stayed to teach and help with agriculture. They were building "communism" there, he said, because they were actually implementing Marx's goal of "from each according to his ability, to each according to his need."[8]

Other Marxists around the world considered communism an economic stage to be reached after many years of socialism and only after the worldwide defeat of capitalism. But according to Fidel Castro and Che Guevara, enthusiasm and revolutionary ideology could actually achieve communism on one island. Fidel Castro told French journalist K. S. Karol that young people on the Isle of Youth were making "a small cultural revolution." They were eliminating "every last vestige of the old mentality. . . It will be the first truly Communist island in the world."[9]

People such as Orlando did contribute mightily to improving education and food production. Today, the island produces a lot of the country's citrus crop. But it hardly became a "truly communist island." The PCC later dropped the whole theory. "I guess they were dreaming," said Orlando.

And therein lies a serious problem. Cuban leaders promoted a super-revolutionary ideology based on egalitarianism that ultimately undercut their own goals. For example, in the city of Cienfuegos I met a "communist construction brigade" building a fertilizer factory. Every worker earned the same pay, 200 pesos a month, regardless of skill. In other workplaces, workers did receive increased pay based on skill and seniority. But the differential was small. At first, revolutionary enthusiasm sustained the workers and farmers. But over time they lost the incentive to work hard or pay attention to quality. Too often, the Cuban leadership hoped lofty rhetoric and revolutionary ideas would transform the economy.

From the beginning, Fidel Castro and the Cuban leadership were highly suspicious of small businesspeople. In March 1968, the government closed all independently run businesses, whether restaurants, bars, groceries, or self-employed artisans. Unlike the chaos of China's Cultural Revolution, Cubans weren't jailed, assaulted, or killed; the suddenly unemployed people were offered jobs in factories or other state-run enterprises. In some cases, they were sent to rural areas to work. But in a matter of a few days, the economy was upended.

Castro considered the petit bourgeoisie (small capitalists) to be a source of counterrevolutionary thinking. He called them a "small segment of the population that lives off the work of others, living considerably better than the rest, sitting idly by and looking on while others do work; lazy persons in perfect physical condition who set up some kind of vending stand, any kind of business, in order to make 50 pesos a day."[10]

Orlando remembered those 1968 events very well. "We were romantic. All the people hanging out at bars were lumpen [criminal underclass] and needed to work. So they sent them to farms to work. Even carnivals were canceled." The closings of bars and clubs proved particularly controversial. Many Cubans disagreed with the policy. A teacher in Holguín told me, "Now young people can only go to cinemas or parks at night. The government could have eliminated the lumpen elements by requiring patrons to show work or student cards when going to a club."[11]

The "revolutionary offensive," as it was called, coincided with a national campaign to create *el hombre nuevo*, "the new man." It was an attempt to encourage new, revolutionary thinking but was also a crackdown on nonconformists. Black Cubans with afros, women with miniskirts, or men with long hair and tight pants became targets. Although the offensive to eradicate unorthodox appearances died down, small business suffered a mortal blow. Food became scarcer, state restaurants often served mediocre food with lousy service, and simple repairs on a house became a major headache. Far from eliminating counterrevolutionary thinking, the policies spurred even greater cynicism. They were partially reversed in 1993.

≡

In the late 1960s, Cuba had launched an ambitious campaign to become self-sufficient in food production. Before 1959, Cuba had been dependent on the United States for its food supplies, and it didn't want to repeat that experience. The government set up large state farms to manage the greenbelt. But over time, that proved a costly mistake. Orlando told me, "State farms aren't very efficient. There's little incentive to produce more and better-quality food. You got a lousy salary, so why work?" Many years later, Cuba did break up these greenbelt state farms as part of economic reforms.

But Cuba never became agriculturally self-sufficient, and in fact, became more dependent on the Soviet Union and Eastern Europe. In 1972, Cuba joined the Council for Mutual Economic Assistance (CMEA), also called COMECON, the trade association linking the Soviet Union to Eastern Europe and Vietnam.

During a 1972 Fidel Castro visit to the Soviet Union, Soviet President Leonid Brezhnev increased the price it paid for Cuban sugar, agreed to defer debt repayments for 15 years without interest, and offered $350 million in interest-free investment credits over the next three years.[12] Cuba provided sugar cane to the socialist camp. In return, the CMEA provided Cuba with two-thirds of its food and 50 percent of its energy needs.[13]

The system worked for about 15 years because the Soviet Union bought Cuban sugar for more than world prices and sold Cuban oil at subsidized prices. Cuba was able to sell some of the oil on international markets to raise hard currency, which in turn allowed it to import food, chemicals, and other much-needed products. On the streets of Havana, Soviet-made Ladas began to replace the clunky old American cars from the 1950s. Hungarian buses plied the streets of major cities, although their poor quality and tendency to break down infuriated Cubans. More food, clothing, and consumer items became available.

Unlike the Soviet Union, Cuba did maintain a sense of revolutionary enthusiasm among at least part of the population. Orlando, for example, graduated from university in 1971. With six months additional training, he went to work as a junior high principal at the age of 21. He told me, "It was hard but it was beautiful. This time, the food was great."

By the 1980s, Orlando was back in Havana working first as an inspector for the school system and later as a manager with the state petroleum company. "I had a company car and plenty of gasoline." He and his wife lived comfortably on their two salaries. They ate food using the ration system (rice, beans, chicken, etc.). But they also had enough money to buy from the free markets, which had reopened on a limited scale. "You could afford to buy at the free markets. There was no second currency, although owning dollars was prohibited." Cubans could stay at hotels and pay in pesos.

Economic statistics showed significant improvement during this era. From 1970 to 1988, Cuba averaged GDP growth of 4.1 percent, compared with 1.2 percent in other parts of Latin America.[14] Infant mortality dropped below 6 per 1000 live births, the lowest in Latin America.[15]

Orlando admitted that even in these relatively good times, certain items were tough to get. Cars were apportioned only to high officials or to a select few who absolutely needed to travel out of town for work. New refrigerators and air conditioners were impossible to buy. "A few lucky people got them through their trade union or work unit for exceptionally good work," said Orlando. The government didn't build enough new housing, and it was hard to make repairs or expand existing units due to a shortage of building supplies. But in the 1980s, the government created "micro-brigades": groups of ordinary people who learned construction skills to build their own housing.

Cuba's economic conditions began to seriously deteriorate as the Soviet Union lurched from crisis to crisis. Soviet President Mikhail Gorbachev eliminated the subsidized trade deals, and by 1990 Cuba was forced to buy petroleum products for hard cash on world markets. In 1991, the old Soviet Union dissolved. Cuba lost 80 percent of its trade.[16] The Cuban economy crashed.

The collapse of the Soviet Union, combined with the tightened U.S. embargo, hit every Cuban hard. In a 1992 interview, Gilda Zerquera told me, "We have to ride bicycles because there's no gas, sometimes carrying kids. Many factory lunch rooms have been shut down. Women have to fend for themselves to find food."[17]

From 1989 to 1993, Cuba's GDP dropped by 35 percent.[18] For Orlando, a supporter of the Revolution, the early 1990s were a disaster. His peso salary was suddenly worthless. From 1989 to 1998, the estimated real salaries of Cubans dropped by 60 percent.[19] It was impossible to buy certain foods. "In the early '90s, there were no fat people in Cuba," joked Orlando. "If you hadn't seen an old friend for a year, you wouldn't recognize him because people had changed so much physically. It was horrible. We had two cars, and we couldn't buy gas. All available gasoline went to hospitals, emergency services, buses, and so on. Our lunch at work was rice, beans, and plantains. We had electric blackouts all the time."

The economic hard times led to the *balseros* (rafters) emigration crisis of August 1994. After a series of boat and plane hijackings, Fidel Castro announced that Cubans were free to leave the island by boat or be picked up by Cubans from Florida. This coincided with a massive wave of emigrants fleeing Haiti, also trying to reach U.S. shores on rafts and makeshift boats. Eventually, the United States interned 14,000 Haitians at Guantánamo Naval Base, virtually all of whom were returned to Haiti. Some 30,000 Cuban *balseros* were also kept at Guantánamo, but they were eventually allowed legal entry to the United States.[20]

Starting in 1991, and faced with its worst crisis since the earliest years of the Revolution, the Cuban government instituted radical economic reforms. Before, the government had deemphasized tourism as a reflection of capitalist dependency. But Cuba signed numerous joint venture contracts with European hotel companies to remodel or build new tourism facilities. Tourism quickly became the number one source of foreign currency, surpassing sugar.

In September 1993, the government legalized small businesses such as restaurants, small hotels, and repair shops. Under the same law, the government leased unused state land to individual farmers. Agricultural co-ops made up of individual farmers began to replace state farms. Farmers markets were expanded and given much greater leeway to buy and sell food. Perhaps most significantly, Cubans living abroad were allowed to directly transmit remittances to relatives inside Cuba. Hundreds of millions, and ultimately over a billion dollars per year, came into the Cuban economy through these remittances.[21] The government established dollar stores in which hard-to-find items could be purchased for hard currency. In 1993, Cubans were allowed to legally possess dollars and exchange them for pesos for the first time.

The Cuban economy showed major improvements. Cuba's GDP was growing at between six and seven percent through the 2000s and hit seven percent in 2008.[22] During my 2008 trip, I was surprised to find shiny new Chinese buses plying the streets of Havana. They had significantly helped alleviate the city's chronic transport problems. During my month-long stay, I experienced only one blackout—a planned three-hour electricity outage. Kiosks called *agros* sold vegetables and pork every few blocks.[23]

Some international developments also helped improve the Cuban economy in the 2000s. High world prices for nickel and cobalt helped propel Cuban foreign currency earnings upward. In 2007, Cuba's nickel industry earned $2.7 billion, and for the first time exceeded tourism ($2.1 billion) as a source of hard currency.[24]

President Hugo Chávez of Venezuela shipped about 90,000 barrels of oil a day to Cuba at favorable prices.[25] Cuba paid for the oil, in part, by sending medical personnel to work in impoverished parts of Venezuela. In addition, by 2008 Cuba was directly drilling about 10 percent of its own oil. It discovered an additional 4.6 billion barrels of oil and 9.8 trillion cubic feet of natural gas offshore. Cuba sold concessions to exploit the reserves to Venezuelan and European oil

companies. Venezuela refurbished and reopened a long-closed petroleum refinery in December 2007, allowing Cuba initially to refine
60,000 barrels a day.[26] China extended favorable trade deals and low-
interest loans to Cuba, although nothing comparable to the old Soviet
subsidies.

===

The market reforms begun in the 1990s were successful but tentative.
Private restaurants became popular: they were named *paladares* after
a restaurant in a Brazilian soap opera. By law they had to employ only
family members and have no more than 12 seats, but some people set
up the restaurants in their homes, secretly hired professional staff, and
expanded beyond the seating limit. The *paladares* certainly served the
best meals at reasonable prices for foreigners. I still remember a lobster
dinner, including rum and beer, for $10 per person. Unfortunately, the
beer, rum, and lobster came from the black market, having fallen off
the back of some government truck. Such theft, combined with sus-
picions about the petit bourgeoisie, led to a crackdown. In December
1996, the government started a campaign to combat theft, rule violations, and evasion of the business tax.

Once again, Fidel Castro expressed his dislike of socialist free markets and small business owners. He sharply criticized the inequalities brought about by Cubans receiving dollars from abroad and from
small business corruption. "How I rue the day foreign-currency shops
were created, just to pull a little of the money that some people were
receiving from abroad and spending on highly desirable goods in
stores when there were tremendous scarcities across the island . . . In
addition some people were charging high prices for things they did
'off the books,' so they were earning several times as much per month
as one of our doctors . . . ."[27]

But the economic gap in Cuba is not between the parasitic petite
bourgeoisie and the working class. It was between Cubans with access

to hard currency and those who don't have it. A taxi driver or a hotel waiter legally earning Cuban Convertible Pesos (CUCs) might take home twice the monthly salary of a cancer surgeon.[28] That situation won't change until the Cuban economy produces more domestic products and is able to raise people's real wages.

Meanwhile, small business owners will have to get used to the risks and rewards that come with entrepreneurship. Over the years, I've met many Cuban business owners who complain bitterly that high government taxes are driving them out of business. Miami conservatives amplify those complaints and say the real purpose of the taxes is to restore the dominance of the state sector hotels and restaurants.

To try to figure out what was really going on in 2008, I paid a visit to an old friend who had operated a bed and breakfast. I met Christina Martínez in 1994, when I wrote a story about efforts to computerize the island's health care system. Later I met her husband, Jorge, an entrepreneur who could always find a discounted bottle of rum or box of cigars. To my great sadness I learned that Jorge, only 67, had died of heart problems the year before. It had happened suddenly, and Martínez remained heartbroken.

For almost a half hour she talked about the tragedy and how she has yet to get over it. They had been married for 35 years. She had closed the small B&B that Jorge and she ran since the 1990s. She explained that she just didn't have the heart to continue. But it was also an interesting example of how free enterprise works in Cuba in 2008. They lived in a nice home in the Miramar District. They converted three bedrooms into living quarters for guests. The government charged a flat tax based on the number of rooms and common areas used for the hotel. The government collected the tax whether or not the rooms were occupied. This has led some Cubans, and a lot of Miami conservatives, to denounce the system's inherent unfairness.

Martínez paid 340 CUCs in taxes per month for each room and an additional 10 CUCs for a garden porch used by customers. By law, owners are taxed on a maximum of two rooms even though, as in Martínez' case, she rented out three.[29] So she paid 690 CUCs per month in taxes. In addition, she had to pay for a housekeeper, natural gas for cooking, electricity, and similar expenses totaling about 50 CUCs per month. The B&B had charged 60–70 CUCs per night, depending on the room. So in order to break even, Martínez had to rent at least one room for 11 nights per month. Everything after that was profit.

Many Cubans, unfamiliar with free markets and tax systems in other countries, are outraged at these costs. Not surprisingly, they want to keep a higher percentage of their earnings. For a comparison, I phoned Angela Weston, owner of the Weston House B&B near Lassen Park in northern California. She was envious of any B&B that could break even after 11 days. It takes her at least 15 days to reach that point. As for the Cuban complaints, she told me, "Welcome to America."[30] Or, to be more accurate, welcome to the free market.

One can argue about whether the business tax rates are too high. But the Cuban government charged a flat rate business tax rather than one based on occupancy, fearing that hotel owners would simply lie about the number of paying guests. That hasn't stopped some entrepreneurs from lying anyway. Some declare that they rent only one room when, in fact, they rent two. Or they don't declare any rooms at all and run the whole operation off the books. Similarly, *paladares* limited to 12 seats suddenly discover chairs and tables for 10 more when enough patrons arrive.

The response by the government has been to crack down on corruption and rule violators, emphasizing the need for "revolutionary ethics." In November 2005, Fidel Castro announced a campaign against the "new rich," and even replaced gas station attendants with young, revolutionary-minded social workers in order to stop gasoline pilferage. But these intermittent campaigns haven't solved the problem.

That's because even the most stalwart revolutionaries must bend the rules to survive. The average salary of 400 pesos per month is the equivalent of about $16. Cubans get free medical care, education, rent, and subsidized utilities. They can buy a limited amount of subsidized food at very cheap prices. But without CUCs, it's almost impossible to find supplies to make household repairs or buy simple consumer goods, and difficult to find enough food.

≡

After the transfer of power in 2006, the acting president, Raúl Castro, began making quiet reforms. In the spring of 2008, Cuba made world-wide headlines by implementing a series of long-anticipated changes: Cuban citizens would now be allowed to stay in tourist hotels and own cell phones, computers, and microwave ovens. For years the U.S. government and conservatives in Miami had blasted Castro for these restrictions, but now that they had been reversed, those same critics quickly denounced the changes as meaningless.[31] You just can't satisfy some people.

How significant were the changes?

Since the beginning of the special period, Cubans were not allowed to rent a room in a tourist hotel. They could enter the hotels to meet with guests or eat a meal in the hotel restaurant. But they couldn't check in to stay overnight. Some Cubans called it "tourism apartheid." In April 2008, the government reversed the policy. But because tourist hotels cost upward of 50 CUCs per night, very few Cubans could afford them. Traveling Cubans continued to use *campismo*. *Campismo* is a generic term that includes what we would call camping facilities but also hostels and economy hotels in urban areas.

Cuba also legalized ownership of cell phones, microwave ovens, and personal computers. Miami conservatives had argued that Cuba restricted some of those items to prevent freedom of communication with the outside world. But Cubans have always been able to receive international phone calls on landlines, and those with hard currency can phone abroad. Some Cubans already owned cell phones by having a foreigner set up the account.

Cell phone restrictions weren't a question of political repression. The government worried about overwhelming the cell phone network if too many people signed up. So it issued administrative rules banning Cubans for owning cell phones. By allowing Cubans to own phones and by charging a high fee, the market regulated what had been previously handled by administrative fiat. Similarly, the government worried about the impact of widespread use of microwave ovens on the electric grid. After testing some energy-efficient models in one small town, the government legalized them for sale in Cuba. Once again, officials figured that the relatively high cost of the appliances would limit widespread use and thus wouldn't overload the system.

The reforms benefited relatively few Cubans, but they did remove some long-festering irritants. Many Cubans believed Raúl Castro would deliver bigger changes in the years to come. And, perhaps most significantly, the new administration tacitly admitted that administrative fiat doesn't always work. Limited free markets do.

Cuba, for all its very real economic problems, ranks fairly high in quality of life compared with other countries in the third world. According to UN statistics, Cuba has the 94th highest GDP per person ($6,000) of 193 countries in the world. It ranks 32nd in life expectancy (77.7 years) and has the second highest literacy rate (99.8 percent) in the world. The UN Human Development Index measures every country by life expectancy, education, and standard of living. In 2008, Cuba ranked 51st, putting it in the top one-third of all the world's nations.[32]

But ranking better than many third-world countries doesn't cheer a lot of people in Havana. Cuba clearly needs to make drastic improvements. The success of the reforms depends to no small degree on whether Cuba can feed itself. The island has become the world's largest experiment in organic farming, which, of course, has produced more controversy.

8

Food, Organic Farms, and Jewish Jokes

SIXTY-EIGHT-YEAR-OLD FERNANDO FUNES LOOKS RATHER unassuming in person. He stands five-feet-five-inches tall and wears frayed blue jeans and eyeglasses. When walking around the country-side, he dons a small, traditional Cuban straw hat. He looks more like a community college teacher than the father of Cuba's organic farm-ing movement. Funes campaigned for organic farming in Cuba even before its widespread adoption in the early 1990s. And since then he's become a hero to peasant farmers, agronomists, and government offi-cials. He also loves to tell jokes.

Funes asked if I had heard the one about a classified ad in the farm-ers' newspaper. It seems that a peasant farmer in Las Tunas province wanted to get married. So he placed a classified ad: "Farmer, age 33, seeks wife, age 30–35, preferably with own tractor. P.S. Send photo of tractor."[1]

I was tempted to tell him my Jewish jokes but decided to wait until we knew each other better.

I had gotten up at 4:30 a.m. and wandered around the darkened outskirts of Havana trying to find Funes's house. He lived on the west-ern edge of the city, not far from the Hemingway Marina. We were planning to drive to the city of Sancti Spíritus, where he was to be the keynote speaker at a conference of agronomists and farmers. Then we would spend some time interviewing organic growers.

Funes's car was in the shop. So I offered to provide a rental car if he could cover the gas expenses. We agreed. I expected we would stop at a gas station, and he would pay for the gas. Nope. When I arrived at the house, he had a 25-liter plastic jerry can full of gas. He also had a one-liter plastic soft drink bottle cut in half to use as a funnel. So, on the street corner near his house, in the dawn's early light, we hoisted the jerry can and aimed the gas in the general direction of the makeshift funnel. We managed to get most of it into the tank.

After breakfast we settled in for what would become a four-hour drive. Funes explained that Cuba has become the largest organic farming experiment in the world. In the 1990s, Cuba could no longer afford to import most chemical fertilizers and pesticides. The entire island mobilized its scientists, farmers, and even the army to develop effective organic production. Significantly, Cuba didn't face the market pressures that come with organic farming in capitalist countries.

In the United States and Europe, organic goods typically cost consumers 20 to 100 percent more than their nonorganic equivalent.[2] Organic food, indeed, costs more to produce because it's labor intensive and produced in smaller quantities. But some organic farmers and retailers want to boost their profits, thereby making organic produce unaffordable for ordinary people.[3] Organic food has become, to a large extent, a niche market aimed at well-to-do shoppers concerned about health and the environment.

In socialist Cuba, where there are no agribusiness interests or supermarket chains, it's a much purer experiment. There is no motivation to make more profit by charging a premium for organic food. Cuban consumers pay the same price whether or not it's organic. But wide-scale organic farming certainly presents problems. Insects and disease kill plants. Workers must be more knowledgeable. Organic farms often produce less per acre, and chemical use can increase production for some crops. Cuba faced a major question in the 2000s: can all-organic methods feed the nation or should Cuba rely at least partially on chemical fertilizers and pesticides?

Fernando Funes and I dug into this question by visiting Sancti Spíritus. But first we had to get there.

═══

If you plan to drive on Cuban freeways at night, I have one piece of advice: don't. You may or may not find street lights in Havana, but the main freeway to Sancti Spíritus has none whatsoever. It also has no signs to indicate curves and few indicating freeway exits. There are plenty of large potholes and lots of fog.

There is some good news. The '50s-era American cars and Russian Ladas from the '70s can only go about 40 miles per hour. So they stick to the slow lane. More good news: the horse-drawn carts pretty much stay to the side of the road, usually coming toward you. Funes told me that his car cracked up on one of the infamous potholes. It was in the shop for three weeks. "I call the body repair man," Funes told me, "and he tells me they don't have acetylene one day, and they ran out of metal parts the next."

That, of course, reminds him of a joke.

He asked if I knew the difference between socialist hell and capitalist hell. Actually I did. It's a joke I had first heard in the Soviet Union in 1990, but it probably goes back even further. I decided to play along. "No," I said innocently. "What's the difference?"

Funes tells the joke. Former Soviet President Mikhail Gorbachev dies and arrives in hell. The Devil tells him he has a choice of living in capitalist hell or socialist hell.

"What's the difference?" asks Gorbachev. The Devil says, "In capitalist hell we tie you to a stake, pour gasoline over you, and set you on fire. That continues throughout eternity."

"That sounds horrible," Gorbachev says with a shudder. "What's it like in socialist hell?" The Devil says, "We tie you to a stake, pour gasoline over you, and set you on fire."

"So what's the difference?" asks an incredulous Gorbachev.

"If I were you," says the Devil leaning closer, "I'd choose socialist hell. Some days we have no gasoline. Other days we have no matches . . ."

As the sun rose and the fog lifted, we pulled into Sancti Spíritus. It's a relatively small city with a population of about 135,000, famous mainly as a stopover on the road to the colonial city of Trinidad. We drove off the freeway and toward the local teacher's college, where the agricultural conference was being held. We passed food processing factories and lots of open fields. Sancti Spíritus reminded me of the agricultural towns of central California, except Cuba still has horse-drawn carts. They compete with cars, bicycles, and motorcycles for control of the streets. For one peso (five cents), residents could traverse the whole city in horse-drawn jitneys.

We pulled into the teacher's college parking lot, and officials quickly swarmed the car. My cautious driving had delayed our trip, and the conference was already an hour late. Some 150 people had been waiting for Funes's arrival. He quickly rushed into the auditorium and began his keynote address. The jocular, diminutive Funes was suddenly transformed. There in front of his colleagues, he became the famous agronomist. And I could see why he earned their respect.

In his speech, Funes placed Cuba's agricultural problems within a world context. Developing countries around the world are facing food crises. Oil prices are up, partly due to the U.S. war in Iraq, he said. Global warming and water shortages are affecting farming everywhere. Capitalist countries are "converting agricultural land to develop biofuels, which is a big mistake."[4] The Cuban government has decided not to convert sugar cane or other crops into ethanol, despite the potentially lucrative market, because of the disastrous environmental impact.[5] "Industrial farming is the world model and also wastes a lot of energy, which the world can ill afford to lose," said Funes. "By contrast Cuba is developing an alternative model of organic self-sufficiency."

As Funes talked, I remembered that in 1968 Cuba had also wanted to become self-sufficient in food. It planned to harvest 10 million tons of sugar cane, the largest in Cuban history. Virtually the entire country mobilized to plant and harvest cane, seriously disrupting other industries and food production. Although Cuba produced a record 8.5 million ton harvest, the effort was a disaster for the economy.[6]

It's not easy for any country to feed itself, let alone an island with limited resources and a hostile neighbor. Beginning in the early 1960s, the United States did everything possible to prevent Cuba from trading with Latin America and Western Europe. It even introduced biological warfare agents in an effort to destroy certain crops (see chapter 2). Partially in response, and partially out of ideological conviction, Cuban leaders turned to the Eastern Bloc.

Funes told me that Cuba copied the Soviet agriculture model in which small farms were almost eliminated in favor of large, state operations, where a single crop was grown with heavy use of chemicals. Those policies contributed to the ecological devastation of parts of the USSR. The ecology of Kazakhstan was ruined, for example, by massive diversion of water and use of chemicals for intensive cotton production.[7] Cuba also imported cattle from the Soviet Bloc with the intention of improving beef and dairy production. It was largely a disaster. "The animals were of very high quality but they came from temperate countries," explained Funes. "They didn't adapt to our climate."

As the Soviet Union declined economically and stopped the subsidized trade, Cuba's agriculture collapsed. Between 1989 and 1998, Cuban beef production dropped by nearly 50 percent because of the unsuitability of the cattle, the lack of feed grain, and the heavy use of bulls as draft animals.[8] Daily caloric intake for the average Cuban dropped from 3,100 calories in the late 1980s to between 1,800 and 2,100 calories in 1993.[9]

At the time of the crisis, the U.S. government could have provided humanitarian assistance. Instead, the United States cranked up the pressure in hopes of overthrowing the Cuban government. In 1992 Congress passed the Torricelli Act, which included a prohibition on food exports to Cuba. Torricelli told Georgetown University students that he wanted to "wreak havoc on the island."[10]

So, out of necessity, Cuba began intense, nationwide organic farming in 1993. In the first few years, pests and disease caused horrific damage. Cuba's vegetable production, for example, fell 34 percent from 1989 to 1994.[11] But Cuba's farmers kept trying. When the soil was properly prepared over time, and the crops were planted using pest-resistant methods, production came back. By late 1999, organic production in vegetables and tubers had returned to pre-1989 levels.[12] By 2005, Cubans were back to eating an average of 3300 calories per day.[13]

But many problems remained, as I found out in meeting with farmers. Funes and I drove out of Sancti Spíritus to a spread owned by organic farmer José Casimiro. We parked the car and walked about a half mile out to his 10 hectares (25 acres) of land. Wearing a straw cowboy hat and a green shirt with epaulets, Casimiro looked like a cross between a farmer and a rural cop. That's because he was. Before taking up farming full time in 1993, he was a highway patrolman. He's also become known as a farmer philosopher because of his impassioned, and sometimes esoteric, declarations about the organic lifestyle.

"We've embraced permaculture," Casimiro told me, using a word that I understood neither in Spanish nor English. He explained that he tries to apply environmentally friendly methods and socialist ideals to everyday living. He promoted permanent, pro-environment culture. "It's more than just organic growing. It goes to the sociology of the people. The women love the idea and participate in the farming.

That counts for a lot. Nothing contaminated leaves the farm, not even a drop of water."[14]

To illustrate his point, we walked outside where Casimiro showed off his land. A peacock strutted proudly next to a dairy cow, proving, apparently, that the animals were also proud of the farm. Casimiro grew mango, yucca, and plantains—and raised dairy cattle—all without the use of pesticides, artificial fertilizer, or hormones.

"In the 1930s and '40s, all the farms were organic by necessity," Casimiro told me as we walked through his fields. "Pesticides didn't exist. The land was very productive. Later they started using chemicals, and farmers thought it was good because it increased production." In that sense, Cuba followed the model of both capitalist and socialist countries, where chemical use supposedly reflected a natural process of industrialization. Casimiro's father had used chemical fertilizers and pesticides on the farm starting in the 1960s. But by 1993, when Casimiro inherited the land, he decided to follow government plans to grow organically.

He noted that some crops in this region, like tomatoes, require a lot of chemicals. Other vegetables, such as squash, grow much more easily in the Sancti Spíritus climate. "The best result for me was learning how to grow naturally. We let weeds grow, but they repel some animals. We use compost as fertilizer. Instead of wooden fences, we have 5,200 meters of fence made from trees and plants." It's called a "living fence."

In the 1980s, 80 percent of Cuban food production came from state farms and 20 percent from small farms working with co-ops. By 2008, it was about 52 percent state farms and 48 percent small farms.[15] Funes argued that small, diversified organic farms work far better than the state farms. "Integrated farms give you the possibility to produce many things together: animals, plants, and trees. For example, the animals give you milk and meat. And they supply dung in order to fertilize the plants."

In the United States, organic production can be expensive because of the high cost of manual labor. In addition, the U.S. agricultural system favors large corporate farms through use of subsidies. In 2008, the U.S. farm bill called for $5.2 billion annually in direct payments to agribusiness despite record harvests and profits.[16]

But in Cuba, labor is cheaper. Funes said that it's actually more costly to use artificial fertilizers and other chemicals because Cuba must import them and pay in hard currency. "Oil costs have skyrocketed. All the inputs, such as machinery, fertilizers, and pesticides, require oil. They are very expensive." Chemicals, Funes argued, also create long-term costs by damaging the environment. "They are destroying all the micro flora of the soil. We are using chemicals that destroy the ozone in the atmosphere. We have this crazy climate change." Funes advocated 100 percent organic production and said the Cuban experience shows it's practical.

But some government officials disagree. And this is where the argument gets interesting.

These officials argue that Cuba doesn't produce enough food at affordable prices. Cuba's economy has improved over the past few years. Tourism and nickel production have generated hard currency. The country can now afford to buy some chemical inputs from abroad. Santiago Yáñez, a Ministry of Agriculture official, supported organic farming but argued that the country must embrace whatever technology produces the most food.

"I think it's harder to use organic methods when you've got a lot of land and a lot of equipment. It's much easier for small- and medium-sized farms. I don't think we can abandon agriculture using chemicals and go all organic. It's impossible. It's possible to use both and still respect the environment."[17]

Funes conceded that intensive use of chemicals can increase production in the short run. But, he said, it's a long-term disaster. "Under the mono-cropping system, you put fertilizers on the land. The earth becomes inert. It becomes like a cement floor because it doesn't have life. You don't have birds around; nothing in the environment helps it live. If you put 200 kilos of nitrogen [on the land], you have to put 225 the next year, and 250 the next year in order to produce the same amount. It's inefficient."

I tried to find out how many farms in Cuba are 100 percent organic. Cuba has an inspection system for the nearly 4,000 organic gardens in the cities. But the island has no official certification system for all farms. Funes estimated that about 30 percent of Cuban farms are completely organic, 40 percent combine organic techniques with some chemical inputs, and 30 percent use mostly chemicals with few organic techniques.

Casimiro concedes that some farms in his area have gone back to partial use of chemicals. "It's the culture we've had for many years. It seemed to function well. You need less manual labor. You don't have to know a lot about agriculture to use chemical methods. But to do organic farming, you have to be very knowledgeable. It's much more complicated."

A pattern is emerging in Cuban agriculture. Large-scale farming, such as sugar cane and citrus, tends to use chemicals. Small- and medium-sized farms grow tobacco, lettuce, and other vegetables using all organic methods.[18] So what does this mean for Cuban consumers?

━━━

During my month-long stay in Havana in March 2008, my food consumption was considerably better than a typical Cuban's. But I visited all the places ordinary Cubans get their food: subsidized food stores, farmers' markets, restaurants, and supermarkets. I came to understand how to shop. In theory, everyone in Cuba gets an adequate amount of food each day. But getting that food, to borrow a Cuban phrase, "es muy complicado."

Some Cubans get subsidized meals at their workplaces, and all

Cubans get a ration book. With it they can buy one kind of bread at government bakeries. These rolls cost one peso each. Friends bought the tasty rolls for me. They are healthy because they don't have preservatives. They also go hard within 24 hours.

Two blocks from my apartment sat a government food store that also required a ration book. A chalk board listed two dozen staples at very cheap prices, ranging from rice to cooking oil to pork. One liter of milk a day was supposed to be available for each child. Cubans often live together in large, extended families. So the combined ration cards, including family members who died or moved away, would provide a lot of food if all the subsidized items were actually available. But during my numerous visits, no more than 10 items were actually in stock, and never the same 10.

So Cubans also shop at farmer's markets. The Army's open-air markets provided the best quality produce at the cheapest prices. In the early '90s, the FAR (Revolutionary Armed Forces) made a decision to grow its own food. By having recruits work on farms, labor was cheap and FAR was able to sell the excess to the public. For the last few years, urban agricultural co-ops have set up kiosks in neighborhoods throughout Havana. The organic vegetables and pork were much fresher and of higher quality than at the state stores. But, once again, availability varied from day to day. One kiosk in my neighborhood sold about 10 fresh produce items, including garlic, lettuce, tomatoes, and pineapples. If there was anything green—whether lettuce or green beans—I bought it immediately because it probably wouldn't be there the next day.

I bought a very large head of lettuce, a clove of garlic, and a large fresh pineapple for 27 pesos (just over $1).

That's a lot of money for a working-class Cuban. I met one woman who wanted to buy a pork roast. It would have cost one-sixth of her monthly wage. So she had the butcher cut it in half. Beef was never available. Chicken, eggs, and fish had to be obtained elsewhere.

And that's where the informal, gray-market system comes into play. Every day, vendors came by my apartment carrying large bags and shouted to the neighbors. They offered everything from fresh fish and lobster to eggs, mangoes, pineapples, and beer. In some cases, they had caught the fish themselves and were selling it legally. In other cases, the food or liquor was stolen. One government official told me that there's tremendous theft from hotels, particularly from the all-inclusive resorts in Varadero, where it's hard to keep an accurate inventory. Food, liquor, and building supplies are stolen, then sold and resold until they reach ordinary people.

Everyone in the neighborhood knew about the vendors and their purloined goods. There's a CDR (Committee for the Defense of the Revolution) block captain down the street. These captains are supposed to guard the neighborhood against crime. I saw no efforts to stop the vendors. Marta Núñez, a professor at the University of Havana, told me that her Communist Party meetings often discuss this question of corruption. The government is trying to crack down on the organized theft rings and not pursue the street vendors. Whether to buy from the vendors "is a very personal decision," Professor Núñez told me. "You buy or do not buy, but you don't turn them in, because they are the lowest point of a chain. You really want the people at the top."[19]

But this widespread, small-scale corruption corrodes Cuban society. Ordinary Cubans face the option of buying stolen goods or not getting enough food. Such options don't do a lot to improve faith in socialism. Cubans with access to CUCs can shop at hard currency stores that offer a lot more choices and much better-quality products. As mentioned before, for many years Cubans couldn't legally possess dollars or other foreign currency. But that only created a black market. The government legalized dollars in 1993, and then in 2004, as the dollar weakened internationally, made the CUC the legal second currency. Cubans can spend pesos or CUCs.

One day I visited the *Supermercado* at 70th Street and 5th Avenue in

Havana's Playa neighborhood. Before 1959, Playa was an upper-middle-class district with fine homes and tree-lined avenues nestled near the beach. It still has some of that quality because the government maintained green street medians and parks. New tourist hotels and office buildings have sprung up near the beach. The *Supermercado* is one of the best-supplied markets in Havana, and as such, is very revealing.

One section is kind of a short-shrift Kmart with towels, bedding, hardware, and all manner of non-food items. Another section sells liquor. The food section is enormous by Cuban standards, with 10 aisles filled with food. An entire aisle on one side had nothing but mayonnaise! That item was hard to find in other stores, and some home cooks made it from scratch using cooking oil and eggs. Other aisles were filled with canned goods, rice, beans, and pasta.

I bought enough groceries for a week. It cost about 25 CUCs, roughly the equivalent of a month's salary for a middle-income worker. So these hard currency markets were very pricey. But they are full of Cubans. I didn't hear a single foreign accent during numerous visits to several such markets. Cubans earn CUCs because they work for foreign enterprises in tourism, or they receive remittances from abroad.

There's a tremendous food gap between those with access to hard currency and those without. The Cuban government is trying hard to increase food production and lower prices. It has increasingly turned to Cuba's 250,000 small farms and co-ops. To see how these reforms are working, I traveled west of Havana to the city of San Cristóbal.

≡

Starting in 1993, the government began leasing out state farmland and other unused government land to individual farmers. Farmers could sell some of their produce to the state and the rest on the free market. The Barrera family in San Cristóbal directly benefited from these changes. I had first met the Barreras in 1992, when I produced a one-hour NPR documentary. In 2008, I rented a car and drove out to see them again. Heading westward, I went from freeway to city street, to dirt road, to rutted dirt road, and finally to a very rutted, dirt road.

The Barrera house sits just outside the San Cristóbal city limit. Roosters crowed and pigs grunted in their pens a few feet from the house. We took a three-minute walk and found ourselves in lush, tropical fields where 85-year-old Fernando Barrera grew yucca and plantains. Like many of his generation, Barrera remained a staunch supporter of the Revolution. For all of today's food shortages and other problems, he remembered life was much worse before 1959. His family has always owned this land, but they were hardscrabble farmers. "We didn't have piped water or electricity on our farm," he told me. "The situation is much better today. We have access to many more things, even things like soap. We got a motor to pump water for our house."[20]

In the early '90s, Barrera leased some extra land from a nearby state farm as part of the nationwide reform. It nearly doubled his acreage. He decided what to plant, then made an annual contract with the local government-sponsored co-op. "The co-op buys our products at fixed prices. All the prices are good. For example, we sell pigs for 1,150 pesos per kilo [$21 per pound]." He said that was a very good price, historically. He could sell the leftover production either to the co-op at the fixed price or to the *agros* at market rates. The co-op also provided transport to get the produce to market. Barrera's standard of living had improved a lot since my 1992 visit, allowing him to expand his house, build new pig pens, and otherwise improve the property.

Raúl Ruiz, a Ministry of Agriculture official, told me that small farms have proven to be more productive for many types of food. "People are able to produce a big quantity of foodstuffs in small places. They are the owners of this production. The salaries and benefits are very high. This is good for the producer, and for the customer, too. The products are fresh, but prices are lower."[21]

That might seem obvious in a capitalist economy, but for socialist Cuba it's a major conceptual breakthrough. For years Cuba had tried technical solutions, such as improved farming methods. But Ruiz says that wasn't the problem. "Maybe it's a social and political problem. You must open the market, open the land, the way a person can grow vegetables, products, and animals. Increasing the market may result in obtaining more products. It's a political solution."

But allowing market flexibility in the context of a centralized socialist economy isn't easy. The Cuban state owns the vast majority of farmland. Even privately owned farms can't be bought and sold. This prevents land speculation, but it also means farmers can only pass their farms on to relatives after they die or trade them for another farm.

The system for supplying farmers was still geared for large state farms or co-ops rather than individual farmers. Barrera gets farm implements, seeds, and other supplies at a co-op store.

But other farmers complained to me that the stores often lack items they need, and there's no other legal place to buy them. In early 2008, the government started allowing farmers to buy supplies with CUCs for the first time.

Deputy Agriculture Minister Alcides López also said that co-ops will get more government credit and have greater leeway in what to plant and where to sell produce.[22] These partial reforms have given rise to a debate in Cuba: how to increase food production without encouraging speculation and corruption.

≡

In the United States and other industrialized capitalist countries, farming was oligopolized long ago. A few large multinational corporations such as ADM and Cargill control the vast majority of agricultural production and distribution. Chain stores such as Safeway and Wal-Mart dominate sales. Big corporate farms are mechanized and use environmentally destructive methods. It's hard to remember what a real tomato tastes like unless you pay double for those grown in special hothouses. Industrial farming practices have led directly to serious pollution and contribute to global warming.[23]

This corporate domination, however, doesn't even guarantee that everyone is fed in America. We have plenty of food in the stores, but the U.S. Department of Agriculture (USDA) reports that 10.9 percent of Americans are "food insecure." That means 12.6 million households were unable to buy necessary food for at least part of the year.[24] That's in part because where incomes are low, food prices are high. For example, in my hometown of Oakland, California, Safeway charged *more* for the same advertised products in the working-class flatlands than in the upscale hill areas. Safeway faced competition in the hills and little in the flatlands. Corporate concentration means higher prices for the poor.

Capitalist food production can also become irrational. During times of economic recession, farmers are forced to destroy food rather than sell at below the cost of production in order to keep prices up. Farmers spilling milk onto highways shocked Americans during the 1930s Great Depression. But it's not just an historical oddity. In April 2008, the Canadian government announced plans to pay pork producers to destroy 10 percent of their breeding stock in order to stabilize prices.[25]

In theory, socialism is supposed to eliminate those irrationalities and inequalities. Without multinational corporations seeking to maximize profits, a socialist government should be able to provide lots of good-quality food at affordable prices. But it hasn't worked out that way in Cuba. Why?

Beginning with Stalin's government in the Soviet Union, traditional Marxists have preferred large state farms. Such agricultural enterprises were supposed to use the best scientific techniques to produce food and pay good wages to farm workers. A central plan would guarantee adequate production but not overproduction. That model was passed along to Eastern Europe, China, and Cuba.

I visited China for the first time in 1981. Some basic foods, such as rice, were in short supply. But within 10 years, after China dismantled the state farms and leased the land to peasant farmers, food production shot up. Whatever other very real problems China faces, it has largely overcome food shortages that had plagued the country for hundreds of years.

Cuban officials have shifted a lot of vegetable and meat production away from large state farms. But state farms continue to produce citrus, sugar cane, and other crops.

Cuba would not be adopting all of the Chinese reforms, officials told me. They seemed prepared to muddle along with a mixed system of state farms and co-ops. Agricultural official Ruiz said, "Chinese culture is very different from Cuban culture. I don't think you can make an extrapolation from the Chinese to the Cuban experience."[26] Ruiz pointed out that China's success relied in part on foreign investment, which, so far, hasn't come to Cuba on a large scale. "Everyone in the world wants to invest in China. That is not the case in Cuba. We have a shortage of investment. It's hard to maintain development with our own resources."

And that's where the U.S. embargo reenters the picture. In 2000, the United States started selling food to Cuba, but the terms were extremely harsh. The United States required Cuba to pay cash in advance, but prohibited Cuba from selling goods to the United States that could earn that cash. As mentioned before, the Helms-Burton Act not only banned American investment in Cuba, but it also sought to prevent other countries from investing as well.[27]

In 2007, Cuba spent $1.9 billion to import food, and the United States did everything possible to make sure Cuba doesn't earn enough hard currency to pay for it. Agricultural Ministry official Santiago Yáñez said those policies hurt Cuba's food supply. "We're very close to

Political prisoners after liberation from Batista's jails, January 1, 1959. Photo: Lee Lockwood

Raúl Castro was an early leader of the Cuban Revolution, as seen here with revolutionary icon Che Guevara. Raúl's independent history as a leader made his 2008 permanent transfer to the presidency much easier. Photo: Lee Lockwood

Militia women arrive from the Sierra Maestra mountains, 1959. Women actively participated in the Cuban Revolution. Cuba has made a conscious effort to guarantee equal pay and fight discrimination, but machismo remains a major problem. Photo: Lee Lockwood

From its earliest days, the Cuban government was able to mobilize over a million people at a time for rallies and demonstrations in the Plaza de la Revolución. Even former U.S. diplomats and anticommunist dissidents admit that the Cuban government retains significant popular support. Photo: Lee Lockwood

Fidel Castro temporarily turned over power to his brother and the country's vice president, Raúl Castro, in 2006. Fidel resigned the presidency in 2008, an unprecedented move by a revolutionary founding father in the modern era. Photo: Associated Press

Members of SDS board the Mexico City plane bound for Havana in August 1968. They departed full of revolutionary enthusiasm and sharp questions about Cuba. Photo: Reese Erlich

Reese Erlich, age 21, during the 1968 SDS trip to Cuba. Reese went on assignment for *Ramparts* magazine. Photo: Reese Erlich

CIA-trained Orlando Bosch fired a bazooka at a Polish freighter in Miami, sent death threats to European leaders, and has been implicated in the 1976 bombing of a Cubana Airline plane. Miami honored him with an "Orlando Bosch Day" in 1993. In this 1965 photo, the FBI had just arrested him on extortion charges. Bosch is now a free man living in south Florida. Photo: Corbis

Police escort Luis Posada Carriles to court in Panama, where he was charged with plotting the assassination of Fidel Castro in 2003. Carriles also admitted to organizing the bombing of Havana hotels in 1993, which killed an Italian tourist. He has been implicated in numerous other terrorist activities, including the 1976 Cubana Airlines bombing. He lives in Miami. Photo: Associated Press

Ernestina Ford, daughter of a seamstress, became a college professor. Black Cubans are among the strongest supporters of the Revolution, even if some remain critical of continuing racism on the island.
Photo: Reese Erlich

Fernando Barrera, 85, owns his own farm near San Cristóbal in western Cuba. He benefitted from the agricultural reforms that leased state land to individual farmers. He sits on his front porch with his great-granddaughter. Photo: Reese Erlich

Agronomist Fernando Funes (left) is the father of Cuba's organic farming revolution. José Casimiro (right) is known as a farmer-philosopher because of his advocacy of organic farming. Casimiro lives near the city of Sancti Spíritus in central Cuba. Photo: Reese Erlich

Reese Erlich interviews farmer Humberto Hernández, who is now partially paid in hard currency for his milk production. Agricultural policy is critical to the survival or fall of the Cuban government.
Photo: Julia Adame

Piano tuner Ben Treuhaft works on a piano at a Cuban music school. His campaign "Senda Piana to Havana" donates pianos to Cuba, combing the tactics of Mahatma Gandhi and Groucho Marx.
Photo: Reese Erlich

The Buena Vista Social Club performs at Carnegie Hall in 1998. The front row (left to right): Eliades Ochoa, Juan de Marcos, Ibrahim Ferrer, and Compay Segundo. Contrary to popular myth, almost all of the Buena Vista musicians were successful artists before the CD. After release of the film, they became internationally famous.
Photo: Associated Press

José Fuster, known as the Picasso of the Caribbean, has turned his Havana neighborhood into a living museum by painting murals and erecting sculptures up and down his street. Photo: Reese Erlich

the U.S. It makes sense to trade. Cuban products could easily ship to the U.S. The U.S. could invest here."[28]

Top agricultural officials admitted that, as of 2008, Cuba imported 50 percent of its total food supply.[29] Ruiz said Cuba is not likely to be self-sufficient anytime soon. "We are trying to provide the foodstuffs at very low prices, trying to maintain the social equity. It is very difficult. I don't think it will be achieved in a short time."

≡

While Cuba wrestled with the very real issue of agricultural reform, Fernando Funes and I returned from our trip to the countryside.

Driving back from Sancti Spíritus to Havana during daylight hours on the same road, we made much better time. Although the potholes were still there, the darkness had created many more in my mind than actually existed. We saw maybe 20 other cars on the road during our entire three-hour return drive, mostly older cars creeping along in the right lane. I got used to driving between two lanes, moving over to avoid possible potholes and then crossing lanes without signaling, all the time hitting 70–80 miles per hour.

I learned that, by law, drivers must stop at railroad crossings. I then learned that some of these railroad tracks cut across the freeway, a first in my experience driving in various parts of the world. Rarely did I see signs indicating a railroad crossing coming up, and nothing as sophisticated as a clanging signal. When I accidentally crossed the railroad tracks at 65 miles per hour amidst a general outcry from Fernando and his friend, there was only one politically correct response: "oh sh-t."

As the afternoon waned, I realized I had just spent two very intense days with Fernando. I felt it was time to tell him a Jewish joke. I realize it's an old joke. You may have heard it at a bar mitzvah. But I was sure it hadn't made the rounds in Cuba.

Two old Jews are standing outside of a temple, I said in my best Spanish. Fernando leaned forward with a critical ear.

I was, after all, going *mano a mano* with a champ.

"I have a sad story to tell," continued the old man. "My son, my only son, I gave him a good Jewish upbringing. He went to Hebrew school, had his bar mitzvah at age 13, and was confirmed at 16. Then he converted to Christianity."

"Funny thing you should mention it," said the other old man. "My son, too. Let's consult with the rabbi to get his advice."

They go inside the temple and tell their sad tales to the learned rabbi. "Funny thing you should mention it," he said. "My son, too. Let's us pray to G-d for guidance."

They pray, bobbing back and forth in the davening motion of orthodox Jews. Suddenly, there's a crack of lightening and an invisible hand rips the roof off the temple. A deep voice comes out of the heavens. "Funny thing you should mention it . . ."

I finished the joke and there was dead silence. Neither Fernando nor his friend from the Dominican Republic said a word. Cuba is an atheist country, and I assumed Fernando was no practicing Catholic. But for a moment I feared that I had deeply offended some lingering Christian sensibility. Then an American traveling with us burst out in laughter, and said, "I get it. G-d is Jewish."

After a moment, both of the Latinos joined the uproarious laughter. They didn't take the joke as an insult to their culture. They just didn't get it.

Sometimes I think Cuban agricultural reform is the same. Cubans are trying to understand a new concept, and they just don't get the joke, yet. But they will.

9

The Real Story of the *Buena Vista Social Club* and Artistic Freedom

DURING ONE OF MY TRIPS TO CUBA IN THE LATE 1990S, I found out something disturbing. Most Cubans had never heard of Desi Arnaz. The Cuban American singer and costar of *I Love Lucy* is a household name in the United States. Yet, he's virtually unknown in Cuba. I was determined to find out why. I asked every Cuban I met—on street corners, at farmers' markets, and in rural towns. I asked workers, farmers, and intellectuals. One woman thought she knew the name, but he turned out to be a neighborhood truck driver, not the puffy-sleeved, conga-drumming maestro.

I began to suspect the worst. Perhaps the government considered Desi Arnaz a counterrevolutionary. His films, TV shows, and even his name had been erased from Cuban history like so many Soviet encyclopedia entries during Stalin's rule. But I kept asking everyone I met. Finally, when I finished interviewing 65-year-old Communist Party official Leonel Borrego about another topic, I casually asked about Desi.

"Desi Arnaz and Lucille Ball, yes, yes, I have seen them in many pictures. [He was a] very famous artist, Cuban artist, the same as Caesar Romero. He was a Cuban also." Borrego noted that Arnaz had left Cuba at a very young age, so the Cuban Revolution never thought of him as a counterrevolutionary. In fact, Cubans were very proud of what he accomplished.[1] Arnaz and Romero were "very, very famous artists and very good ones. All those pictures were broadcast in Cuba." As it turned out, younger Cubans had never heard of Desi Arnaz because Cuban TV never reran *I Love Lucy*. Think about it: how many Americans would know about Desi without the benefit of reruns?

Mystery solved. I filed a story for the public radio show *Common Ground*, and everyone got a good chuckle.[2] But the incident got me thinking. I could have stopped investigating after half a dozen interviews and filed a speculative story about government suppression of the memory of Desi Arnaz. That happens all the time with reports from Cuba. Take, for example, the widespread myths about the *Buena Vista Social Club* CD and film.

═══

Eliades Ochoa, the cowboy-hat wearing singer/guitarist from the *Buena Vista Social Club* CD and movie, welcomed me into his Havana house in 2008. He had flown in from Santiago the day before and was off to the Dominican Republic the following day. So I was lucky to catch him. Standing at about five-foot-five and with a weathered face, Ochoa looks like a short, aging cowboy. The image is complete when he dons his black Mexican cowboy hat, which also makes him look about five inches taller.

For about an hour I chatted with Ochoa about the vast changes facing Cuban artists. Cubans usually talk about before and after the 1959 Revolution. Ochoa talks about before and after the *Buena Vista Social Club* CD. It catapulted him from a successful career into the stratosphere of world renown. He now owns houses in Santiago, Havana, and Madrid, where he stays part of the year while on European tours.

Such wealth was rare before the 1990s. Although musicians were relatively freer than other Cubans, the government still restricted international travel. "I didn't work abroad for the first time until 1981," Ochoa told me. "I did a Caribbean tour. It was impossible to dream about traveling the world. Now the dream has come true."[3]

The government lifted most travel restrictions on Cuban musicians in the 1990s as part of an effort to garner more political support and earn hard currency. American mainstream media and politicians would have us believe that Cuban artists still face massive human rights violations and would defect from the island at the first opportunity. But, interestingly enough, none of the Buena Vista Social Club musicians have ever done so. Because they can travel freely, Ochoa and many other artists remain in Cuba. "I don't think about living in another country," Ochoa told me. "I have everything here: my family, my house. I feel good here. I have no desire to live elsewhere."

The Buena Vista story, and the myths that grew up around it, reveal a lot about the relationship between the government and the arts in Cuba.

The Buena Vista Social Club is the single most internationally recognizable face of Cuban music. The 1997 CD and 1999 documentary film not only took the United States by storm, but also made traditional Cuban music famous around the globe.[4] The original *Buena Vista Social Club* CD happened by accident. Blues guitarist and record producer Ry Cooder went to Cuba in 1996 to record another project. When that fell through, he got together with Cuban producer and band leader Juan de Marcos. They assembled some veteran musicians, many of whom played classic songs from the 1940s and '50s.

Cooder, who admitted he knew nothing about Cuban music at the time, simply selected tunes that he liked. The CD is an unexpected mix of Cuban musical styles, something like issuing an American CD with country, pop ballads, and Dixieland jazz. Many people think that Buena Vista Social Club was a band. It wasn't. The musicians were assembled just for that recording, and they played their own styles.

But international audiences loved it, and the CD went on to win a Grammy in 1997.

Cooder then convinced German director Wim Wenders to shoot a documentary around the recording of an Ibrahim Ferrer CD and the musicians' performance at Carnegie Hall. Interspersed with concert sequences, Wenders shot absorbing footage of Old Havana and interviews with the seasoned musicians, who talk at length about their careers.

There's a great shot near the beginning: 92-year-old Compay Segundo, outfitted with his ever-present Panama hat and eight-inch cigar, arrives in the Marianao district of Havana in the back of a vintage convertible. He tells the camera it should be easy to find the building that housed the Buena Vista Social Club from 1932 to 1962. As it turns out, no one can quite remember where it was.

Then there was the sequence with Ibrahim Ferrer singing softly in his cramped apartment, pouring a libation of rum at the small Santería shrine on his mantle.[5] The film came to U.S. theaters in 1999 and was an immediate art-house hit, hailed by critics as "magical" and "life affirming." The Buena Vista Social Club has evolved into a brand name, with many individuals and groups grabbing a piece of the action. Anything with the name draws huge crowds. Ochoa told me, "Now the whole world knows me. If a concert poster says 'Eliades Ochoa, one of the Buena Vista Social Club,' the theater is full."

The Buena Vista phenomenon resulted in lots of positive publicity for Cuba, but after the release of the film, another story began to emerge. The U.S. media focused on the rags-to-riches tale of impoverished musicians whose wonderful music had been forgotten. *New York Times* critic Peter Watrous wrote, "When Cooder first encountered these musicians in Cuba in 1996, they were disillusioned. Some had abandoned music altogether . . . A year later they had won a Grammy."[6] Watrous even blamed the Castro government for the decline of traditional Cuban music. "The music, which predates the Cuban Revolution, was ignored by the state . . ."

It makes for a great back story and neatly fits into anticommunist stereotypes about Fidel Castro. There's only one problem: it isn't true.

For starters, almost all of the Buena Vista participants were successful working musicians. Several were outspoken supporters of the Cuban Revolution, if reporters had ever bothered to ask. It's true that traditional Cuban music had lost popularity, but that reflected changing musical tastes, not a government conspiracy. So how did these myths about the Buena Vista get started? They began with the Wim Wenders documentary and attendant publicity.

The film follows a definite pattern. As Wenders interviews the musicians, they describe their careers prior to 1959. Then the film skips the next 37 years and describes the impact of the *Buena Vista* CD. Audiences are left with the impression that the musicians had no careers after 1959 and that they were forgotten until Cooder's CD rescued them from the crumbling slums of Havana. In publicizing the film, Wenders emphasized the rags-to-riches storyline, which was quickly picked up and further distorted by some reporters.

A reviewer for the Mr. Showbiz.com website wrote, "Amazingly, many of these musicians haven't picked up an instrument in years. They were wandering the streets when Cooder happened upon them." U.S. critics, and other reporters who filed reams of follow-up articles, rarely bothered to ask the Buena Vista Social Club musicians themselves. So what's the real story?

One member of the original Buena Vista ensemble, Ibrahim Ferrer, was indeed poor and retired. He had been reduced to shining shoes for neighbors to supplement his meager musician's pension. Pianist Rubén González, who performed actively until the mid-1990s, had retired at age 75 and lived modestly. But everyone else was a working musician. Several, such as Eliades Ochoa, Omara Portuondo, and Compay Segundo, were quite famous in Cuba and performed abroad. I've spent years tracking down the Buena Vista Social Club musicians to ask what they thought of their portrayal in Wenders's film and its wider impact on perceptions of Cuba. Their responses might surprise you.

≡

Back in 1999, I found pianist Rubén González at his newly painted apartment in central Havana. The street was filled with people, bikes, and kids. The paint had long ago faded on most of the homes, but the wrought-iron balconies were intact, wonderful examples of the city's 150-year-old Spanish colonial architecture. González passed away in 2003 at the age of 84. But back in 1999, tourists would stop by his home unannounced. He was easy to find. If you were within two blocks of the apartment, you just asked anyone standing in the street. They'd point the way.

González and his wife, Eneida Lima, welcomed me into their home and left the front door open, hoping for some fresh air on a hot Havana afternoon. Their house was decorated with kitschy knick-knacks they'd picked up during their world travels. González looked a bit scraggily, his wiry arms poking out of his T-shirt. He was friendly and loquacious, like everybody's favorite grandpa. But his memory was slipping, the first signs of the dementia that would eventually overtake him. Sometimes he couldn't remember a question I'd asked moments ago. But he was absolutely lucid on certain topics. He said he could remember every piano piece he'd ever played. And he sat down at his electric keyboard to prove it.

The *Buena Vista Social Club* CD did reenergize his career, but he was well known before its release, particularly among the older generation. González told me he had been a supporter of the July 26 Movement in the 1950s and sent money to Cuban revolutionaries from Venezuela, where he was living at the time.[7] He had a successful career in the 1950s and became even more famous in the '60s and '70s.

After retirement, his old piano fell apart. So for about a year before *Buena Vista*, González had practiced daily at a neighbor's apartment. He also regularly visited the nearby Egrem recording studios. He didn't know that record producers Ry Cooder and Nick Gold were there one day planning what would become the *Buena Vista Social Club* CD. They pulled up chairs and sat in rapt attention as González played the piano for them.

"I didn't utter one word," González told me, pausing for effect. "I didn't leave, either."

Cooder was impressed enough to feature González on several tracks and on some of the numerous spin-off CDs he produced later, including one ironically titled *Introducing Rubén González*. Cooder has earned the Buena Vista musicians' admiration because, González told me, he respects Cuban music and because he made sure they received royalties from their recordings.

Whereas the musicians respected Cooder, they were far less pleased with Wim Wenders. "Frankly, I don't like the film," said Eneida Lima, González's wife of 46 years. She leaned forward in her vinyl-covered chair and wagged her index finger sideways in a familiar Cuban gesture for "no." She said the film gives the impression that the musicians were all poor and despondent prior to recording the CD. She told me that Rubén was performing, including tours of Mexico, until he retired at age 75.

Lima also criticized Wenders for focusing on the older, dilapidated neighborhoods of Havana, the streets strewn with trash and stray dogs. "What was the reason behind shooting the worst parts of the city, the worst neighborhoods, with people in the worst dress?" she asked.[8]

Mario Jorge Muñoz, a cultural reporter for the Havana daily newspaper *Juventud Rebelde* (*Rebel Youth*), thought he knew the answer. In 1999, Muñoz ushered me into his office, where an ancient, window-mounted air conditioner wheezed chilled air into the newsroom. A few reporters pecked away at 386-PCs, which passed for hi-tech in Cuba in those years. Muñoz wore a traditional shirt known as a *guayabera*. He said Wenders shot mostly in the oldest parts of Havana and favored grainy, black-and-white cinematography in an effort to recreate the atmosphere of prerevolutionary Cuba. "He saw only old Buicks, Fords, and Chevrolets," Muñoz said. "He's stuck in a time warp in the 1950s, which I think is the Havana remembered by some Cubans living outside of Cuba."[9]

Muñoz was an easygoing 30-something reporter, but he was anything but easy on Wenders. He criticized the film for leaving out mention of Cuban music and musicians after 1959, which, he said, led some film critics in the United States to draw the conclusion that the Cuban government had discouraged them from playing music.

I don't know if Wenders went out of his way to distort the musicians' histories through omission. Perhaps he thought talking about Cuban music under socialism would be too controversial. But by leaving out that side of the story, and filming mainly in the run-down parts of Havana, Wenders ended up distorting the Cuban reality, even if unintentionally. He also did a disservice to Ry Cooder, who kept his own musical presence on the CD to a minimum. Cooder is front and center in the film, way out of proportion to his musical contribution.

Even singer Ibrahim Ferrer, who generally liked the movie, still had misgivings. I interviewed him in 1999. During the filming of the documentary, he was retired and living in a small apartment. In the film, he sounded resigned, even fatalistic. But his life improved markedly in subsequent years. Ferrer died in 2005 at the age of 78.

After the phenomenal success of the original CD, a solo CD called *Buena Vista Social Club Presents Ibrahim Ferrer*, and numerous foreign tours, Ferrer earned enough money to move out of his old apartment and into a roomy house. But he still didn't have a phone, a common problem when people changed homes in Cuba. So, of necessity, I showed up at his house unannounced at 9:30 on a Tuesday morning. Bad timing.

The 72-year-old Ferrer and his wife had been up until five in the morning, partying at a friend's house. But after much pounding on the front door and a hurried explanation, he agreed to an interview.

We sat down in his comfortable living room. It was clearly going to be another humid, 95-degree day, and the lanky Ferrer was relaxed and bare-chested in his loose-fitting sweatpants.

Before the *Buena Vista* CD, Ferrer never enjoyed the same popularity as Rubén González or Eliades Ochoa. He was a backup singer for many years with a moderately well-known band called Los Bocucos. He retired in 1995 at the age of 68. He said the movie accurately describes his impoverished situation at the time. In general, he told me, he liked the film but thinks it failed to put his and other Cubans' economic situation into a wider context.

"Yes, I was bad off," he said. "It's due to the U.S. government economic blockade of Cuba. If it weren't for the embargo, there would be more musical activity. We would have more opportunities, and the economic situation would be better. The American public has to realize that it's partly because of the U.S. embargo that we're in such a bad situation."[10]

≡

A number of the *Buena Vista* CD songs are traditional *son* (pronounced *soan*), the rhythmic Cuban music that Americans best remember from the 1940s and '50s. Think of men with puffy sleeves shaking maracas as they did on *I Love Lucy*. Mambo and modern salsa have their origins in Cuban *son*. But traditional *son* is a lot more popular internationally than it is in Cuba. Ferrer said in the film that *son* is in danger of disappearing altogether in Cuba.

Actually, it's a bit more complicated than that. During each of my trips since 1968, I've heard traditional *son* played on the radio and performed live. The Cuban government promotes *son* in tourist spots because it remains popular with foreigners. Walk through Old Havana and virtually every restaurant features a live band playing *son*. After the success of Buena Vista, some young Cubans started listening to *son* once again. But most prefer *reggaeton*, *timba*, and other modern dance music.[11] Many Cubans see *son* as old sombrero, much the way Americans look at Dixieland jazz.

González, Ferrer, and others involved in the Buena Vista Social Club were pleased with the renewed international interest in their music—even if they were puzzled by it. "I don't know how it happened because I had done those songs 17 years before," Ferrer told me. "They were remakes of old songs. I just can't explain why they became popular." At the Smithsonian Institution in 1986, Ochoa and Compay Segundo performed exactly the same kind of music later featured on *Buena Vista*, but the Smithsonian didn't even bother to issue a CD at the time.[12]

Ochoa remains philosophic about Buena Vista's success. "The *Buena Visa Social Club* came out at a particular moment. The promotion was very good. And the film helped a lot. The sales of CDs shot to over a million after the film."

I think the CD became a hit for a number of reasons. The tunes are timeless. Audiences don't have to understand Spanish to feel the rhythm of "Chan Chan" or to be moved by the unashamed romanticism of "Dos Gardenias." The CD evokes nostalgia for a seemingly less complicated era. It also was released just as Americans were becoming more aware of Cuba. The Clinton administration was loosening the embargo slightly. More Cuban musicians were touring the United States; more Americans were visiting Cuba. The *Buena Vista Social Club* came just in time to ride the wave of renewed interest in the island.

But for all its success and publicity, one part of the story remains virtually unknown internationally.

The original Buena Vista Social Club was a nightspot that opened in 1932 in the Marianao district of Havana. It was a segregated, all-black club. With American support, successive Cuban governments made sure that Cuba's posh nightspots, casinos, and hotels admitted whites only.

"In response, Afro-Cubans formed their own social clubs," says journalist Muñoz. Some of the great black musicians of Cuba played at the Buena Vista and at other clubs formed by Afro-Cubans.

Afro-Cuban retiree Lázaro Martínez told me he used to visit the Buena Vista. "We had social clubs, but they were divided according to color and income. Black working people like me had to go to the Buena Vista Social Club to enjoy ourselves. In those days, meetings or dancing between whites and blacks wasn't welcomed. Whites were on one side, blacks on another, and mestizos on another."[13] The Cuban government closed the segregated social clubs by 1962 and decreed that Afro-Cubans could enter any club or hotel. The Buena Vista Social Club closed, as did the era of segregated night spots.

The wonderful musical traditions embodied in Buena Vista now continue in Cuba's innovative music education system. Teachers find talented youngsters at an early age and encourage them to apply to specialized music academies. Kindergarten through university studies are high quality and free.

The government converted the old Havana Country Club into two music schools. The clubhouse once echoed with the sounds of the spiked golf shoes of dictator Fulgencio Batista and Vice President Richard Nixon. In those days, of course, the club was all white and all male. These days, the racism and sexism have gone the way of the fairways and putting greens.

The old country club houses the National Music School (high school) and the Superior Art Institute (ISA, university). During a visit to the high school, conga drummers competed with clarinetists in a cacophony of individual practice sessions. Fifteen-year-old Giselle Garía exuded the enthusiasm typical of students. She told me she wanted to graduate and study at the ISA. "I want to get my degree in piano music. Piano, piano, always piano! That's what thrills me. I want to be a professional pianist playing classical music. I may end up being famous, I don't know."[14]

The school's assistant director, Violetta Pérez, told me, "Art in Cuba is for everyone, without barriers. Starting at age 8, they can study piano, violin, and cello. At age 10 they can study percussion and guitar. We recruit from around the country based on competitive exams. The ones who do the best are the ones with the most talent. And then they are qualified to study here."[15]

These schools have graduated some of the country's finest musicians, including pianist Chucho Valdés. In a radio documentary I produced for NPR's *Jazz Profiles*, Valdés told me that when he studied at ISA, he consciously prepared to be a teacher as well as a professional musician.

"We prepare the students not just to be musicians but teachers as well," said Pérez. "They study a full range of courses from esthetics, to psychology and Spanish. They study music theory, as well as their own instruments.

As with many institutions in Cuba, the school's infrastructure needs a lot of work. Students don't have enough instruments. Student Garia told me, "The quality of the pianos isn't very good. Some are really old. Others are out of tune." Students from out of town were housed in crumbling student dorms. The rooms hadn't been painted in a long time, and the plumbing leaked. The campus needed a lot of maintenance.

That's a pretty good description of Cuba's subsidized arts system in general. The government pays artists good salaries and they produce high-quality art that ordinary people can enjoy. But you have to look beneath the surface and understand some of the history.

Since the early 1960s, all Cuban writers, painters, musicians, and other artists belonged to associations such as the National Cuban Writers and Artists Union (UNEAC). These associations judged if the young university graduates were qualified to join, based on their work.

Once members, they received a salary commensurate with their age and experience. Until the early 1990s, talented artists enjoyed excellent salaries by Cuban standards.

In return for their government salaries, musicians performed inside the country without additional compensation. Painters exhibit their works; filmmakers make films. Government support for the arts means low admission prices at the box office. In 2008, Cubans could attend world-class jazz, popular music, ballet, or symphony concerts for five pesos; foreigners paid five CUCs.

When musicians traveled abroad, they collect salaries, but the state took a hefty chunk. The government associations argued that the artists received regular salaries, so the associations were entitled to a large share of any fees earned. There was no system for receiving domestic royalties. Until recently, artists, with a few rare exceptions, could not independently sell their art outside the country.

In the early 1990s, the government revamped the system. Cuban artists still received their peso salaries in return for work inside Cuba. Those salaries had become almost worthless, however, and artists sought to make money abroad. For the first time, the government allowed them to negotiate their foreign appearances. Government-sponsored companies began to act as international agents. A festival manager or club owner in Europe, for example, paid money to such a company, which kept a fee, usually about 20 percent. The musicians received the rest. A similar system existed for university professors teaching or speaking abroad, with the university keeping up to 50 percent of the fee.[16]

At the end of the year, artists, like other Cubans, pay income tax on foreign and domestic earnings. One musician showed me his income tax form, which consisted of two pages. It's a progressive tax system. Anyone earning less than 2,400 CUCs a year pays nothing. Those earning 2,400-6,000 pay 10 percent with a sliding scale upward; people earning 60,000 CUCs or more pay the maximum, 50 percent.

I'm sure that all Cuban artists—like their counterparts around the world—report their income honestly and completely on their tax forms. There doesn't seem to be much effort by the government to verify it though.

≡

Cuba has never followed the Stalinist model of strictly controlling the arts, where even listening to unauthorized music could land citizens in jail. In a 1961 speech, Fidel Castro coined a famous phrase that art, and political opinions in general, "within the Revolution" would be encouraged, whereas art that was "against the Revolution" would be suppressed.[17] But the definition of what was "within the Revolution" has shifted over the years. In 1968, the country was in the midst of a vibrant, revolutionary experiment in the visual arts. Cuban posters had become famous throughout the world, as had films such as *Lucía* (1968) and *Memories of Underdevelopment* (1968).[18]

But that period also witnessed repression. I came across an unusual example that was typical for the era. The Cuban Jazz Club was founded in the 1940s by a group of Havana residents enamored of American jazz. The mostly black Cubans met in each other's homes to listen to bebop, then considered avant-garde. Paulina Ugarte, who helped establish the club, was a retired teacher when I interviewed her. "We listened to Dave Brubeck, Stan Getz, Stan Kenton, and Charlie Parker. We got records from the States with some of those great musicians. We used to have listening sessions. We'd ask, 'What do you think of this drummer, of this bassist, or this pianist?' But we also enjoyed dancing very much."[19]

The Cuban Jazz Club grew in popularity and started meeting in clubs. But then in 1960, the revolutionary government formally disbanded the group. Jazz club member and retiree Lázaro Martínez explained. "Many members of the government believed that to be fond of American music was some kind of betrayal of the Revolution. So we had to keep away from the club. People were afraid to be involved in something where you could be considered an American agent."[20]

Jazz was considered counterrevolutionary music, a view that had percolated down from the Soviet Union under Stalin. No one was jailed for listening to jazz at home, but the music schools, radio stations, and concert halls were prohibited from playing it. That ban ended with the emergence of Irakere in the early 1970s. That band featured young musicians who later went on to fame: Chucho Valdés, Enrique Pla, Oscar Valdés, Paquito d'Rivera, and Arturo Sandoval. Irakere combined jazz with elements of Afro-Cuban and other indigenous music.

As guitarist Pablo Menéndez later told me, "Suddenly jazz was transformed from the counterrevolutionary music of imperialism to the lyrical sounds of the oppressed black masses of the United States."

Thus, jazz became acceptable, but the government had forgotten about the Cuban Jazz Club. Members continued to meet in private homes, wearing out the grooves on their LPs. Then things changed in the early 1990s. Cuba was in turmoil. Tens of thousands of *bolseros* left the island on rafts. The Cuban government changed a number of policies in order to bolster popular support. The Cuban Jazz Club was reconstituted in 1994, along with dozens of similar groups.

They met at community centers, played old LPs or cassettes, and danced the jitterbug or disco. Martínez told me that no other music has quite captured the combination of melody and rhythm that they hear in '50s jazz. "That music is magical. Every person has his own problems. We have many problems. Once we hear this music, we forget about them. We get together, we dance, we sing, and we do things that really are very special."

For a contemporary view on artistic freedom in Cuba, I visited José Fuster, known as the Picasso of the Caribbean. He lived in the Jaimanitas district of Havana, a seaside community on the far western flank of the city. Seagulls whooshed overhead and the smell of the sea wafted through the streets. He had decorated some dozen homes on the street near his house with huge ceramic murals. Large arches in front of each house combined the surrealism of Pablo Picasso with the architectural beauty of Spain's Antoni Gaudí.

Fuster told me that starting in the early '90s, censorship of the arts had loosened up for those working "within the Revolution." Havana boasted a number of independent art galleries that were allowed to sell paintings to Cubans or foreigners. "There are limitations on art in Cuba. No one can open a gallery with pornographic art. You can't speak badly about the government." I asked him what happens to artists who criticize the government. They aren't thrown in jail, he said. "Nothing happens to them. They don't have to close their galleries."[21]

On the other hand, their work isn't publicized or promoted through official channels. "I know artists whose works were critical of the government," said Fuster. "The Cuban press just says, it's 'interesting work.' They don't give any details. And they won't show it on TV."

Artists working within the Revolution have joined other Cubans in complaining about the country's economic situation. That was apparent at the UNEAC convention in 2008, the first such meeting in 10 years. Dalia Acosta, a reporter for the Inter Press Service (IPS), wrote "Among the problems discussed were hard currency-only sales of Cuban music and films, the lack of venues for dance music and singing, meager royalty payments for authors, and the lack of resources which threatens Cuban television production."[22]

By 2008, Cuban artists said they were much freer to create than in previous eras. This certainly didn't square with the image in the United States of brutal repression and artists anxious to defect at the first opportunity.

In the cable TV movie, *For Love or Country: The Arturo Sandoval Story*, the embattled trumpeter flees political persecution for freedom in the United States. The fictional film, based on the life of Cuban trumpeter Arturo Sandoval, is typical of the tales that fuel mainstream U.S. media, about artists who face totalitarian human rights violations on the island and seek political asylum at the first opportunity. [23]

Before the 1990s, some Cuban artists and intellectuals did leave the island under very difficult circumstances. The Cuban government limited travel abroad, and the musicians were accompanied by government officials who sought to deter defections. All Cubans who emigrated without permission were banned from returning. Later, the policy was changed to prohibit visits home for five years.

Some musicians and dancers have publicly defected in recent years. In November 2004, 43 members of the *Havana Night Club* show defected publicly while in Las Vegas.[24] Salsa singer Isaac Delgado left Cuba to live with his family in Florida at the end of 2006.[25] Other musicians have left quietly to live in Mexico or Europe.

The vast majority of Cuban artists leave the island for the same reasons people from other underdeveloped countries leave their homelands. Money and career advancement are a powerful lure. Bill Martinez, a San Francisco attorney who has helped countless Cubans arrange for visas to perform in the United States, told me the bright light of hope quickly dims. "Cubans are driven by the attraction of better money. But when they get here, it's not that easy."[26]

Cuba has modified its travel policies for musicians since the early 1990s. Politically outspoken critics of the government, such as trumpeter Arturo Sandoval, are still banned from visiting. But noncontroversial exile musicians, including such well-known performers as jazz pianist Gonzalo Rubalcaba and drummer Horacio "El Negro" Hernández, have returned to play in recent years.[27]

Ironically, the American government prohibits virtually all Cuban musicians from performing in the United States. Toward the end of the Bush Jr. administration, Cubans were free to play anywhere in the world except the United States of America.

10

Women, Gays, and Machismo

THE WOMEN STOOD IN THE KITCHEN BOILING VEGETABLES and brewing strong, syrup-sweet coffee. Outside, the men prepared to slaughter a pig and do other manly things. It was 1992 in an old house just outside San Cristóbal in western Cuba. Thirty relatives of the Barrera clan had gathered for a family reunion, and I was invited.

Family matriarch Aracéliz Barrera stood at the center of this bustling activity. Her plain cotton dress and lined face made her look older than she was. She commanded the respect of the family with a firm voice. "We're doing various jobs here. Somebody's preparing the garlic. Outside, the women are peeling the yucca. Others are preparing the pork skin to make *chicharrones*."[1]

Roberto chased an ill-fated pig around the yard. Roberto had a craggy face and beard almost as prickly as the pig's tough, hairy skin. The chubby porker didn't stand a chance once Roberto grabbed its leg. José Luis Hernández had carefully sharpened his knife. It takes skill to kill a pig quickly, and Hernández had done it many times. Proudly, he thrust once, directly into the pig's heart.

Other men were also quite busy—playing dominoes. As a friendly gesture, they asked me to join the game. In Cuba, dominoes is not child's play. It's intense and very competitive. Normally Cubans are very friendly to foreigners. But when I played a domino out of turn, the stares became very frosty. I also got strong reactions when I asked why only men were playing.

"Usually men and women play dominoes," said one Barrera cousin. "But in a situation like this, where the women are cooking, then this happens. This isn't a question of discrimination. This is a Cuban idiosyncrasy." The Barrera men are touchy because Cuban law actually requires men to share equally in the housework and child rearing. Passed in 1975, the Family Code guaranteed women's and children's rights and called for full equality in marriage. So the men didn't want to appear to be violating the code. But they clearly felt guilty.

Women have made tremendous advances in Cuba since 1959. Burdened with a long history of machismo and discrimination on the island, the Cuban Revolution faced an uphill battle.[2] Before 1959 only 20 percent of women worked;[3] by 2002, it was 45.6 percent.[4] By 2007, some 65 percent of college graduates were women, as were two-thirds of all professionals.[5] Figures such as these led Fidel Castro to boast, "We are the least *machista* [macho] country . . . in the hemisphere. We have created a culture of equality and respect."[6]

But many dozens of interviews with Cuban women suggest that's an overstatement. Many Cubans are struggling to survive economically, and women face the added burden of working, doing the housework, and raising the children. Divorced couples sometimes continue to live in the same apartment because of the country's housing shortage. Prostitution, once virtually eliminated, has permeated the big cities and tourist locales.

But I also found an optimistic attitude among many Cuban women. They recognized the real progress being made and saw their lives improving economically; they also were continuing the struggle for women's rights. To understand this phenomenon, we have to return to that rural house outside San Cristóbal.

≡

During that visit in 1992, I accompanied Barrera family members on a drive through a seemingly interminable number of back roads in San Cristóbal. Even back then we stopped periodically to utilize the Cuban equivalent of Google Maps: we would slow down and ask passersby, "Where's Panchita's house?"

The Barreras had no phone, so in 2008 I had no idea how to reach them. I phoned a professor in Sydney, Australia, who was married to the daughter of Panchita's cousin. Follow me so far? The good news was he remembered me and the 1992 visit. The bad news was he had divorced his Cuban wife. But they remained on good terms, and she and I exchanged some emails just days before my trip to the island.

She gave me a phone number in Havana for her mother who was Panchita's cousin, I think. Cuban family trees get quite complicated. Anyway, I phoned Ernestina Ford, her mother, and the number didn't work. By now, I'm despairing of ever finding the Barreras. At that point I decided to simply drive out to Ford's house in Villa Panamericana, a half-hour drive east of Havana.

The town was built to house athletes from the 1991 Pan American games. It boasted a new sports stadium and neatly laid-out, carefully numbered streets. The government later gave the concrete apartments to working-class Havana residents as subsidized housing. But the town hadn't been maintained much in the intervening years. So by 2008 the streets were cracked and full of potholes; the apartments definitely needed repairs and coats of paint.

I also figured out why Ford's phone didn't work. Getting telephones installed has been a major headache in Cuba. Residents sometimes wait years to get a new landline. But a Cuban-Italian joint venture company built up a cellular network in the early 2000s, and the government began providing residents with a special, low-cost cell phone that could be used only in the home. Ford had just received one, but the service hadn't yet started.

Ford well remembered our 1992 venture to San Cristóbal. She immediately agreed to go there again because she hadn't visited those relatives for two years. I agreed to rent a car and come back to her apartment the following Sunday. I gave her a plastic bag with some laundry detergent and shampoo, items in short supply at the time. She thanked me and suggested I put together some gifts for the Barreras as well.

Early Sunday morning we jammed six people into a compact Kia, filled the trunk with gifts, and went careening around Villa Panamericana in search of the highway. Ford knew the way to the Barrera house—at least in theory. We immediately made a wrong turn trying to find the *carretera* (freeway). We drove a few blocks and then stopped to ask some pedestrians. They said we had been on the right road after all. So we made another U-turn and went back the way we came. We meandered through several small towns until we found the freeway. I know we meandered because on the way back, we returned in about half the time.

Several hours later, we were welcomed into the Barrera home as long-lost family. Everyone remembered the 1992 visit and even brought out photos from the event. I left a bag of presents on a table. It included laundry detergent, cookies, and rum. Someone discovered the rum and asked if it was for them. They proceeded to pour straight shots for anyone interested. The bottle was gone within an hour. It was 11 a.m. I had seen the same phenomenon in other visits throughout the island. Back in the early '90s, I thought that people were desperate for a drink because of the rum shortage. But now that rum is readily available and cheap, I realize that some people just like to start drinking early.

I started catching up on what everyone had been doing over the past 16 years. Their lives had certainly improved economically. Aracéliz Barrera worked as a nurse in Caracas, Venezuela, on a two-year contract. Her husband, the famous pig killer José Luis Hernández, was a manual worker in a tobacco processing plant. Aracéliz Barrera received enough money to live in Caracas plus 50 CUCs per month banked in Cuba, a fortune by Cuban standards. She bought hard-to-find items in Caracas and brought them home during vacations. So the family had a laptop computer, a new refrigerator, and a television set. Hernández proudly showed me his cell phone. "Our lives have gotten much better."[7]

Other Barreras, though not as successful as Aracéliz, had improved their lives economically. The government had raised prices for their crops, and they were able to sell more to the farmers' markets. Barrera's parents had added a room to their house and were making other repairs. But after spending a day with the Barrera clan, I concluded that relations between the sexes seemed to be about the same as in 1992. Women still did the cooking. The men brought in yucca from the fields and oversaw the barbeque. Panchita Cuni, age 72 and mother of Aracéliz, told me, "My husband works hard. But no, he doesn't help me in the kitchen. He's macho and doesn't help," she said laughing. "It's the same for my sons. They don't like to cook."[8]

Passage of the Family Code was supposed to educate the population to combat machismo, but it wasn't implemented in practice, according to Mariana Ramírez, head of the Women's News Service for Latin America and the Caribbean, an independent feature news service in Havana. Men may help with a particular task but don't provide the on-going assistance necessary to genuinely share housework, she said. "Men continue to say, I am going to *help* you with the kids or with housework. But it's not really a matter of *sharing.*"[9] Professor Marta Núñez, another expert on women's rights, disagreed.

≡

I had first met Professor Núñez when she was a sociologist at the University of Havana researching women's rights issues. During a 2008 visit, I walked up to her house in the Vedado section of Havana. It was freshly painted. We sat in the living room, windows open, enjoying a late afternoon breeze. In the intervening years, Núñez had worked as a Cuban diplomat in Moscow in the 1990s and then returned to the University of Havana as a consulting (adjunct) professor.

Back in the late '80s, before the country's economic crisis, Núñez spent 60 days living with and studying male-female relations among 75 poor families who worked in farming, food processing, and fishing. Back then, she told me, "things were changing. I'm seeing the seeds being germinated," to implement the Family Code.[10]

She observed that husbands shared certain household tasks but that wives made the assignments. "They were the ones to decide who is in charge of what household chores. They don't completely trust the quality of men's work. Some of their husbands and children did the shopping. Very few men washed clothing."

Then came the economic crisis of the early '90s. "It was a very tough moment for society as a whole, but especially for women," said Núñez. "We had to figure out how to wash without detergent and sometimes without water. We had to learn to cook food without almost anything. We had to learn to medicate people without any medicine. We made it through with many different survival strategies. I interviewed professional women and asked them what they had done. We sold ice. We made sweets and sold them. Some used their cars as taxis. Some of them rented rooms. Some typed theses."[11]

Núñez acknowledged that men and women are still not equal at home or in the workplace. But she saw the glass as half full, not half empty. She argued that women's roles were strengthened after surviving the depths of the crisis. "As we came out of the special period, the women felt an increase in self-esteem. It was acknowledged by the rest of society. It gave us a kind of pride to be able to help our families during all those years."

She emphasized that the Family Code needed updating, particularly concerning gay rights, an almost taboo subject in the 1970s. "There is a need to acknowledge homosexual relations. The Family Code talks about a union founded by a man and woman. Now the Family Code should include a union by two people." Some Cuban leaders had already endorsed expansion of gay rights. Culture Minister and Politburo member Abel Prieto said, "I think that marriage between lesbians, between homosexuals, can be perfectly approved and that in Cuba that wouldn't cause an earthquake or anything like that."[12]

=====

The Cuban government's early policy toward homosexuals was reactionary and repressive. Starting in 1965, the government rounded up many homosexuals and other people who didn't serve in the armed forces and sent them to UMAP (Military Units to Aid Production) camps, where conditions were quite harsh. Gays were purged from the University of Havana. The writers and artists union (UNEAC) and foreign leftists sharply criticized those actions. The UMAP camps were dissolved in 1968.

In his 2006 spoken autobiography, Fidel Castro continued to justify those early actions, although admitting some mistakes. He argued that in the early '60s, because Cuba faced immediate military threats from the United States, the government needed to mobilize the entire country. Homosexuals were excluded from mandatory military service, but they had to serve the country in some way. Gays, along with some members of pacifist religious groups, were sent to UMAPS.

Castro said, "In a visit I made to Camagüey, touring one of the agricultural installations, I became aware of the distortion the original plan had been subjected to, because I can't deny that there were prejudices against the homosexuals. I personally asked for a review of that issue. Those units lasted only about three years."[13]

Castro admitted that Cuba's culture of machismo magnified prejudice against homosexuals. But, he asserted, "I can most assuredly tell you that the Revolution never encouraged those prejudices. On the contrary, we encouraged a struggle against various kinds of prejudice."[14] But that's not what Castro told American journalist Lee Lockwood in 1965. Then, Castro said, "I will be frank and say that homosexuals should not be allowed in positions where they could exert influence on young people." He said that homosexuals couldn't be communists because "a deviation of that nature clashes with the concept we have of what a militant communist should be."[15]

Castro was expressing homophobic prejudices common in that era. Communist parties of all ideological tendencies rejected membership by gays, and homosexuality was considered deviant behavior. In the United States at that time, government agencies and most employers would fire gays. An openly gay politician could not be elected to major office. In many states, homosexual sex remained a crime, unless you were J. Edgar Hoover.[16]

But it is simply historically inaccurate for Castro to say that the Revolution never encouraged those prejudices.

In later years, Cuban policies on gays changed significantly. By 1979 sodomy was decriminalized. In 1992, gay sex among consenting adults was legalized. The 1994 film *Strawberry and Chocolate* represented a cultural breakthrough because, for the first time, a Cuban film portrayed a sympathetic gay character. The lead character uttered the line, "I'm part of this country, like it or not. And I have the right to work for its future."

The 2006 Cuban soap opera *La Cara Oculta de la Luna* (translated as *The Other Side of the Moon* or *The Dark Side of the Moon*) looked at the lives of people with AIDS. One segment featured a married, bisexual construction worker who falls in love with his next-door neighbor—a man. The theme was shocking for some Cubans and led to heated discussions. Rafael Lahera, an actor in the soap opera, said *The Other Side of the Moon* made him famous around the island. Ironically, he also faced some of the same problems as the fictional characters. "People think I'm gay," he said. Lahera complained that he had been turned down for acting jobs because employers did not want a role to be played by a homosexual.[17]

Mariela Castro, daughter of Raúl and revolutionary leader Vilma Espín, played an important role in advancing the debate about sexual minorities. She headed the National Center for Sex Education (CENESEX). She helped get Cuba's free health care system to perform sex-change operations. And she promoted greater tolerance toward transsexuals and transvestites. Each May CENESEX sponsors an anti-homophobia educational event. Castro told Reuters that her father agreed with her views. "I talk with my father whenever I have the chance. He is one of those in the party that supports our work. He thinks it is useful, good, just."[18]

One late Saturday night in 2008, I was returning to my apartment via the Malecón, the large avenue along Havana's seawall. Dozens of obviously gay men had gathered to party, drink rum, and generally act like young men on a Saturday night. There was no harassment from either the police or passersby. Journalist Ramírez told me that although there's much room for improvement on gay rights issues, Cuba has made significant progress. "They are allowed to gather as long as they don't burst into flames, as long as they're not making love on the street."[19]

≡

In 1992, I visited Santiago, Cuba's second largest city, located in the east of the country. The government was trying to revitalize tourism and had built a multimillion-dollar entertainment complex named after Havana's famous Tropicana nightclub. European and Canadian tourists watched shows that combined glitz, glitter, show tunes, and plenty of bare skin. Male singers with '50s-era puffy sleeve shirts belted out songs on a darkened stage. Showgirls in sparkling, skin-tight costumes walked down a roadway extending into the audience.

The show organizers consciously recreated the stereotypical pre-revolutionary Cuban nightclub. In the old days, the dancers often doubled as prostitutes. But Tropicana announcer Georgiana Bota told me that modern showgirls aren't like those before the Revolution. "The women dancers wear the same costumes, but they don't have the same attitude toward life. Today's dancer is a far cry from the old kind. They didn't hold to a moral code. Today they certainly do."[20]

The Tropicana showgirls may well have had good morals, but prostitution has become a serious problem elsewhere in Cuba. The government once denounced it as shameless exploitation of women, a holdover from the evil, capitalist past. The prevalence of prostitution in the first decade of the 21st century showed how the country's ongoing economic problems can overwhelm government policy.

Prostitution is legal in Cuba, although pimping and pandering are not.[21] In the early days of the Revolution, the government encouraged prostitutes to find legitimate jobs or go to school, sometimes moving them to new housing so they wouldn't face shame among their former neighbors. In 1968, while visiting the city of Holguín in eastern Cuba, I found out about the one remaining prostitute in town, who apparently plied her trade at a *posada* (love motel) without interference by local authorities.[22] In traditional Latin American culture, so-called good girls were supposed to be virgins before marriage, and so-called good boys gained sexual experience by visiting a prostitute.

In the early years of the Revolution, prostitution was virtually eliminated through a combination of improved economic conditions, education, and police crackdowns. But that all changed in the early 1990s. Cubans had become desperate for even the bare necessities. Women, including college students and professionals, prostituted themselves for a bottle of shampoo or a new blouse. During my trips in 1992 and 1994, I saw dozens of beautiful women hanging out in front of the Nacional, Havana Libre, and other major hotels, offering themselves to tourists. The hotels banned the women from entering tourists' rooms, but through bribing hotel staff or using local apartments, the trysts occurred anyway. Journalist Ramírez remembered that walking through tourist areas of Havana in those days "you'd see all the old men with young girls. It was like Father's Day."

Ramírez said the government cracked down in the late 1990s and cleared the women off the streets. "They started picking up the girls and taking them to special schools where they would try to see what their needs were, why they were doing that. Women did it to help their families. If they brought in $100, they would give $50 to their mothers."

"The government tried to educate them," said Ramírez, "but many of them are educated. They come from universities. Many of them are professionals. They decided that was an easy way to live, an easy way to get some hard currency."

Prostitution certainly became less visible in the 2000s.

Improvements in the economy helped. But as sociologist Núñez told me, the problem will continue for the foreseeable future. "As soon as the crisis goes, so will prostitution. I don't think it will be completely erased. It has been decreased, not by repression, but by improved economic conditions. You have more options to work, not just to sell your body."

≡

Marxists refer to a society's economic system as its "base" and its customs and way of thinking, or ideological framework as the "superstructure." In Marxist theory, socialism eliminates the basis for exploitation and allows the superstructure to move forward toward real equality. Women under socialism should enjoy greater economic independence and freedom. That, in turn, should help reduce the amount of sexism.

Cuba has made important strides at the base. About 66 percent of Cuba's professionals are women. Some 34 percent are managers, such as factory heads, department chairs at universities, and school principals.[23] In the 2008 national assembly elections, 43 percent of the seats were won by women, compared with 25 percent in 1979.[24]

Every year the UN publishes the Human Development Index, a

ranking of every country's accomplishments in life expectancy, education, and living standard. In 2008, Cuba ranked 51 out of 193 countries. The UN then adjusts the statistics to see how each of those categories affects women, and calls the result the Gender Development Index. Cuba ranked 2 in the world.[25]

Journalist Ramírez, who has sharp criticisms of conditions facing women in Cuba, nevertheless said that they have made great progress. "They can study whatever they want. They can get the same job as a man. They can apply for science jobs that used to be just for men. There are more women doctors than men. You see a lot of surgeons, even neurosurgeons. My father was a neurosurgeon, and he wouldn't let me study to be a neurosurgeon. 'It's not for women.' And my father was a very smart man."

But the participation of women decreased as they went up the pyramid of power. In 2008, only 6 of 27 cabinet ministers were women.[26] Professor Núñez criticized the attitudes that prohibit women from making more gains. Since women made up two-thirds of professionals, why were they only 34 percent of managers, she asked. The macho attitudes persisted. And that carried over to personal relationships, she told me.

"Sometimes men are afraid of professional women, afraid of getting into a relationship with them, but at the same time they're attracted by them. A professional woman . . . would be a prize for them. They want it and are afraid of it. The men still want to be in control."

Many Cuban couples didn't even bother to get married anymore. There was no social disapproval of couples simply living together. The children were given the last name of the father. The marriage rate in Cuba was 5.5 per 1,000 couples, and the divorce rate was 4.5, which led to its own set of problems. Because of the acute housing shortage, married couples frequently lived with in-laws until an apartment, usually assigned by the government, became available. And in the case of divorce, they frequently continued living together in their old dwelling. "If you're divorced, you can stay living with your wife and children if you don't have a parent that would allow you to live with them," explained Ramírez. "That is still very strong problem. It's very tough."

Cubans own their own apartments and houses, but they can't be bought and sold. Owners may trade domiciles for ones of similar size. So some couples traded their large house for two smaller ones, or two apartments. "It is difficult but they do it all the time," said Ramírez. The housing shortage meant large extended families frequently living together under one roof. Women tended to take on the household tasks. Cuban American sociologist Marisela Fleites-Lear noted that "in many households, grandmothers and their daughters help to perpetuate the status quo by reinforcing sexist ideas . . . It is even thought that teaching boys to cook or clean might foster homosexuality."[27]

Núñez noted that the U.S. blockade hurt the fight for women's equality in Cuba. For her it became very personal. She used to lecture at U.S. universities, and had even received an invitation to speak at Harvard. But academic travel to the United States has been virtually frozen since 2003. Núñez was diagnosed with breast cancer in 2000. The specialized radiation machinery to treat the cancer is manufactured in the United States and thus can't be sold directly to Cuba. Cuba finally did obtain the equipment by purchasing it through a third country. But Núñez asked, "How many innocent women suffered or went untreated because of the U.S. blockade?"

Cuban women seemed determined to push forward the battle against machismo. But much depends on economic improvement in the society as a whole. And that applies just as strongly to Cubans of African descent.

Racism in Cuba?

ONE AFTERNOON I ENTERED THE SIDE DOOR OF HAVANA'S
Roldán Theater to the strains of Beethoven's Fourth Piano Concerto.
The music grew louder as I walked down a long hallway and up a
staircase to the balcony. Cuba's National Symphony Orchestra was
rehearsing for one of its weekly concerts. Fifty musicians sat on stage
dressed casually in jeans or skirts. A portly man with long, unruly
hair and wearing all black waved his baton furiously. Francesco Belli
was a guest conductor from Rome. After the rehearsal, we sat down
in his cramped office in the theater basement. We quickly figured out
that neither his English nor my Italian were sufficient to communicate. So we settled on Spanish. Belli had come to live in Havana for
a month and prepare four concerts. He told me that "musicians here
are of very high caliber. Cuba has the best symphony orchestras in
Latin America. Without doubt, they play on a level comparable to
some good European orchestras."[1]

Something else stood out that day. Nearly 40 percent of the musicians were black and mixed race, and almost 45 percent were women.
The featured pianist was black, and the orchestra included women
playing such nontraditional instruments as bass and bassoon. Luis

Aragú, a 74-year-old classical musician whose father founded the symphony in 1930, told me that before the Cuban Revolution of 1959, the orchestra was overwhelmingly white and male. "Before, there was discrimination against black Cubans."[2] Black musicians were allowed to perform popular music but not the European classics, he said. Similarly, women only played the "feminine instruments. Before, they played piano, harp, and violin. Not now. Women didn't play wood-winds very much. Now they do. There are women trumpet, flute, and oboe players—all with very high standards."

And it's not just symphony orchestras. Enter any Cuban hospital, university, library, or similar institutions and you will see large num-bers of black Cubans in positions of authority. Considering that black Cubans were barred from many jobs and rarely attended university before 1959, the change is striking. According to the 2002 census, 10 percent of Cubans were classified as black and 25 percent as mulatto.[3] Cuba has taken serious steps to reduce racism and discrimination, but it still has a long way to go. In an otherwise highly critical article about race relations, even the *Miami Herald* admitted, "Today's Cuba is more racially and socially integrated than the United States, but it is far from color-blind."[4]

Despite such advances, black Cubans frequently complain that they live in poor housing, face a disproportionate incarceration rate, and suffer police harassment. Those problems are compounded, they say, because back in 1962 the government officially claimed it had eliminated racism. That makes dealing with today's problems even more difficult. Black Cubans are struggling to put the issue back on the table.

During my 1968 trip, I remember meeting with a group of sugar refinery workers—both black and white. When we asked if Cuba had any current problems with racism, the workers literally shouted back that "there is no racism in Cuba." Our guides later explained that Cuba's history was different from the United States and that the

Revolution has taken care of the issue. Cuba and the United States do have somewhat different histories on the issue of race. Cuba didn't abolish slavery until 1886, 21 years after the United States, and well after almost all other countries in the Americas.[5] Because slaves were still arriving from Africa in the late 1800s, black Cubans' ties with Africa were stronger than in the United States, where African languages and customs had been suppressed for generations.

Spain was an old and teetering colonial power by the end of the 19th century. Unlike the United States with its constant inflow of European immigrants, Spain had a hard time getting Spaniards to immigrate to the Americas. So it adopted a different attitude toward people of mixed race. Although still considered inferior to white settlers, mulattos were given relatively greater freedom and power.

Devyn Spence is an African American woman who wrote her dissertation on black Cubans and taught at Williams College. She told me, "There was more racial mixing and more opportunities to buy your way out of slavery in Spanish colonial countries. The population was more mixed. There was a greater space for being a mulatto, and they were able to move up more. [1890s Cuban independence leader] Antonio Maceo was a mulatto, as were other leaders."[6]

Compare that situation with the one in the United States in the same era.

Homer Plessy, a Louisiana Creole who was one-eighth black, sued the East Louisiana railroad for not allowing him to sit in the segregated carriages reserved for whites. The political activists seeking to outlaw Jim Crow segregation intentionally pursued a legal test case with a mixed-race person in order to show the absurdity of the separate but equal doctrine. But in 1896, the U.S. Supreme Court, by a 7–1 vote, ruled in the now infamous *Plessy v. Ferguson* case that Jim Crow was constitutional. The United States enshrined in law discrimination against mixed-race as well as dark-skinned African Americans.[7]

By contrast, Cubans boast of their 1940 Constitution, which outlawed racial and gender discrimination. The United States didn't pass such antidiscrimination laws nationally until 1964. Some ultraconservative Cuban Americans use these examples to claim that racism didn't exist in pre-1959 Cuba. Not coincidentally, advocates of this view are white. The *Miami Herald* noted, "Some Cuban exiles think Castro invented the problem of racism. 'In Cuba we all got along,' they say."[8]

The reality is quite different. The United States occupied Cuba in 1898 and dominated the island politically and economically for the next 60 years. U.S. military officers and businessmen also imported many of America's racist practices. University of Havana professor Esteban Morales, a leading expert on racism, told me, "All but a few blacks were barred from working in American companies. They did not work at the telephone company or the electric company or in general in foreign companies. They couldn't get jobs even as manual workers."[9]

The system of racial discrimination was more than just personal prejudice. By barring black Cubans from certain jobs and denying them higher education, U.S. business leaders and the Cuban elite maintained a permanently oppressed group that could be paid less money and used to foment divisions between blacks and whites. It was the old divide-and-conquer strategy. Cuba's rulers magnified and encouraged people's existing prejudices to create even more divisions. Black Cubans were characterized as lazy, shiftless, incapable of working skilled jobs, and prone to criminality. So why would a white Cuban want his daughter to marry a black man? Even the *paseos* (evening strolls) were segregated. Following the Spanish tradition, Cuban families took walks along streets in major cities in the evenings. It was a way to meet friends, and for young people to find future partners. Before 1959, "blacks and whites had to walk on opposite sides of the park during courtship," said Spence.

Similar customs existed in the countryside. Few black Cubans

owned their own farms; they were mainly agricultural workers. Ismael
Barrera, one of the Barrera clan who lives near San Cristóbal, told me
about the *soga*, or rope, used to divide the races. "During festivals,
there was a *soga* stretched down the street. Blacks were on one side
and whites on the other. It was like a border."[10] Cuba never passed Jim
Crow–style segregation laws. But de facto segregation existed in most
aspects of daily life.

Professor Marta Núñez grew up in the Vedado section of Havana in
a big house. She's white, and her father was a public relations man for
Braniff Airlines in the 1950s. No black Cubans lived in her neighborhood. "Some Afro-Cubans worked as domestic workers in Vedado.
Some houses even refused to hire them as domestic servants. And
of course they couldn't live in Vedado or Playa [middle- and upper-
middle-class areas of Havana]. They lived in slums, mostly in Old
Havana."[11]

≡

In 1992, I visited Old Havana to interview 77-year-old Ángela Jiménez,
a black Cuban who still had vivid memories of the pre-1959 years of
segregation. Jiménez was an imposing and impressive matriarch. She
was the mother of Ernestina Ford, whom we met in the last chapter.
Jiménez passed away in 2006.

"I came to Havana in 1923," Jiménez told me. "I had to work as a
domestic servant from the time I was a child. My three brothers
worked in the streets selling newspapers, peanuts, anything to eke out
a living so we could survive. In those days, we didn't have any rights
at all."[12]

Jiménez recalled an incident that typified the conditions facing
black women in those days. "I remember once I went to see my cousin,
who was also working as a domestic. She opened the front door and
took me upstairs to where she was working. Afterward, the white mis-
tress gave her a terrible time because she let me in through the front

door. She said I should have gone in through the back door where people wouldn't see me."

Ángela's daughter Ernestina Ford picked up the family story. "My mom worked fixing people's clothes in the street, kind of a street corner seamstress. She also worked as a political agent for one of the political parties."[13] The parties ran Cuba like Tammany Hall, buying votes and paying local ward heelers to keep voters in line. Party loyalists got rewarded with low-level government jobs or other perks.

"I remember, when I was 10, my mom and dad mixed up a bucket of glue," said Ford. "They went out at night, because you had to be discreet, and plastered up political posters." As a reward for their activities, they got her into a better school. Her particular school in old Havana included "blacks and whites—all poor. We were all in the same situation. There were private schools that were all white. There were no private schools for blacks."

As you might imagine, Ángela Jiménez was pretty cynical about politicians. So the promises of some bearded guy in the hills named Fidel Castro didn't mean much to her back in 1959. "We didn't know much about him," said Jiménez. "He sounded like another politician with phony promises. But we realized very quickly he was different. First of all, he organized a union for black domestic servants. We got organized and improved our conditions at work. And those that were intelligent were allowed to study and find good jobs."

Jiménez's world also changed rapidly when she got her first garment factory job. Working in a small sewing cooperative may not seem like much by U.S. standards, but for a woman who could only look forward to life as a maid or street vendor, it was a big step. She had tried to get factory work before 1959 but was turned down. "A friend of mine was working in a sewing shop, and they were looking for people. I went there and told him I could sew. I had never worked with an industrial sewing machine, however. They said that was no problem because there's plenty of work to do. They said I could sew the buttons on or cut cloth. They found some work to do. There were plenty of opportunities."

Jiménez worked for over 20 years at that sewing shop and later received retirement benefits from the state. She told me the Cuban Revolution changed her life. "Now that I'm retired, I love my state pension. I was able to aspire to a better life. I have free health care. I have my life set."

＝

During the first few years of the Revolution, the new government worked hard to create equal opportunities for blacks and whites. "Fidel Castro made a number of speeches in 1959 that we're going to end racial discrimination," according to Spence. "He said, we don't have to make any laws. The Revolution is going to get rid of laws by putting blacks and whites in classrooms, by ending segregated social clubs, by giving everyone opportunities and jobs. The government didn't advocate affirmative action."

As wealthy white Cubans fled the country, the government turned many of their houses into schools for impoverished children from the countryside. Because black Cubans made up a disproportionate number of the poor, they also benefited. Ernestina Ford told me, "There were a lot of new schools in Havana." She had been able to attend university, the first in her family to do so, and she became a teacher at one of the schools while still a university student. "We taught all day long and then studied for our classes at night."

In addition, she said, "Many of the white, private schools became public schools. The children of Old Havana or Central Havana went to these schools. They attended without racial discrimination." The revolutionary government stopped the segregated *paseos* and took down the *sogas* in the countryside. It closed the segregated social clubs. Spence said, "The interviews I've done with Afro-Cubans suggest that most people felt that was okay in 1959–61."

But such actions didn't always please white Cubans. "There was a backlash," said Spence. "People say this is not something we necessarily want to see happen. Are you saying you want to see blacks and whites dancing together at the yacht club?" Fidel Castro defended himself and the Revolution by saying there would be no forced intermixing. In a 2006 interview, he looked back on that period and said, "People started saying that we were going to force people to marry people from other ethnic groups—whites marry blacks and vice versa . . . And not a few people were scared to death by that lie that stirred up prejudices . . ."[14]

In the context of the times, promoting genuine equal opportunity was indeed revolutionary. Politicians in the United States and most European and Latin American countries were arguing that it would take generations for minority residents to become equal. Even many white liberals in the United States argued that Negroes should concentrate on getting an education, rather than participating in illegal and confrontational civil rights demonstrations. American civil rights leaders of that era advocated policies similar to Castro's. If discriminatory laws were eliminated and economic discrimination overcome, they reasoned, social relations and racist ideas would decline. Some Marxists had the same orientation.

In 1961, the United States sponsored the Bay of Pigs invasion of Cuba. By 1962, the country was facing the Cuban Missile Crisis and the possibility of nuclear war. The Cuban leadership didn't want what they perceived as divisive debates about race at a time when the country was under attack. Spence said the government emphasized that "we all have to be Cubans." By 1962, Fidel and the mostly white Cuban leadership had declared that the country had overcome racism. In an interview that appeared in Lee Lockwood's 1967 book, *Castro's Cuba, Cuba's Fidel*, Fidel Castro said, "We ourselves went through the experience of discrimination. Discrimination disappeared when class distinctions disappeared, and it has not cost the Revolution much effort to resolve that problem."[15]

Not only was that untrue, it would prove to be a costly mistake. Professor Morales told me, "At the beginning of the Revolution, Fidel attacked the problem of racism very strongly. But then in 1962 he said the problem is solved. Fidel was an idealist. He was a voluntarist. A solution to this problem is very difficult."[16] Simply improving the economic conditions of black Cubans and ending formal segregation wasn't enough. Morales told me, "It's not only an economic problem, it's a cultural problem. We have a lot of people in Cuba today with prejudices. First of all, black people are poor, and second of all they're discriminated against. For a long time, we didn't talk about it and didn't pay any attention to it. So we are in a situation today of racial discrimination."

Although discussion of racism stopped, programs helping the poor continued. Marta Núñez remembers as a white child the wrenching changes in the education system in the early 1960s. She had attended an "American" school in which children of expatriates and the Cuban elite studied in English. It was, of course, all white.

"The American school was nationalized in January 1961. But I left in December 1960 because the principal told my father that it would be closing soon. Out of my class of 25, there were only two or three students left. I continued my education at a public high school. The quality of the teaching was very, very good. But it was a shock because from a classroom of 20 or 25, I had to go into a classroom of 60. I was in a classroom with blacks as well as whites. For me that was *really* a shock. I started living a completely different life than I did before."

Ernestina Ford was experiencing the same upheaval as the daughter of a black seamstress. "I finished high school. After the Revolution, everything for education was free: tuition, books, school uniforms, shoes, everything. After that I went to a school for teachers. We participated in the literacy program in Holguín Province. It was the first time I was out of the house. It was far away."

In the 1960s and '70s, tens of thousands of black Cubans who would never have finished high school were graduating from college. Then, black Cubans' lives were affected by a most unexpected development.

From 1974 to 1991, Cuba dispatched over 300,000 troops to Africa, about half of whom were black.[17] To bolster support at home and justify his actions to other parts of the third world, Fidel Castro began to emphasize that Cuba was an "Afro-Latin" nation. In 1981, for the first time since the Revolution, the government conducted a national census that included racial statistics. The official count indicated Cuba was 66 percent white, 21.9 percent mulatto, and 12 percent black, although critics argued that people of color were undercounted.[18]

The government also finally admitted that racism did indeed exist in Cuba. Fidel Castro said in 1986, "The correction of historic injustice cannot be left to spontaneity. It is not enough to establish laws on equality and expect total equality. It has to be promoted in mass organizations, in party youth . . . [19]

Castro proposed a modified affirmative action program for a period of time. Black Cuban participation in parliament and major Communist Party organs increased from about 25 percent in 1980 to 35.5 percent in 1986.[20] But Cuba soon ran into a deep economic crisis and all but abandoned such programs. By 1991, blacks constituted only 20 percent of the national parliament.[21]

In 1992, I telephoned a friend of a friend to set up an interview. That's how I first met Urbano Canizares and his wife Gilda Zerquera, the black Cuban couple living in the heart of dilapidated Old Havana (see chapter 1). We made an appointment to meet at my hotel, which was about seven miles from Old Havana. Much to my surprise, they arrived an hour early. The buses were so crowded and infrequent that they had walked the whole way. They were really worried about missing me, so they left extra early.

The Canizares were in dire economic shape. He was an English instructor at Havana's only dental university, and she was a secretary.

But their combined salaries were only enough to cover about half their expenses for a month. I took them out for dinner and visited their apartment near the train station in Old Havana. Zerquera had inherited the one-bedroom apartment after her mother passed away. I walked up the narrow, winding staircase barely wide enough for one person. Their second-story balcony looked out on the old colonial-style apartment buildings that had housed black Cubans for decades. Inside they had a 1940s Gibson, a Sherman tank of an American refrigerator, which continued to work into the late 1990s. They never did get rid of the Gibson, even after it finally broke down, because it wouldn't fit through the narrow staircase. It became a storage cabinet.

The early 1990s economic crisis devastated many black Cubans. White Cubans were more likely to have relatives in the United States or Europe who could send remittances. Less than two percent of black Cubans had relatives abroad.[22] In the early 1990s, the government reinvigorated the tourism industry, building dozens of new hotels as joint ventures with European companies. Tens of thousands of new jobs opened up in hotels, restaurants, clubs, and travel agencies. Cubans considered these jobs particularly desirable because they earned tips in hard currency. But black Cubans complained of discrimination and said they weren't getting enough tourism jobs.

Spence said, "Maybe the lingering aspects of things not dealt with at the beginning of the Revolution have come back. I've talked to a number of Afro-Cuban scholars, and they used the analogy of running a race. The problem was, Afro-Cubans were behind the starting line. So it became impossible to ever catch up, especially when you ran into the special period."

≡

If you take a walk along Havana's Malecón or hang out in an Old Havana park, you'll inevitably meet some disaffected youth. Many young black people complain about lack of work and consumer goods, as well as harassment by the police. Whereas Ángela Jiménez remembered the segregation of the old system, today's youth know only the problems of the current one.

I met Pablo Michel through a mutual friend one night. He's solidly built and wore the international youth uniform of jeans, T-shirt, and a baseball hat. The 29-year-old black student insisted that I use his real name. Despite his sharp criticisms of the government, he said he didn't fear retaliation. He studied communication at a local university. His situation was typical for Cuban students. All his tuition and books were free. He received 150 pesos per month as a stipend. He lived at home with his mother. Students from outside Havana got free room and board in dorms. Michel worked as a driver's helper to earn extra money. The truck driver made government deliveries from Havana to nearby rural areas. There they unofficially picked up meat and vegetables to resell in Havana.

Michel expressed anger about the lack of good jobs and the discrimination he faced as a black youth with dreadlocks. "My main aspiration," he told me bluntly, "is to leave the country. I want to marry my French girlfriend and leave after graduation." Michel told me about two incidents in which he said police unnecessarily harassed him as a black youth. He was standing in front of a disco with two Austrian women and a black Cuban friend. The police asked the men for their IDs. He was stopped for perhaps five minutes and then continued walking with the tourists. He said police frequently hassle black Cubans in the tourist areas. But in his residential neighborhood, he wasn't hassled because "when the police know you, there are no problems."

In another more serious incident, he accompanied two foreign tourists to the Havana airport. As soon as he entered, police asked for his ID. "They asked me questions about my relationship with the foreigners, and why I had come to the airport." The foreigners "tried to explain and help me out. She said she was my girlfriend. But they ended up missing their flight. Whites taking foreigners to the airport don't have the same problems," Michel said with finality.

Cuba has faced a real problem of hustlers and petty criminals harassing tourists. In the 1990s and early 2000s, it was impossible to walk through the tourist sections of Old Havana without dozens of people trying to sell you cigars and trinkets, or fix you up with a prostitute. The government cracked down, posted police on every corner in some neighborhoods, and did a lot of ID checks. Police don't need probable cause to stop people on the street. And Cubans can't effectively challenge such actions through the courts. By U.S. standards, however, the harassment is relatively mild. In hundreds of interviews over the years, and after researching media accounts, I have found that black Cubans aren't thrown up against the wall, handcuffed, or arrested without reason. I've never met a black Cuban who had been physically assaulted by police, let alone shot.[23]

But harassment it is, and it's fiercely resented in a country that strongly condemns police brutality in the United States. Professor Morales told me, "The problem of police stopping blacks disproportionately to ask for our IDs is real. They don't understand the psychological impact on blacks. Some institutions consider blacks less sophisticated, less educated, and not smart. There's a certain prejudice."

In 2006, as part of his spoken autobiography, Fidel Castro made some startling admissions. "The Revolution . . . has not had the same success in its fight to eradicate the differences in social and financial status for the black population of the country. Blacks don't live in the best houses; you find that they still have the hardest, most physically wearing, and often worst-paid jobs, and that they receive much less help from their family members no longer in Cuba, in dollars, than their white compatriots."[24]

Black Cubans and experts that I interviewed make even harsher comments. Incarceration rates are considerably higher for black Cubans than for whites. When Ernestina Ford started working with prisoners in the 1960s, the prison was about 60 percent white and 40 percent black. By 2008, the percentage was reversed. Black Cubans lived in formerly all-white sections of major cities, and poor Cubans received priority housing when new apartments were built in the 1980s. But the impoverished barrios that existed before 1959 still existed, and they were overwhelmingly black. Streets were rarely repaired, and basic city services were more likely to break down.

Professor Morales said that although black Cubans have entered the professions and provide leadership in some institutions, a legacy of segregation remains. For example, "institutions more connected with international issues are more white," he told me. "The institutions having to do with production are black. People working in the sugar industry, for example, are black." Although black Cubans participate heavily in certain entertainment fields, such as sports, music, and dance, they have far less representation in film and TV. UNEAC, the artist's association, has launched an education campaign called "Cuban Color" to encourage increased black participation in those areas.

Castro argued that Cuba remains committed to changing the situation facing blacks. "I am satisfied with what we're doing in terms of discovering the root causes, which, if you don't make a determined effort to do something about them, tend to prolong people's marginalization down through subsequent generations."[25] Cuba began implementing a version of affirmative action in which students from poor backgrounds and ethnic minorities are given special training and preparation in order to enter universities. The government reduced the amount of time some young people had to serve in the army and gave them an extra year at boarding school to train for university entrance. There they received intensive instruction. Professor Morales said such programs don't rely on quotas or lowering admission standards. "We must help blacks arrive at the same level. After that they have the opportunity, because in general whites have more opportunity and possibilities."

Professor Morales has seen success at the University of Havana as significantly more black students have entered, starting around 2005. "In the last 10 years, most people coming to the university have been white and women. Over the last three or four years, more blacks have come," he said in 2008. Cuba boasted that black Cubans' literacy and life expectancy rates were almost the same as those for whites.[26]

The continuing entrance of black Cubans into universities and the graduation of black professors accounts for one of the reasons why the National Symphony Orchestra is so integrated. The black professors encouraged their black students to explore different musical styles and study all kinds of instruments. As more black musicians joined orchestras, their numbers reached a critical mass. It was no longer unusual to find black musicians playing the European classics. Professors, musicians, and orchestra conductors focused on finding the best-qualified person to perform. But Cuba has yet to accomplish that same critical mass for society as a whole.

≡

I was particularly interested in how Canizares and Zerquera compared their racial experiences in Cuba and the United States. They had left Havana for Buffalo in 2001. Canizares told me that darker-skinned people in Cuba definitely face discrimination but as a light-skinned person, he did not. So when he shuffled off to Buffalo and started applying for work, he faced discrimination for the first time in his life. "When you apply for a job, they don't say anything [discriminatory], but they don't call you back. I applied for a job and when I showed up, there was not a single person of color. And they never called me back."[27]

Canizares was shocked by what he described as "Balkanization" in the United States, something he never saw in Cuba. "The East side here in Buffalo is predominantly black. Our neighborhood is predominantly Latino and Puerto Rican. The white people have moved to the suburbs." He told me that although blacks face discrimination in Cuba, "It's even worse here [in the United States]. If you're a black, especially dark-skinned, you're automatically thought of as a criminal. It's unfair. Some people say they bring it on themselves because they're involved in criminal activity more than the rest of the population. I don't think so. It's a mindset. It's unjust and unfair."

Canizares and Zerquera left Cuba for both political and economic reasons. They are struggling to survive as a working-class couple in a difficult situation. They stay in Buffalo because, on the whole, their lives are better than in Havana. But it is ironic that in seeking the American dream, they found the American reality.

12

Dissidents, Democracy, and the Internet

ON A BRIGHT AND SUNNY AFTERNOON, I VISITED ONE of Cuba's most well-known dissidents. Martha Beatriz Roque, 62, lived in a modest apartment building in Havana. The pastel colors and black railings reminded me of 1950s Miami. I walked down a narrow outside corridor with a concrete wall on the right and apartment entrances on the left. Hostile neighbors had hung a big poster of Fidel on the wall directly opposite her apartment. In turn, she had festooned her door and windows with posters and bumper stickers supporting dissident causes. It reminded me of Bay Area friends who proudly display their political proclivities outside their homes. Only in her case, it was like a Bush supporter putting up posters in the People's Republic of Berkeley.

Roque once taught math at the University of Havana and thought of herself as a supporter of the Revolution. She later became a full-time dissident. The government had imprisoned her twice and continually harassed her. The Bush administration featured Roque in an unprecedented March 2008 videoconference between the president, leading U.S. officials, and three dissidents.[1]

In her interview with me, Roque complained that opponents of the regime have no freedom of speech, freedom to assemble, or other means to organize for political change. Those who oppose the government, she said, face harassment and jail. "Here in Cuba you can't be against anything. You have to be like the government wants you to be." When I asked Roque what kind of system she would like to see in Cuba, she said, "I'm a person of the right. I want to liberate the economy. I support free-market capitalism. It's the way to develop."[2]

She praised Miami's conservatives who left Cuba for the United States in the 1960s. "They used to live in a democratic country."[3] Cubans in Miami "have ideas about how to come to Cuba and change the Cuban government. I think they want good things for Cuba. They love their country. They want freedom for Cuba. Perhaps when we are in a free country, they can come to Cuba and give us money and resources that we need for development."

Roque denied that she received money from the U.S. Interests Section. She was on good terms with all foreign diplomats, she said, and the only money she received was from relatives living in Miami. She wanted to see peaceful change in Cuba and didn't support ultrarightists who engage in armed struggle against the Cuban government. "I am a pacifist. I don't want war. I do not support those who want to come to Cuba to make war."

Dissidents such as Roque play a vital role in the propaganda war between the two countries. The U.S. Interests Section publicizes their views and encourages American journalists to interview them.[4] Their plight becomes known, and Americans become convinced of the repressive nature of the Cuban regime. But U.S. diplomats don't publicize their own role in the process.

In May 2008, Cuban authorities dropped a bombshell on Roque and some other dissidents. In a series of press conferences for the foreign media, they revealed recorded phone conversations, surveillance tapes, and emails showing that she accepted money from a Miami ultrarightist, delivered by the chief of the U.S. Interests Section. The press conferences showed Roque had accepted $1,500 a month from Miami resident Santiago Álvarez. Álvarez had been arrested for stockpiling weapons to attack Cuba and, in another matter, was serving 10 months in a Florida jail for refusing to testify in the illegal immigration case of terrorist Luis Posada Carriles.[5]

The authorities provided reporters with email exchanges between U.S. Interests Section Chief Michael Parmly and Roque in which she arranged for relatives to deliver Álvarez's money to Parmly at the Miami airport. Parmly had given her his personal cell phone number. When a reporter called the number, Parmly answered, but refused to comment.[6] When I contacted Roque, she had no comment either.

According to Cuban officials, the United States was also passing money to 22 members of the Ladies in White, a group of wives of political prisoners who demonstrate Sundays in front of a Havana church.[7] The Ladies in White have received a great deal of favorable international publicity comparing them to human rights groups that opposed the 1970s military dictatorship in Argentina. A Ladies in White leader later confirmed that they did receive regular payments from Álvarez but denied getting money from the U.S. government.[8]

When questioned at a Washington press conference, Thomas A. Shannon, assistant secretary of state for Western Hemisphere Affairs, never denied the accusations that Parmly had carried funds from Álvarez to Roque. In fact, in roundabout diplomatic language, Shannon confirmed them. "[A]assistance that moves from the United States to Cuba under official auspices in this regard does so for humanitarian purposes. It really is aimed at helping dissidents and the families of political prisoners who operate under enormous stress in a society in which their loved ones have been locked away."[9]

Parmly's actions are a blatant violation of Cuban law. They also apparently violate U.S. law, which limits remittances to no more than $1,200 per person annually. Parmly's actions also violate international diplomatic norms. Can you imagine the reaction in the United States if the chief of the Cuban Interests Section in Washington had been caught passing funds to American revolutionaries?

Don't expect an FBI investigation anytime soon.

≡

I also interviewed Eloy Gutiérrez Menoyo, a dissident from the other end of the political spectrum. Gutiérrez had led an armed guerrilla group opposing the Batista dictatorship. He considered himself a social democrat, politically aligned with the socialist parties of Europe. In 1959, Gutiérrez broke with Fidel Castro and fled to the United States, where he founded Alpha 66, a group dedicated to overthrowing the Cuban government by armed force. Alpha 66 launched terrorist attacks against Cuban civilians. Gutiérrez landed in Cuba with a small Alpha 66 group intending to wage guerrilla war, was arrested in 1965 after only a month, and spent 21 years in a Cuban jail.

After getting out of jail in 1986, Gutiérrez went to live in Miami. Fed up with ultraconservative domination there, however, he returned to Cuba to carry out legal political struggle in 2003. Ultrarightists in Miami denounced Gutiérrez for working within the Cuban system, and Cuban authorities viewed him suspiciously, refusing to give him permanent residence.

I had trouble finding Gutiérrez's apartment in the San Agustín section of Havana. I knew that the government tapped his phone and watched his apartment. I would ordinarily have asked the taxi driver to wait and drive me to my next appointment, but I worried that the driver might get hassled. So I found the apartment on my own. Gutiérrez lived on a pedestrian-only street without clear street signs or addresses. Neighbors pointed the way. Gutiérrez told me my concerns about the taxi driver were unfounded. As a dissident, he freely talks to foreign journalists. I wasn't hassled going in or out. Family members who live with him are not harassed. But Gutiérrez said that when he meets with people outside his apartment, the intelligence service visits them later to ask what was discussed.

Gutiérrez told me he returned to Cuba "to establish some independent political space, including setting up an office and creating other political parties." But the government has not allowed such activities. He wanted to separate himself politically from the ultrarightists in Miami, who support the U.S. embargo and such undemocratic measures as the coup against President Hugo Chávez of Venezuela.[10] "How can you support a coup and then claim to be for democracy here?" he asked.[11] He accused the United States of manipulating the dissidents by doling out cash. "I won't have anything to do with the U.S. Interests Section. I don't have anything in common with the State Department or its Cuba policy."

Dealing with the United States, he told me, is "like a drug addict who says I don't like the drugs from Colombia. But I like them from Russia. No. Drugs from one are as bad as drugs from another." In retaliation for his political views, the United States has accused Gutiérrez of unauthorized travel to Cuba and threatened him with a 10-year jail term and $250,000 fine.[12]

I asked Gutiérrez a critical question: if somehow Cuba allowed free elections tomorrow, would the dissidents and their supporters win? He paused for a long moment. The dissidents are too closely identified with the Miami exiles, he said. "The people of Cuba don't want the ultraright from the U.S. They think they will take their houses." The dissidents "wouldn't win" free elections, he said. "The government would win."

That's a startling admission from a man who has spent his life opposing Cuba's communist dictatorship. Gutiérrez is not alone in his assessment that the Communist Party has a significant base of popular support. Jay Taylor headed the U.S. Interests Section in Cuba from 1987 to 1990. During the time he was in Cuba, he told me, "25 to 30 percent of Cubans probably supported Castro quite strongly. They would vote for him in an election. About the same number of Cubans really hated him. There's a group in the middle who grabs another 30 percent or so.[13]

A 2006 Gallup poll of Cubans offered an even more fascinating picture. Gallup conducted personal interviews with 1,000 residents of Havana and Santiago. The poll indicated 49 percent approved of Cuba's leadership, 39 percent disapproved, and 13 percent offered no response.[14] Other polls show that Cubans are far more concerned about economic problems on the island than about political freedoms or democracy.[15]

The U.S.-backed dissidents have little popular support. The United States actively seeks out dissidents who ideologically agree with U.S. policy, which further isolates the dissidents because U.S. policy remains unpopular with the vast majority of Cubans. "We don't care if it hurts the dissidents," said former diplomat Wayne Smith. He told me the United States seeks to make propaganda points. "The more the Cuban government reacts to them [the dissidents], the more we like it."[16] Some of the dissidents were simply seeking a fast track to emigration. "Some may have seen it as a way to get to the States," Taylor told me. "They could get status eventually if we thought they were genuine dissidents. If they were facing difficulties, we could get them visas."

The United States has played this game for a long time. During the Cold War, it publicized the plight of selected Soviet dissidents and welcomed some as heroic opponents of totalitarianism. When elections were held after 1992, however, no dissident promoted by the United States was ever elected to a significant office in Russia.[17]

═══

Beginning in 1998, Christian Liberation Movement leader Oswaldo Paya initiated the Varela Project. He and his supporters circulated a petition calling for changes in the Cuban Constitution: freedom of the press, speech, and assembly; amnesty for political prisoners; and the right to start private businesses. The Varela Project said it collected over 11,000 signatures and called for a national referendum. President George Bush Jr. declared support for it, and in a May 2002 speech televised in Cuba, former president Jimmy Carter praised the project as well.

The Cuban government said the Varela Project was a creation of U.S. imperialism, and that the U.S. Interests Section had given money and gifts to project organizers. Cuban officials argued that the Cuban Constitution already provided for civil liberties and that the real thrust of the project was restoring capitalism. National Assembly chair Ricardo Alarcón said the petition was also procedurally flawed because no Cuban law allows for a citizen petition to become a national referendum. "I challenge you to show me just one constitution of any country that can be modified at the request of some citizens," he said. "I have found many constitutions in the Western world that can be modified, but none that recognizes a citizens' initiative."[18] The Cuban National Assembly accepted the petition but tabled any action.

Interestingly enough, the ultrarightists in Miami denounced Project Varela as too moderate. Ninoska Pérez Castellón, whom we met in chapter 5, was spokeswoman for the Cuban Liberty Council. She told the *Miami Herald*, "If you accept these baby steps, you are legitimizing the system. They are steps, but steps in the wrong direction."[19] The ultraright feared that political initiatives inside Cuba could take away from their domination of the anti-Castro movement and dash their hopes of eventually coming to power.

Less strident groups, such as CANF, realized that Miami had little impact on Cuba and saw supporting the Varela Project as a means to exert their own influence. CANF recognized the Varela Project as an initiative from within the island that could ultimately push forward the Miami agenda. "Forty years ago, the debate was in the streets of Miami," said Joe García, then executive director of CANF. "Now we have to take the debate to the streets of Cuba."[20]

The Cuban government saw the Varela Project as a direct challenge to the socialist system. It gathered thousands of signatures for its own petition drive, and the National Assembly voted to hold a referendum:

Cubans voted overwhelmingly to make the socialist system a permanent part of the constitution.[21] The government also cracked down,
arresting 25 of the Varela Project organizers in March 2003 as part of
a wider effort. While the United States was preparing to invade and
occupy Iraq in March 2003, the Bush administration talked about
spreading American democracy elsewhere in the world. Cuban leaders feared their country could be next. The government rounded up
opponents, gave them quick trials and threw 75 in jail. Martha Beatriz
Roque was among those arrested. Cuban officials accused the dissidents of receiving funds from the United States. They charged that
chief of Interests Section James Cason financed the dissidents, including organizing a private meeting at his diplomatic residence. Cason
didn't deny the charge. In a Miami speech, he said his actions "were
fully consistent with U.S. policy and with diplomatic protocol."[22]

The crackdown had serous negative consequences internationally
for Cuba. Groups such as Amnesty International and Human Rights
Watch complained that the opposition figures were given show trails
and faced horrible conditions in jail.[23] The European Union (EU)
voted to limit diplomatic visits and cultural exchanges with Cuba.
In retaliation, Cuba evicted Spain from its Cultural Center in Old
Havana and erected a huge, antifascist billboard nearby. For two
years, diplomatic relations remained cool between Cuba and Spain,
Italy, and some other European countries.

Relations began to warm again when the EU suspended the sanctions in 2005 and then formally lifted them in June 2008. The Cuban
government had released 23 of the 75 dissidents by then. The releases
were interpreted as a response to international calls for greater respect
for human rights.[24] Cuba also signed two international human rights
treaties and promised to allow international human rights monitors
into the country starting in 2009.

≡

In a now infamous 1979 article, "Dictatorships and Double Standards," Jeane Kirkpatrick drew a distinction between authoritarianism and totalitarianism. Kirkpatrick later became U.S. ambassador to the UN under President Ronald Reagan. She defined totalitarian regimes as one-party dictatorships that controlled every aspect of people's lives through propaganda and terror. Authoritarian regimes were less repressive dictatorships, which were more unstable and therefore subject to democratic change. Not coincidentally, all her totalitarian regimes were Cold War opponents of the United States (USSR, China, Cuba) and the authoritarians were allies (Indonesia, Saudi Arabia, Iran under the Shah).[25]

The theory didn't make any sense even when written. Why was the relatively free-wheeling Yugoslavia somehow more repressive than Saudi Arabia with its all-controlling religious police? And since the end of the Cold War, the theory has been even further discredited given that—by U.S. standards—many parts of former Yugoslavia and Eastern Europe made the transition to democracy but Saudi Arabia remains a dictatorship.

But there is one crevice of U.S. foreign policy where Kirkpatrick's theory still holds sway: Cuba. U.S. officials argue that America can neither lift the embargo nor have full diplomatic relations because Cuba remains a totalitarian state. Former chief of Interests Section Taylor described himself to me as a "moderate liberal, a tough-love liberal." He disagreed with Bush administration policy on Cuba, but he still called Cuba totalitarian. "It is a more pervasive dictatorship. If you have thoughts and express them you can get into difficulty." Taylor said Cuba's totalitarianism is disguised by the island's relaxed atmosphere. "The climate and the sun and the beaches, it's not like you live in dreary old Romania. When I arrived [in 1987], it was a totalitarian regime that had pretty much repressed spontaneity."

It's true that Cubans don't have free speech, freedom of assembly, or a free press. One party rules the country. But I've traveled in totalitarian states such as Myanmar (Burma) where the military junta controls every aspect of life and people won't talk politics with strangers. In Cuba, by contrast, you'll meet people who vigorously criticize the government. Filmmakers, musicians, and writers criticize ruling policies. I've had numerous conversations throughout the country in which people complain about the economy, poor transport, lack of food, and a host of other problems. None of them ended up in jail.

The United States always points to the political prisoners held in Cuban jails as a sign of totalitarianism. According to a leading, pro-U.S. human rights activist in Cuba, Elizardo Sánchez, at the end of 2007, there were 234 political prisoners, down from thousands in earlier decades. The number has steadily declined over the past few years.[26]

I think U.S. diplomats label Cuba totalitarian in order to justify present policies, a holdover from the Jeane Kirkpatrick era. I think the designation will disappear as soon as the United States decides to trade with Cuba, much as happened with China and Vietnam. Former chief of Interests Section Wayne Smith agreed. I asked him to rate Cuba's level of repression on a scale of 1–10, with one being the least repressive. "It's down on the lower end. It can be repressive. There's no real freedom of expression or assembly. On the other hand, Cubans are very patriotic. I think the Cubans are loyal to the Revolution."[27]

In 2007, acting President Raúl Castro called for a wide-ranging debate about solving problems on the island. In February 2008, a video delivered to the foreign media displayed a fascinating example of that debate. Several students at the University of Computer Sciences challenged Communist Party Political Bureau member and National Assembly chair Ricardo Alarcón at a campus forum. They asked sharp questions about why ordinary consumer goods cost so much, why they can't freely travel outside Cuba, and why they don't have full access to the Internet. Foreign media accounts characterized the interchange as an unusual discussion of uncomfortable issues.[28] Some reports later falsely maintained that one of the students had been arrested.[29]

But reading the entire question-and-answer session from the video reveals that the students were clearly trying to improve Cuban socialism, not challenge the system. And several of the criticized policies—such as the inability to stay at tourist hotels—were, in fact, changed soon thereafter.

There's actually a long history of such interchange with government officials. I remember in 1968 students at the University of Havana telling me that Fidel Castro would periodically show up for nighttime bull sessions, engaging any students who happened to be around at the time. Cuban leaders have always maintained an unusual frankness and direct interchange with the people. On his frequent visits around the country, Fidel would be peppered with requests to improve something or right some injustice. Unfortunately, Cuban leaders have never institutionalized a means of democratic control. Nor do they allow full access to information in this Internet age.

In 2008, the international media gave a great deal of publicity to Yoani Sánchez, an Internet blogger who posed as a tourist to enter hotels and write her daily blog. She mostly wrote about her personal life and reactions to developments in Cuba, and she was hailed as an intrepid example of Cuba's younger, dissenting generation. When the Cuban government eventually made her blog inaccessible, critics called it government repression.[30] It illuminated a wider issue: as Martha Beatriz Roque told me, "Cubans don't have access to the Internet."

As with almost everything in Cuba, it's a lot more complicated than that. Broadband Internet connections don't exist except in a few government offices and hotels. Few Cubans have access to dial-up Internet service at home. Cubans can go to the post and telecommunications offices or to tourist hotels, although the cost is very high. Connection fees ranged from 3 CUCs per hour for slow access to 10

CUCs per hour for DSL-like connections at some tourist hotels. Yet virtually every young person I met had an email address. So what's going on?

Cuba was cut off from high-speed communication because the United States won't allow a fiber optic upgrade to the existing underwater phone lines between the two countries.[31] So Cuba used a very expensive satellite system for all its international Internet traffic. This drove up the cost of Internet connections for Cubans and required the government to ration access. Cuba and Venezuela have plans to lay a fiber optic cable between the two countries, but it was not scheduled to begin operating until 2010.

Late one Friday afternoon, I entered an air-conditioned office at the International Press Center in Havana to meet Juan Fernández, a professor at the University of Information Science and advisor to the Communications Ministry on Internet issues. He said that the U.S. embargo hurt Internet use in many ways. U.S. companies control a lot of the computer hardware needed for modern Internet connections. He told me, "The U.S. is very close and could sell everything very cheap. Yes, we can buy it in Asia, but it's more expensive."[32]

I asked him if Cuba limited access to certain websites such as Google or the website of the *Miami Herald*'s Spanish-language newspaper, *Nuevo Herald*. He said that each college, office, or other institution determined which Internet access would be available. For example, people can't play computer games during work hours or access porn sites. He pointed out that certain travel sites advertising trips to Cuba are blocked in the United States. But I hadn't asked about travel sites, porn, or games. He never directly answered the question about limiting access to media. He used the same argument Cuban authorities have long used to limit access to information. "Cuba isn't a normal country. We face great pressure, practically an economic war, from the most powerful country in the world. Every day the United States tries to make our system disappear. For 50 years the United States has

been trying regime change in Cuba." He never explained how access-
ing Google would endanger Cuban socialism.

After interviewing many college students, professors, intellectuals,
and ordinary Cubans, it became clear that Cubans have access to the
Internet, but it's limited. Some artists who regularly travel abroad are
given free dial-up access in order to communicate with bookers. Some
medical personnel get home dial-up with access to a specialized medical intranet that allows limited international access to medical websites. Many Cuban young people obtain email addresses and check
their accounts when they can afford to use the telecommunications
office. The satellite link is a serious cost issue for Cuba. If socialism
disappeared tomorrow, and the Miami ultrarightists returned to
power, they would not be able to provide cheap Internet connections
for Cubans until the United States allowed the laying of new cables.

But Cuba clearly does block some websites and worries that un-
limited access to foreign websites will have a negative ideological
influence. As a practical matter, Cuban authorities can't completely
block unpopular or controversial news. For example, every student
and professor I spoke with was aware of the computer students sharp
questioning of Alarcón. Many had received the entire transcript of the
session via email. When sports stars defect to the United States, word
circulates quickly via cell phone, text messaging, or the Internet.

≡

In his famous 1961 speech to writers and artists, Fidel Castro formu-
lated how the Revolution would deal with criticism, ". . . within the
Revolution everything; against the Revolution nothing." In theory
that meant supporters of Cuban socialism were free to criticize its
shortcomings so long as it was done constructively. That's not always
been the reality.

In the late 1960s, the University of Havana Philosophy Department
taught the classics of Marxism but also a wide range of contemporary

Marxist authors. Marta Núñez, a member of the department, told me, "We were against the Soviet manuals that were very popular at the time," finding their interpretation of Marxism too narrow. "We were in the midst of revolutionary fervor, we were very much interested in understanding what was happening in our country and the world. The students really did study the essence of Marxism."[33]

But as Fidel Castro and top officials decided to bring Cuba closer to the Soviet orbit, the free-wheeling ideological discussions shut down. The Soviet teaching manuals came back. And in 1971, the university closed the Philosophy Department altogether. It wasn't a purge because professors kept the jobs by moving to other departments. But it was a top-down decision conforming to the Soviet ideological view, which tolerated no deviation from its version of Marxism. As good members of the Communist Party, Núñez and other faculty didn't protest. "We accepted the decision. There was a discussion, but we accepted it. Perhaps one or two of us left the country. Everyone else stayed."

Ironically, some of the contemporary Marxist philosophers discarded in the 1970s are being taught once again. Cuban intellectuals are taking another look to see if they offer some help in figuring out Cuba's current difficulties. American poet and author Margaret Randall had similar experiences. She lived in Cuba from 1969 to 1980. She wrote a fascinating memoir, *To Change the World: My Years in Cuba*, in which she reexamines some of her experiences on the island. In her book, she described herself as a supporter of Cuban socialism and a critic of its deficiencies.

Randall wrote about "Magin," a group of women revolutionaries and Communist Party members who came together in the 1990s. They saw the growth of feminist movements around the world and wanted to bring the positive aspects of that movement to Cuba. Magin held workshops and "published studies revealing the ongoing gender bias" in Cuba.[34] They met with delegations of foreign women and maintained contacts with feminist groups abroad. Then in 1996 the Communist Party Central Committee ordered Magin to disband and cease all publication activities. Randall wrote, "The reason given was patronizing in the extreme: in light of the ongoing efforts of the U.S. government to destroy the Cuban Revolution, party officials said, they were afraid these women might be duped into making contacts or doing work which inadvertently played into the enemy's hands."[35]

No one was jailed. But some women lost their jobs; others were refused permission to travel abroad. The cause of Cuban women was certainly set back. Randall wrote, "As it has done rather consistently through close to half a century of revolution, the Cuban Communist Party used the ever-present threat from the north to legitimize a lack of support for diverse efforts and justify repressive measures . . . [T]here have been many situations in which trusting the insights and intelligence of its own best citizens rather than relying on such insulting excuses might have pushed true revolution forward. This was one of them."[36]

≡

An old joke made the rounds in Havana. "In America, you are free to shout 'Down with Bush.' In Cuba we have freedom of speech as well. We, too, can shout 'Down with Bush.'" The joke reveals a lot about how Cubans view their government. Let's look at some of the Cuban government's defenses of its political system.

Cuba is a democracy because people vote by secret ballot for local councils and the National Assembly. Cuba has elected legislatures at the local and national levels. The Communist Party formulates policy and offers guidance, but formally, these elected bodies make all decisions affecting government.

In reality, decisions are made by a relatively small number of leaders at the top of the Communist Party.

I've covered the legislative elections, and voters don't have much of a real choice. There are no campaigns. Candidates post their photos and qualifications at the polling place. Government supporters argue that Cuba doesn't have the phony, money-driven elections typical in the United States. But Cuban candidates don't even pass out leaflets or hold rallies as would be fitting for a grassroots democracy. The candidates don't take positions on issues, so the lively debate that goes on in every Cuban household doesn't get reflected in the electoral process. The National Assembly, especially in recent years, does have genuine debates. But top leaders still make the critical government decisions. Those policies may be more or less popular, but they are not made through an institutionalized democratic process.

Human rights include not just political rights, but the right to work, education, health care, and a secure life. In that sense Cuba has a very good human rights record.

U.S. leaders narrow the definition of human rights to issues of civil liberties. Many countries include the right to a job, for example, as part of their constitutionally guaranteed human rights. And the U.S. government conveniently ignores its own violations of political rights. In that broader, international definition, Cuba does respect many human rights. But that doesn't excuse Cuba's very real shortcomings in the realm of institutionalized democracy, press freedom, and other civil liberties.

Cuba has press freedom because the country has two national daily print newspapers, many online publications, and broadcast news programs that put forward a revolutionary perspective.

The Cuban press is among the worst in the world, and it's really boring. The daily Communist Party paper, *Granma,* is almost unreadable, and believe me, I've read a lot of turgid rhetoric in my day. The evening news broadcasts are often days behind breaking events, rarely take on controversial stories inside Cuba, and tend toward the "heroic workers harvest new rice crop" style of journalism. Film directors and musicians offer better critiques of Cuban society than do the news media.

Since Raúl Castro effectively became president, the *Juventud Rebelde* (*Rebel Youth*) newspaper has published some impressive investigative stories about corruption and economic mismanagement. In 2008, the government was discussing how to improve TV broadcasts as well. However, as long as the Cuban media don't provide better journalism, Cubans will get their information through rumors and foreign sources.

Cuba has been in a virtual state of war with the United States for the past 50 years, and this war has restricted its ability to widen democracy.

True, the United States has remained hostile and still seeks to overthrow the Cuban government. But it is not about to invade Cuba. Nor would it allow an invasion by Cuban exiles under current circumstances. Cuba is a stable country, with a solid base of support from a sizeable sector of the population. Exactly when will Cubans be able to have a larger influence on their country's affairs? When will they be allowed the civil liberties appropriate for a self-described socialist democracy?

≡

Cuban authorities offer a devastating critique of democracy in the United States, from the money-dominated campaigns to the Florida fraud of 2000. Who wants a so-called democracy like the one imposed on Iraq? If ultrarightists in Miami represent democracy, then Cubans will have none of it. But lack of democracy elsewhere doesn't get Cuban authorities off the hook. Democracy has a much more profound meaning: rule by the people. And it's not an abstract issue. If Cubans had full democratic rights, they might have chosen greater self-reliance back in the 1970s and less dependence on the USSR. That, in turn, might have lessened the impact or even avoided the economic disaster of the early '90s. I think that economic reforms are far more important than political liberalization at the moment. Mikhail Gorbachev made the serious error of putting political change first, and chaos ensued.

But if Cuba is to come through the difficult period when both Castro brothers eventually die, Cubans will need to participate more in the political process. Cuba should make a distinction between advocacy and subversive acts. If people accept money from foreign agents or facilitate armed attacks, they should be tried and punished. But no one should be jailed for advocating unpopular views. The media needs a serious revamping, with reporters free to uncover wrongdoings and help facilitate change. As technical conditions improve, the government should open up low-cost Internet cafes with no blocking of political and media websites. The government should allow candidates for office to campaign and disagree. Let grassroots activists organize to improve the society.

Of course the U.S. government and Miami ultraconservatives will seek to take advantage of such changes. But Cuba is sufficiently stable, and if the political and economic changes are positive, the government has nothing to fear. And, as we'll see in the next chapter, those economic changes will be key to Cuba's future.

13

Prospects for Change

ON JULY 31, 2006, THE WORLD WAS SHOCKED TO LEARN that Fidel Castro was ill and had temporarily turned power over to his brother and vice president, Raúl Castro. Fidel was about to undergo intestinal surgery, and following in the footsteps of the United States and European countries, he formally assigned power to his designated successor. The decision was surprising on two levels. First, no one outside Fidel's inner circle knew he was ill. Second, temporarily turning over power was unprecedented in the socialist camp. In the past, people such as Soviet leader Yuri Andropov kept their illnesses secret and stayed in office until taken out in a box.[1]

Fidel came closer to death than reported at the time. He had several operations and developed an intestinal infection. A Spanish surgeon was flown to Havana, and Fidel underwent yet another operation, which apparently was more successful.[2] Fidel never recovered his full strength and, again in an unprecedented move, chose not to continue in office. The National Assembly elected Raúl Castro president in February 2008. It was an orderly transition from one leader to another without upheaval.[3]

Since 2006, Raúl had been making incremental changes in farm policy aimed at producing more food. He continued to expand on those reforms. He also called for a wide-ranging dialogue among Cubans to discuss how to solve the country's problems. But there were no major policy shifts. The transition was smooth, in part, because Raúl was a familiar leader with a long revolutionary history. He had fought in the Sierra Maestra mountains and headed the army since the beginning of the Revolution. But Fidel (born 1926) and Raúl (born 1931) will both die in the not-so-distant future. So, what happens in Cuba when two of the founding fathers pass on?

Since 1991, the U.S. government has fostered numerous university and think-tank projects aimed at planning Cuba's imminent transition from communism to democracy. Over the years, the University of Miami, Florida International University, the RAND Corporation, and a plethora of academics in the greater Miami area joined the effort. The Cuban government didn't collapse, of course, so most of the academic tomes have ended up collecting dust on library shelves.

But the various studies are revealing and share a common characteristic. Beneath the rhetoric about self-determination and respecting the rights of Cubans on the island, they describe means by which the United States can once again reassert control of Cuba. In 2004, the Bush administration's Commission for Assistance to a Free Cuba issued an elaborate report.[4] It assumed that a new Cuban government would welcome U.S. assistance in every conceivable field, from education to infrastructure to legislation. For example, the report states, "The U.S. Government should be prepared to work with the Cuban people and their chosen representatives, should they ask, to lend assistance in drafting laws and regulations, preparing a new constitution, and establishing a system of checks and balances . . ."

The United States would assist in developing the police and security services, and building roads, bridges, and airports. Of course, the report assumes Cubans will welcome capitalism and U.S. foreign investment. The new Cuba would sign a U.S.-Cuba free trade pact, and join the International Monetary Fund and World Bank. "The U.S. Government and the IFIs [international financial institutions] should be prepared to assist a free Cuba in developing a new investment regime that fosters foreign investment and investor confidence, consistent with appropriate free market mechanisms . . ." Cuba would have to settle outside claims "as expeditiously as possible," according to the report. Thus Cuban Americans who say their property was nationalized would either get the property back or potentially receive hundreds of millions of dollars in compensation.

According to these reports, if Cuba follows such pro-U.S. policies, its people would finally breathe the free air of democracy and eat the golden fruits of capitalism. Let's sketch out a more realistic transition plan based on the actual historical experience in Cuba and the former Eastern Bloc.

≡

Let's say an economic crisis hits Cuba, and the Cuban government makes a series of serious political blunders. Cubans start fleeing to Florida by boat and raft; others demonstrate in the streets of Havana. Without either of the Castro brothers as leaders, the Communist Party splits. Some leaders take up the banner of democracy, whereas others try a military crackdown. The situation worsens. The old power crumbles and new leaders come to power, much as happened in the Soviet Union at the end of 1991. Cuban exiles from Miami hop the first planes to Havana, promising freedom, democracy, and an end to economic injustice. At least initially, people welcome the exiles and hope the new system will meet their needs.

But very quickly a number of unforeseen elements of democracy emerge. The new government won't actually hold elections until political parties are organized and election mechanisms are in place. And they can't do that until the state-controlled media are privatized and the Communist Party institutions dismantled. The United States, through its Miami surrogates, will make sure the pro-U.S. parties are well funded and receive overwhelming media coverage. If Cubans opposed to the new system hold demonstrations, let alone take up arms, the new democratic regime would be forced to suppress them. The pro-U.S. political parties form militias to protect their interests, as they did before 1959.[5] The United States sends in armed private contractors, military advisors, and possibly troops, depending on the situation. The new government won't hold elections until the turmoil subsides.

Even U.S. diplomats concede that the Cuban Communist Party has considerable popular support. Cuban communists, unlike many of their brethren in the Eastern Bloc, retain an ideological commitment to Marxism and an ability to mobilize ordinary people. The Cuban army will certainly have set aside caches of weapons to wage guerrilla war. But even if armed insurrection and mass upheaval don't occur, the new regime will face massive problems.

Until now, Cuba has escaped the scourge of heroin and cocaine that has spread through Latin America. The Cuban government has adopted very tough policies to keep out the international drug cartels. But Cuba occupies a perfect geographic location to become a transport hub for drug lords, not to mention a lucrative new market. The Miami Cubans won't be the only ones on the first planes to Havana. Mexican, Colombian, and other drug lords will send kilos and cash. The old, New York–based mafia will also seek to return to operate drug, gambling, and prostitution rings. But they've been out of touch for 50 years, so the drug lords of Colombia and Mexico have a natural advantage. A few violent gang wars should sort everything out. It took 10 years of horrific clashes in Russia in the 1990s, but eventually a few strong gangs emerged triumphant.

But won't the new democrats and the U.S. drug enforcement officials stop the mafia? The United States has conflicting interests on this issue. The drug trade is the perfect source of cash for pro-U.S. political parties and their armed militias. Sectors of the Miami elite already have lots of experience working with drug lords.[6] In general, the United States would not like to see drug lords achieve new markets and share political power. But if the drug lords help pro-U.S. political parties, they become a tolerated evil. That's how the United States operated in Batista's day, when some of Batista's cabinet members were directly involved in cocaine smuggling.[7] And this is not just ancient history. The United States immediately started cooperating with drug-running cabinet members in the Hamid Karzai government in Afghanistan after the U.S. invasion of 2001.[8]

The newly democratized and privatized Cuba would also face tough choices about how to handle the country's extensive social services. I conducted a revealing interview with CANF president Pepe Hernández in Miami. I asked if the current system in Cuba had produced anything worth saving. He admitted Cubans enjoyed universal health care. "In the future the Cuban people should have universal health care provided for them at a low price. Nobody in the future should go without medical coverage."[9] He advocated a mixed system of public and private medical providers.

Would this be possible in a new Cuba modeled on U.S. free enterprise?

The Cuban government currently puts major efforts into educating doctors. They learn not only medical skills but are also inculcated with a spirit of helping ordinary people. After graduation they serve two years in underserved communities. Government-run hospitals and clinics provide the only new jobs in the medical field. Cuba's medical infrastructure does need improvement. The U.S. embargo and Cuban government mistakes have degraded parts of the system. The country needs new equipment and new buildings. After the collapse of socialism, U.S. hospital chains could set up branches in Cuba with modern equipment. They would also attract the best doctors by offering better salaries.

Some Cuban doctors would open lucrative private practices. The government could continue to fund public hospitals, but how long would it take for the best doctors to migrate to the private sector, leaving the poor with second-class care? And how long would it take for the cash-starved government to slash the health care costs to balance the budget? Good-quality, free health care would become a distant memory. We don't have to speculate on this scenario. Russia's health care system went into cardiac arrest after Boris Yeltsin seized power in 1991. Partly as a result of poor medical care, life expectancy in Russia has actually *declined* since the early 1990s.[10]

Black Cubans would suffer the most in this transition. The new, all-white elite from Miami would have little concern for them. Without health care, education, transportation, and other subsidized programs, black Cubans would see their economic conditions plummet far faster than those of whites.

Even if you don't believe everything that I've sketched above, many Cubans do. The prospect of a pro-U.S. Miami elite running Cuba terrifies them. So what constitutes a more realistic prospect for Cuba's future?

The Cuban leadership closely studied the experiences in the USSR and Eastern Europe. They blame Mikhail Gorbachev for unleashing political change while doing little to improve the economy. The Cuban leaders will make few changes in the political system while making some incremental changes economically. Since 1991, Cuban officials have paid many visits to China and Vietnam. Those countries have gone much further than Cuba in liberalizing markets, cutting wasteful government subsidies, and requiring enterprises to be profitable. China has eliminated state ownership in whole sectors, such as agriculture, preferring to control the top economic institutions and maintain political control through the Communist Party.

But many Cubans don't like the rampant corruption, consumerism, and loss of revolutionary ideals they see in China. Instead, Raúl Castro and the Cuban leadership built on the programs developed by the Cuban army during the special period. The army had to become virtually self-sufficient, earning money from businesses to pay for supplies and even growing its own food. Carlos Lage, vice president of the Council of State, referred to this system as *perfeccionamiento empresarial,* or perfecting the company system, that is, providing better management to state enterprises.[11] Raúl wanted local managers to have greater control and workers to receive more pay for more work. The government officially lifted caps on worker salaries and called for more bonuses for good work. For example, the oil industry will remain state owned in order to prevent foreign corporations from dominating energy supplies. But managers at oil drilling sites or refineries will have more decision-making power over wages, incentives, and use of supplies.

Cuba may also experiment with additional market reforms, including limited buying and selling of houses. The government hopes to eliminate the dual currency system by earning more hard currency through exports. The Cuban Central Bank has already proposed cutting back on "indiscriminate government subsidies" to reduce state expenditures and strengthen the peso.[12] The government has floated plans to allow Cubans to freely travel abroad and return without penalty. In the short term, this reform would allow for greater remittances as Cubans obtain employment abroad. In the long run, it could generate greater political freedoms beneficial to the entire society.

But these are clearly incremental reforms. At what point would they be sufficient to change Washington's policies toward Cuba?

≡

The decision to alter U.S.-Cuban relations will depend on developments in Washington, not Havana. Future administrations could decide that the changes in Cuba are significant and therefore initiate negotiations. The decision would certainly be opposed by the Cuba Lobby and entrenched anticommunists in the State Department and security agencies. On the other hand, a growing number of elected politicians, businesspeople, and grassroots activists favor opening up relations with Cuba. The question is: will they be able to reach a critical mass?

To some extent, the Cuba debate cuts across traditional political party lines. In recent years, conservative Republicans and moderate Democrats have joined together to maintain the status quo on Cuba. A strong majority of Republicans and Democrats voted for both the 1994 Torricelli and 1996 Helms-Burton laws. George Bush Jr. tightened the embargo once again in 2004, with bipartisan support from senators John McCain and Hillary Clinton.[13]

Many progressives hoped President Bill Clinton would lift parts of the U.S. embargo during his second term when he no longer faced political pressure to get elected. He did informally loosen the embargo by not pursuing civil fines against Americans traveling to Cuba. He also allowed Cuban musicians and artists to perform in the United States. But otherwise, he continued the same stringent policies against Cuba as previous administrations. During her 2008 campaign for president, Sen. Hillary Clinton took a strident hard line against Cuba. She courted the Miami ultraconservative vote by saying she would keep Bush's 2004 restrictions in place. Her position on Cuba was identical to that of Sen. John McCain.

Sen. Barack Obama differed with Bush on some Cuba policies. He opposed the 2004 restrictions, reflecting the views of many Cuban American Democrats in Florida. He voted against funding TV Martí, saying it was a waste of taxpayer money (Sen. Hillary Clinton voted in favor of that bill). But Obama's differences were incremental. He campaigned in Miami using strident, anticommunist rhetoric. "Throughout my entire life, there has been injustice in Cuba. Never, in my lifetime, have the people of Cuba known freedom . . . This is the terrible and tragic status quo that we have known for half a century—of elections that are anything but free or fair; of dissidents locked away in dark prison cells for the crime of speaking the truth. I won't stand for this injustice, you won't stand for this injustice, and together we will stand up for freedom in Cuba."[14]

Obama also tried to sound hawkish by telling a Chilean newspaper he would favor UN or OAS sanctions against Venezuela because of President Hugo Chávez's alleged support for Marxist guerrillas in neighboring Colombia.[15] Neither international body is likely to vote for such sanctions, but it made Obama sound tough.

Ironically, some conservative Republican leaders—not running for national office—sounded more conciliatory. Sen. Kay Bailey Hutchison, a conservative Republican from Texas, said, "I have believed for a while that we should be looking at a new strategy for Cuba and that is opening more trade, especially food trade, especially if we can give the people more contact with the outside world, if we can build up an economy that might make the people more able to fight the dictatorship. I think that's something that we should have considered a while back, honestly."[16] Hutchison reflected the views of many politicians from farm states. Agribusiness could be making a lot more profits if the United States lifted the trade embargo.

Given the dynamics of Washington, it seems unlikely that any president will take the lead in changing Cuba policy. Pressure to change will have to percolate up from the grassroots to the House, Senate, and eventually to the White House.

≡

In September 2003, the House of Representatives voted 227–188 to eliminate the ban on Americans traveling to Cuba, and a month later the Senate voted to lift the ban by 59–38.[17] Those majorities consisted of farm state legislators, liberals, and libertarian-minded Republicans who opposed unilateral sanctions. Under the threat of a veto by President Bush, however, Congress dropped the bill. Strong critics of U.S. policy included progressives such as Rep. Barbara Lee (D-CA) and Rep. Charles Rangel (D-NY) but also conservatives such as Rep. Jeff Flake (R-FL) and Sen. Pat Roberts (R–KS).

Philip Peters, a former State Department official and now a fellow at Washington's Lexington Institute, told me House Republicans play a crucial role on any Cuba vote. He divided them into three categories. "About a third votes in favor of lifting sanctions. A third is genuinely opposed to it. And another third votes to maintain the sanctions, although their real opinion is opposed. These are the same legislators who favor trade with China and . . . Vietnam."[18]

That one-third and their Democratic counterparts are subject to tremendous lobbying. For example, the U.S.-Cuba Democracy PAC, funded by wealthy Cuban Americans from Dade County, Florida, contributed $446,500 to Congress members in 2006–07, including a minimum of $1,000 to every 2006 freshman representative.[19] Rep. Denny Rehberg (R-MT) had supported loosening the embargo in order to help agricultural exports from his state, but he switched sides and received $10,500 in campaign contributions from the PAC.[20] Three ultraconservative Cuban Congress members from South Florida constituted a key link for the Cuba Lobby: Ileana Ros-Lehtinen and Lincoln and Mario Díaz-Balart. But in 2008, for the first time, the Díaz-Balart brothers faced serious challenges from Cuban American Democrats. Former CANF leader Joe García ran against Mario Díaz-Balart, and former Hialeah Mayor Raúl Martínez ran against Lincoln.

Both challengers were conservative Democrats who strongly denounced the Cuban government and supported the embargo. They differed with the hard-liners by opposing Bush's 2004 measures. The two Democrats hoped to mobilize support from American-born voters of Cuban descent and more recent Cuban émigrés. They also hoped to capitalize on the Díaz-Balart brothers' reputation for sleazy activity. The *Miami Herald* revealed, for example, that the Díaz-Balart brothers sponsored a bill benefiting a Maryland prosthetics maker and received

$10,000 just before introducing the bill, and a total of $130,000 over several months. Melanie Sloan, executive director of the Washington nonprofit Citizens for Responsibility and Ethics, said "Members are here to serve the public interest and not the interests of a private corporation."[21] The Díaz-Balart brothers denied any wrongdoing.

A defeat for any of the three ultraconservative congressional representatives would be perceived as a significant loss for the hard-liners, according to Professor Andy Gomez, senior fellow at the Institute for Cuban and Cuban American Studies at the University of Miami. "It will be a changing of the guard. Maybe Cubans will look at the issue differently. They would lobby to lift the travel ban. We are beginning for the first time to have real challenges for the seat of power."[22]

If conditions change in Miami and Washington, and the United States wants to have relations with the post-Fidel government in Cuba, how will Cuban leaders respond?

Cuban officials said they are willing to normalize relations with the United States under certain circumstances. They won't accept the current demands that the country abandon socialism prior to starting talks. "If the American government continues to insist that Cuba has to make dramatic change to its economic and political system, that's a nonstarter," said Josefina Vidal, the Foreign Ministry's director of North American Affairs. "The same way we won't discuss the American way of government, ours is not open for discussion."[23]

Cuban leaders focus on what they consider certain key issues. They want the United States to stop terrorist attacks on the island launched from Florida. They oppose the "wet foot/dry foot" policy that encourages illegal and dangerous emigration from Cuba. Cuban leaders want the United States to return the Guantánamo Bay Naval Base, which they see as Cuban territory seized by the United States during the years of unequal relations between the two countries. And finally, they would like greater cooperation on interdiction of drug traffickers.

A U.S. president will not pull troops out of Guantánamo in the current political climate, but there should be room for talks on the other matters. Diplomats interviewed for this book told me that the narcotics issue holds a lot of promise. Col. Lawrence Wilkerson, former advisor to Colin Powell, told me, "The Cubans are our best partners in the counter-drug and counter-terror war in the Caribbean, even better than Mexico. The military looked at Cuba as a very cooperative partner."[24] He said agreements on fighting narcotics could lead to cooperation elsewhere. The United States has completely reversed course and reached agreements with other Cold War enemies. That experience could apply to Cuba as well.

≡

Republican and Democratic administrations have vilified North Korea for 50 years. The totalitarian regime oppresses its own people and poses a direct military threat to U.S. troops stationed in South Korea. In 2002, President Bush referred to North Korea as part of the Axis of Evil, along with Iran and Iraq. While the United States was busy invading Iraq in 2003, however, North Korea withdrew from the Nuclear Non-Proliferation Treaty and began developing nuclear weapons. Two former Defense Department officials advocated bombing North Korea's missile sites.[25] The Bush administration tried to bring economic and diplomatic pressure on North Korea through Japan, South Korea, and China. But China balked at proposed U.S. plans for a stringent economic embargo, let alone a military attack. In October 2006, North Korea conducted a successful underground test of a nuclear weapon.

So in 2007, the Bush administration radically changed course. The State Department under Condoleezza Rice negotiated with North Korean leaders. The Koreans agreed to stop further development of nuclear weapons in return for economic aid from the United States, the lifting of some economic sanctions, and the removal of Korea from the U.S. list of state sponsors of terrorism. North Korea didn't agree to give up its *existing* nuclear weapons, let alone change its political and economic system.[26] Conservatives called the agreement a sellout because they claimed Korea would never give up its nuclear bombs. But Secretary of State Condoleezza Rice referred to it as "an important, if initial, step."[27]

The settlement left Cuba the only country in the world subject to sanctions under the Trading with the Enemy Act, the law that prohibits Americans from spending money in Cuba. The North Korea settlement reflected a major shift in U.S. policy disguised as a pragmatic victory. Ironically, the Bush administration wouldn't even meet with leaders of Cuba but sat at the table with people it considers to be nuclear-armed, totalitarian terrorists.

Of course, there are differences in the two situations. From Washington's viewpoint, North Korea presents a real military threat. North Korean artillery and missiles can hit U.S. military bases inside South Korea. President Bush also had greater flexibility to negotiate. The president could unilaterally lift economic sanctions against North Korea. The Helms-Burton Act constrains any president's powers to lift sanctions or even negotiate without congressional approval. Nevertheless, the United States could take a similar approach with Cuba, which presents no immediate military threat and doesn't sponsor fundamentalist or any other kind of terrorism. U.S. farmers could export more food, and U.S. companies could participate in joint ventures to develop the oil and gas fields off Cuba's coast.

For the United States to change course on Cuba, several factors would have to come together. Washington leaders would have to perceive Raúl Castro's economic reforms as significant. U.S. business interests would need to pressure Congress and the president to lift the embargo. And the Cuba Lobby would have to face some political setbacks. Colonel Wilkerson said Cuban Americans are starting to break with hard-line, anti-Cuba policies. "Ultimately that's the straw that will break the camel's back. But it will take time. Once we get Cuban Americans feeling differently about Cuba, we will get a sea change. Let's face it, we have a stupid policy toward Havana."

And if the U.S. policy doesn't change, attorney and lobbyist Robert Muse told me, Cuba can afford to wait. "We're isolated on Cuba. Cuba needs a rapprochement with the U.S. far less than it did 15 years ago." Thumbing its nose at the United States, he said, "gives Cuba stature in the world."[28]

So the ball is in the U.S. court. The question remains whether U.S. leaders are willing to play.

Notes

Chapter 1

1. Before 1959 Cuba had been better off economically than most countries in Latin America in terms of life expectancy, medical care, and education for city dwellers. But rural farmers and workers, the majority of the population, lived in poverty and without access to many of those services. The Cuban Revolution improved the lives of all Cubans. Today the island enjoys the second highest literacy rate in the world (99.8 percent). Life expectancy in Cuba went from 55 years in 1955 to 77 years in 2005, according to UN statistics. See http://globalis .gvu.unu.edu/indicator_detail.cfm?IndicatorID=116&Country=CU. For a discussion of conditions in pre-1959 Cuba, see Richard Gott, *Cuba: A New History* (New Haven: Yale University Press, 2004), 165.

2. In the United States, Cuba is usually called a communist country. Cubans consider the island to be socialist. In Marxist theory, socialism is the long period of transition after capitalism but before communism. In this book I will call Cuba a socialist country because that's what the people themselves prefer. Similarly, I refer to residents of the United States as "Americans," even though people in Latin America often resent the term because they are Americans as well.

3. *Ramparts* magazine began as a progressive Catholic lay publication in 1963. It became the most famous investigative reporting magazine of its era under editors such as Warren Hinckle, Robert Scheer, and Adam Hochschild. I was hired at *Ramparts* as a late-night typist, and then moved up to researcher, research editor, and staff writer.

4. By 1968, SDS had a membership in the tens of thousands with four hundred chapters nationwide. It was an anti-imperialist organization that opposed the Vietnam War and supported black power and women's rights. It split in 1969

into several factions. The Weatherman faction carried out bombings and other ultraleft actions, which quickly isolated them politically. I opposed the Weatherman faction from the beginning.

5. A *mojito* is made with white rum, crushed mint, sugar, and soda water. It has been popular in Cuba for generations but only caught on in the United States in recent years. Think of it as the Buena Vista Social Club of rum drinks.

6. I don't use the term "terrorist" loosely. As you will read in detail in chapters 3 and 4, the CIA trained Cuban exiles to shoot, bomb, and murder civilians in an effort to bring about regime change in Cuba.

7. The U.S. government calls its policy an "economic embargo"; the Cuban government refers to it as a "blockade" because it seeks to cut Cuba off from all trade, even with third countries, and destroy the Cuban economy. I use the term embargo because it remains more familiar to American readers.

8. Che Guevara and Fidel Castro supported a theory that small, determined guerilla bands (*focos*) could spark revolution throughout Latin America. When pro-Cuban movements put the theory into practice, however, it failed to spark a single revolution. Since the 1960s, the *foco* theory has lost credibility and is no longer promoted by Cuba.

9. Ted Gold and two other Weathermen died while assembling a bomb in the basement of a Greenwich Village townhouse in 1970. The explosion disillusioned many Weathermen and their supporters, leading to even further political isolation.

10. For months leading up the October Olympics, Mexican students had been holding demonstrations to demand freedom for political prisoners, an abolition of a brutal tactical police unit, and an end to repressive legislation. Students peacefully occupied the National Autonomous University in Mexico City. On October 2, 1968, police and army units fired live ammunition into a peaceful rally being held at Plaza Tlatelolco, killing hundreds. The massacre remains a hot-button issue even today because no high-ranking Mexican officials were ever jailed for ordering the assault.

11. After 1959, the new government built on the existing health care system to provide free medical care throughout the country. Cuba's comprehensive system of preventative care and public health has been praised by the World Health Organization and many other international groups.

12. Julio Palamino, interview with author, August 31, 1968, Havana.

13. Fidel Castro, "Castro Comments on Czechoslovak Crisis," (speech), August 24, 1968, translated by FBIS, http://lanic.utexas.edu/la/cb/cuba/castro/1968/19680824.

14. Orlando Aloma, interview with author, August 30, 1968, Havana.

15. Raúl Roa Kouri, interview with author, September 21, 1968, Havana. Roa Kouri went on to become Cuba's ambassador to the UN and then ambassador to the Vatican.

16. Reese Erlich, "An unexpected star forward," *Ramparts*, November. 30, 1968.

17. In December 1978, Vietnam invaded neighboring Cambodia and toppled the Khmer Rouge government led by Pol Pot. China, which was allied with the Khmer Rouge at the time, angrily denounced the invasion, and there was a series of artillery exchanges along the Chinese-Vietnamese border. On February 17, 1979, Chinese troops invaded Vietnam, faced heavy resistance, and withdrew on March 16.

18. *New York Times*, "32 Cubans reported to drown in sinking," July 24, 1994.

19. Fidel Castro and Ignacio Ramonet, *Fidel Castro: My Life* (New York: Scribner, 2006), 343–44. Fidel Castro confirmed the details of the incident but said the boat collision was accidental.

20. Urbano Canizares and Gilda Zerquera, interview with author, January 27, 2008, Buffalo, New York.

Chapter 2

1. Richard Gott, *Cuba: A New History* (New Haven: Yale University Press, 2004), 102.

2. Ibid., 101.

3. Jim Zwick, ed., *Mark Twain's Weapons of Satire: Anti-Imperialist Writings on the Philippine-American War* (Syracuse: Syracuse University Press, 1992), http://www.historywiz.com/primarysources/marktwain-imperialism.htm.

4. See my interview with dissident Martha Beatriz Roque in chapter 12.

5. Fidel Castro and Ignacio Ramonet, *Fidel Castro: My Life* (New York: Scribner, 2006), 112.

6. In 1953 the CIA engineered a coup against the popularly elected government of Prime Minister Mohammad Mossadegh in Iran and installed the Shah

(king) as dictator. In 1954 the CIA instigated a military coup against elected President Jacobo Árbenz. Both were nationalists and favored neutrality in the Cold War, but neither were Marxists (see n. 15).

7. For a pro-U.S. government view of this period, see Bill Rogers, "Fidel Castro—A Profile," Voice of America website, August 1, 2006, http://voanews .com/english/archive/2006-08/2006-08-01-voa7.cfm?CFID=17053380&CF TOKEN=57543103.

8. Tad Szulc, *Fidel: A Critical Portrait* (New York: William Morrow and Co., 1986), 51.

9. U.S. Senate, "Alleged Assassination Plots Involving Foreign Leaders," November 1975, www.aarclibrary.org/publib/church/reports/ir/html/ChurchIR _0043a.htm.

10. Castro and Ramonet, *Fidel Castro*, 253 (see n. 5). Only future historians will be able to verify the number of assassination plots against Castro, but certainly they numbered in the hundreds.

11. U.S. Senate, 75 (see n. 9).

12. Castro and Ramonet, *Fidel Castro*, 253 (see n. 5).

13. Ibid., 262.

14. In 1973, General Augusto Pinochet overthrew the elected Chilean government of Salvador Allende. Pinochet, U.S. officials, and military leaders in the southern cone of South America created Operation Condor, which assassinated political opponents living abroad. CIA-trained Cuban exiles played a prominent role in this clandestine activity. In 1976, the Chilean intelligence agency (DINA) paid an agent to plant a car bomb in Washington DC, killing Letelier and Moffitt and severely wounding Moffitt's husband.

15. Elected president of Guatemala in 1951, Jacobo Árbenz was a capitalist reformer. He passed an agrarian reform law that offered to compensate landowners on the basis of the land value as declared on tax roles. United Fruit Company, today called Chiquita Brands International, had paid taxes of $3 per acre. It suddenly demanded compensation at $75 per acre. The CIA instigated a coup against Árbenz in 1954, claiming communist influence in his government. The new, U.S.-backed military government cancelled the land reform, and Guatemala remained under military rule for many years. Cuba implemented a similar land reform, with a similar reaction from U.S. corporate landowners.

16. K. S. Carol, *Guerrillas in Power* (New York: Hill & Wang, 1970), 17.

17. Ibid., 14.

18. Seymour Hersh, *The Dark Side of Camelot* (New York: Little, Brown & Co., 1997), 208.

19. W. H. Lawrence, "President says policy of nonintervention has its limits," *New York Times*, April 20, 1961. Kennedy was referring to the 1956 Soviet invasion of Hungary.

20. Pierre Salinger, "Kennedy, Cuba and cigars," *Cigar Aficionado Magazine*, November/December 2002.

21. CIA, Minutes, TOP SECRET, "Minutes of Meeting of the Special Group (Augmented) on Operation Mongoose," 4 October 1962, National Security Archive, George Washington University, www.gwu.edu/~nsarchiv/nsa/cuba_mis_cri/docs.htm.

22. Brig. Gen. Edward Lansdale, "Review of Operation Mongoose," Phase One, July 25, 1962, National Security Archive, www.gwu.edu/~nsarchiv/nsa/cuba_mis_cri/docs.htm.

23. Eloy Gutiérrez Menoyo, interview with author, March 28, 2008, Havana.

24. Hersh, *The Dark Side*, 355 (see n. 18).

25. Ibid., 361.

26. Castro and Ramonet, *Fidel Castro*, 278 (see n. 5).

27. Francis X. Clines, "A Khrushchev is pledging new allegiance," *New York Times*, July 11, 1999.

28. Wayne Smith was chief of the U.S. Interests Section in Havana 1979–82. I interviewed him January 28, 2008, in Washington DC.

29. *San Francisco Chronicle*, "CIA link to Cuban pig virus reported," reprinted from *Newsday*, January 10, 1977.

30. Quoted in Stuart McMillan, "Biowarfare over Cuban skies," *The Manatoban*, February 25, 1998, www.themanitoban.com/1997-1998/0225/feat.html. A complete list of biological attacks against Cuba can be found at www.poptel.org.uk/cuba-solidarity/CubaSi-January/Bio.html.

31. Castro and Ramonet, *Fidel Castro*, 252 (see n. 5).

32. Stuart McMillan, "Biowarfare" (see n. 30).

33. Ibid., chap. 3.

Chapter 3

1. Col. Lawrence Wilkerson, interview with author, January 29, 2008, Washington DC.

2. On February 20, 1980, President Carter submitted a belligerent report to Congress criticizing Cuba. Jane Franklin, *Cuba and the United States: A Chronological History* (New York: Ocean Press, 1997), 150.

3. Quoted in David W. Engstrom, *Presidential Decision Making Adrift: The Carter Administration and the Mariel Boatlift* (New York: Rowman and Littlefield, 1997), 162.

4. Wayne Smith, "End the Travel Ban to Cuba," International Policy Report, The Center for International Study's Cuba Program, November 2001, www.ciponline.org/cuba/ipr/TravelBan.htm.

5. Wayne Smith, interview with author, January 28, 2008, Washington DC.

6. U.S. Department of State, "Country Reports on Terrorism 2007," issued April 2008, 172, www.state.gov/documents/organization/105904.pdf.

7. Castro said, "Cuba . . . was the first country to express its solidarity with the people of the United States on Sept. 11, 2001, [and] was also the first to warn that . . . the extreme Right in the U.S. . . . was a danger to the world." Fidel Castro and Ignacio Ramonet, *Fidel Castro: My Life* (New York: Scribner, 2006), 562.

8. Ibid., 211.

9. The Saudi government was a key financer of the mujahedeen and Osama Bin Laden when they were using terrorist tactics to fight the Soviet occupation of Afghanistan in the 1980s. Nineteen of the 9/11 hijackers were citizens of Saudi Arabia, and Saudi diplomats allegedly financed at least one of them. See Desmond Butler, "Saudis withdraw Berlin diplomat after Germans cite possible militant link," *New York Times*, April 25, 2003. Pakistan's military and intelligence services have cooperated with Taliban attacks on Afghanistan and fundamentalist attacks on Indian-occupied Kashmir.

10. Catherine Wilson, "Jury mulls Cuban espionage case," Associated Press, *Miami Herald*, June 5, 2001.

11. Cuban exile Luis Posada Carriles admitted organizing the 1997 bombing of Havana hotels in order to scare away foreign tourists. One Italian tourist was murdered during the bombing campaign (see n.11, chap. 4).

12. Wilkerson, interview (see n. 1).

Chapter 4

1. Col. Lawrence Wilkerson, interview with author, January 29, 2008, Washington DC.

2. USA Today/Gallup Poll, February 2008, www.pollingreport.com/cuba .htm. This website also provides data from various polling organizations going back to 1998. American public opinion has gradually shifted to oppose the U.S. embargo and favor full diplomatic relations with Cuba, among Democrats, Republicans, and independents.

3. 2007 poll conducted by the Institute for Public Opinion Research and the Cuban Research Institute of Florida International University, www.fiu .edu/~ipor/cuba8/ExecutiveSummary.htm.

4. Ann Louise Bardach, *Cuba Confidential: Love and Vengeance in Miami and Havana* (New York: Vintage Books, 2002), 116.

5. Ann Louise Bardach and Larry Rohter, "Life in the shadows: Trying to bring down Castro," *New York Times*, July 13, 1998.

6. Peter Kornbluth, "The Posada File: Part II," National Security Archive, June 9, 2005, www.gwu.edu/~nsarchiv/NSAEBB/NSAEBB157/index.htm.

7. Bardach and Rohter, "Life in the shadows" (see n. 5).

8. In 1974, Cuban exile leader José Elías de la Torriente was murdered in his home after disobeying orders for a planned invasion of Cuba. That same year, Hector Díaz Limonta and Arturo Rodríguez Vives were murdered during internal power struggles. See Jim Mullin, "The burden of a violent history," *Miami New Times*, April 19, 2000.

9. Jim McGee, "Lawmen see firebrand turning to crime," *Miami Herald*, Dec. 30, 1983.

10. Mullin, "The burden of a violent history" (see n. 8). Alpha 66 was founded by Cuban exile Eloy Gutiérrez Menoyo and carried out a series of terrorist attacks inside the United States and in Cuba. See also chapter 11.

11. Luis Posada Carriles was arrested on immigration charges in 2005 after sneaking back into the United States, but an immigration judge later dropped the charges, and Posada was released. In August 2008, a federal appeals court reinstated the charges. Venezuela's Ambassador to the United States, Bernardo Álvarez, said the United States had ignored his country's extradition request for Posada. A federal grand jury in Newark, New Jersey, met in 2008 to consider conspiracy charges against Posada for his role in killing an Italian tourist in Havana in a 1997 hotel bombing. Posada admitted to the attack in a *New York Times* interview and investigators have other hard evidence, but it remains to be seen if the next presidential administration pursues the case.

12.   *Miami Herald* journalist Andres Oppenheimer, a harsh Castro critic, details Reagan administration efforts to form CANF. Andres Oppenheimer, *Castro's Final Hour: The Secret Story Behind the Coming Downfall of Communist Cuba* (New York: Simon and Shuster, 1992), 329.

13.   Sen. Joe Lieberman was a conservative Democrat who later became Al Gore's vice presidential running mate in 2000. Lieberman became an independent after losing the Connecticut Democratic primary to a peace candidate in 2006. He supported John McCain for president in 2008.

14.   Ann Louise Bardach and Larry Rohter, "Key Cuba foe claims exiles' backing," *New York Times*, July 12, 1998. Posada later denied that he had received CANF money, but the reporters had recorded the original interviews.

15.   Ibid.

16.   Bardach, *Cuba Confidential*, 117, 199 (see n. 4).

17.   Anne-Marie O'Connor, "Trying to set the agenda in Miami," *Columbia Journalism Review*, May/June 1992.

18.   Cuban Information Archives, Document 0146b, "Broadcasting to Cuba," 1991–94, http://cuban-exile.com/doc_126-150/doc0146b.html.

19.   Human Rights Watch, "Restriction of Free Expression in Miami's Cuban Exile Community," 1994, www.hrw.org/reports/1995/WR95/HRW GEN.htm.

20.   Francisco Aruca, phone interview with author, February 26, 2008.

21.   Jay Taylor, interview with author, January 29, 2008, Arlington, Virginia.

22.   Philip Peters, interview with author, January 31, 2008, Washington DC.

23.   Taylor, interview (see n. 21). Torricelli's favorable comments about Cuba were also reported by Scott Orr, *Newark Star Ledger*, November 24, 1988.

24.   Paul Anderson and Christopher Marquis, "N.J. congressman makes Castro's demise his crusade: Get-tougher bill pushed by Torricelli," *Miami Herald*, February 2, 1992.

25.   Robert Muse, interview with author, January 28, 2008, Washington DC.

26.   Sen. Jesse Helms (1912–2008) was a hard-line conservative even within the Republican Party. He was a staunch supporter of racial segregation in the 1950s, called Nelson Mandela a terrorist in the 1970s, and refused federal funding for AIDS in the 1980s because he disagreed with the homosexual lifestyle.

27.   Jane Franklin, *Cuba and the United States a Chronological History* (New York: Oceans Press, 1997), 363. Sanchez testified before the House of Repre-

sentatives in 1998 as a spokesperson for Bacardi-Martini Corp, http://judiciary .house.gov/Legacy/42011.htm.

28. Francisco "Pepe" Hernández, interview with author, February 25, 2008, Miami.

29. Bardach, *Cuba Confidential*, 71 (see n. 4).

30. Cuban Research Institute, "FIU/Cuba Poll," Institute for Public Opinion Research, School of Journalism and Mass Communication, Center for Labor Research and Studies, Florida International University, October 19, 2000, fiu.edu/orgs/ipor/cuba2000/exsumm.htm.

31. Ninoska Pérez Castellón, interview with author, February 27, 2008, Miami.

Chapter 5

1. Zachary Coile, "Back to 'Elian Times' in Miami: Bush campaign organizes protest to challenge Miami-Dade officials," *San Francisco Chronicle*, November 23, 2000. There were numerous examples of vote irregularities and outright fraud in Florida. But the U.S. Supreme Court ordered all vote recounts halted, and Bush became president. A consortium of news organizations later did its own vote recount, showing Gore won statewide.

2. U.S. Government Accountability Office, B-229069, September 30, 1987, 66 Comp.Gen. 707, http://redbook.gao.gov/13/fl0061375.php.

3. The United States and Israel supplied tens of millions of dollars in military equipment to Iran in the 1980s and used the profits to illegally arm the Contras fighting the elected government of Nicaragua. Abrams was involved in arranging illegal money transfers. For a general description of the scandal, see Reese Erlich, *The Iran Agenda: The Real Story of U.S. Policy and the Middle East Crisis* (Sausalito: Polipoint Press, 2007), 66–67.

4. Ed Vulliamy, "Venezuela coup linked to Bush team," *The Observer* (London), April 21, 2002.

5. Lawrence M. O'Rourke, "Bolton faces tough questioning from Democrats," McClatchy Newspapers, April 11, 2005.

6. Col. Lawrence Wilkerson, interview with author, January 29, 2008, Washington DC.

7. Norman Solomon and Reese Erlich, *Target Iraq: What the News Media Didn't tell You* (New York: Context Books, 2003), 110.

8. Joe García, interview with author, February 25, 2008, Miami.

9. GAO Report, "Foreign Assistance: U.S. Democracy Assistance for Cuba Needs Better Management and Oversight," November 2006.

10. Paul Richter, "Cuba USAID program gets overhaul," *Los Angeles Times*, May 7, 2008.

11. Karen DeYoung, "GAO Audit finds waste in Cuban aid program," *Washington Post*, November 16, 2006.

12. Pablo Bachelet, "A Bush Cuba advisor resigns over alleged funds misuse," *Miami Herald*, March 28, 2008.

13. In 2005, Sen. Ted Stevens (R-AL) was strongly criticized for pork barrel projects, including the Gravina Island and Knik Arm bridges, known as the "bridges to nowhere." In 2007, the bridges were canceled as too costly.

14. Prof. Andy Gomez, interview with author, Feb. 27, 2008, Miami. Professor Gomez, senior fellow at the Institute for Cuban and Cuban American Studies, interviews Cuban refugees after their arrival in Florida, and he told me none had ever seen TV Martí.

15. Laura Wides-Munoz, "Mission of U.S.-funded broadcasts in Cuba debated," Associated Press, May 20, 2008.

16. Ninoska Pérez Castellón, interview with author, February 27, 2008, Miami.

17. Anthony Boadle, "Vatican broaches Cuba prisoners with Raul Castro," Reuters, February 27, 2008.

18. Miguel Bustillo and Carol J. Williams, "Cuban-Americans' attitudes shift," *Los Angeles Times*, February 26, 2008.

19. Bendixen & Associates, "Survey of Cuban and Cuban-American Resident Adults in Miami-Dade and Broward Counties," September, 2006. www.ndn.org/hispanic/memos/Cuban-Exile-Poll.pdf.

20. Prof. Andy Gomez, interview with author, February 27, 2008, Miami.

21. Institute for Public Opinion Research and the Cuban Research Institute of Florida International University, March 26, 2007, www.fiu.edu/~ipor/cuba8/ExecutiveSummary.htm.

22. It's difficult to determine the precise percentage of registered Cuban Americans because voter rolls don't include ethnicity. So analysts rely on public opinion polls. See Ed Kilgore, "Time for Dems to play Cuba card in FL?" *Democratic Strategist*, August 23, 2007, thedemocraticstrategist.org/strategist/2007/08/time_for_dems_to_play_cuba_car.php.

23. Shannon Colavecchio-Van Sickler, "State universities fear brain drain is setting in," *Los Angeles Times*, January 23, 2008.

24. Mary Ellen Klas, "Families protest crackdown on Cuba travel," *Miami Herald*, June 11, 2008.

25. Garcia, interview, (see n. 8).

26. Ann Louise Bardach, *Cuba Confidential: Love and Vengeance in Miami and Havana* (New York: Vintage Books, 2002), 141.

27. Rod Leveque, "Ferro gets five years; Upland man sentenced to prison for weapons stockpile," *Inland Valley Daily Bulletin*, August 27, 2007.

28. Tristram Korten and Kirk Nielsen, "The coddled 'terrorists' of South Florida," *Salon.com*, January 14, 2008.

29. *Miami Herald*, "Some Miami Cuban exiles said linked to migrant smuggling in Mexico," June 26, 2008.

30. Carol Williams, "Cubans heading to U.S.—Via Mexico," *Los Angeles Times*, July 18, 2008.

31. Francisco Aruca, phone interview with author, February 26, 2008, Miami. Aruca was host of the daily radio show "Ayer en Miami" on WOCN-AM and also owned Marazul Travel, an agency specializing in travel to Cuba.

32. Medea Benjamin, phone interview with author, May 27, 2008.

33. Wayne Smith, interview with author, January 28, 2008, Washington DC.

Chapter 6

1. The embargo allows journalists, academic researchers, Cubans visiting family, and certain other categories of people to travel legally.

2. *Guardian* (London), "Bush allows Americans to send mobile phones to Cuban relatives," McClatchy Newspapers, May 22, 2008.

3. *New York Times*, "U.N. votes against U.S. embargo on Cuba for 16th year," Reuters, October 30, 2007.

4. Milton Friedman, phone interview with author, May 23, 1994. Economist Friedman (1912–2006) became popular with conservative world leaders because of his argument that free market capitalism produces political democracy. His adherents included Ronald Reagan, Margaret Thatcher, and Gen. Augusto Pinochet of Chile.

5. Wayne Smith, interview with author, January 28, 2008, Washington DC.

6. Michael Skol, phone interview with author, June 3, 1994.

7. The Cuban government doesn't release figures on the number of Americans visiting Cuba. This MSNBC article estimated 150,000 Americans visited in 2007. Christopher Elliott, "Traveling in a post-Fidel Castro Cuba," MSNBC.com, Feb. 21, 2008.

8. Skol, interview (see n. 6).

9. Author interview with official at U.S. Interests Section, October 12, 2003, Havana. Under standard State Department policy, the official would not let her name be used. She confirmed that Cuban musicians may only receive travel reimbursement and per diem because they were "employed by the Cuban government."

10. Roy Hargrove, interview with author, 1998, Oakland.

11. *Granma,* "Cuba denounces effects of U.S. economic blockade," September 18, 2007.

12. See Venceremos website, www.venceremosbrigde.org, and Pastors for Peace, www.ifconews.org.

13. Jessica (Decca) Mitford wrote *The American Way of Death* and numerous other investigative exposés.

14. Small portions of this chapter originally appeared in my story for the *Christian Science Monitor,* "Crack in Cuban embargo is wide enough for pianos," January 9, 1996.

15. Reese Erlich, "US piano tuner in Havana strikes sour note with feds," *Christian Science Monitor,* May 10, 1996.

16. Tom Miller, letter to the editor, *San Francisco Chronicle,* May 7, 1996.

17. CBS Evening News, July 16, 1996.

18. U.S. Government Accountability Office, "Economic Sanctions: Agencies Face Competing Priorities in Enforcing the U.S. Embargo on Cuba," GAO-08-80 November 30, 2007.

19. Smith, interview (see n. 5).

20. Robert Muse, interview with author, January 28, 2008, Washington DC.

21. Philip Peters, interview with author, January 31, 2008, Washington DC.

Chapter 7

1. Fidel Castro and Ignacio Ramonet, *Fidel Castro: My Life* (New York: Scribner, 2006), 580.

2. In 1973 Vice President Spiro Agnew resigned in a bribery scandal. The

Watergate scandal forced the resignation of President Richard Nixon in 1974, and Gerald Ford became president. Vietnam won the war in 1975 in a humiliating defeat for the United States. By the mid-1970s, the U.S. empire was weakened militarily and politically.

3. Peter Kornbluh, ed., *Conflicting Missions: Secret Cuban Documents on History of Africa Involvement*, National Security Archive Electronic Briefing Book No. 67, www.gwu.edu/~nsarchiv/NSAEBB/NSAEBB67/index2.html.

4. Stephen Zunes, "The US invasion of Grenada: A twenty year retrospective," *Foreign Policy in Focus*, October 2003.

5. *New York Times*, "60 soldiers leave Grenada; Last of U.S. invasion force," Associated Press, June 13, 1985.

6. Castro and Ramonet, *Fidel Castro*, 333 (see n. 1).

7. Orlando Bosch Salado, interview with author, March 20, 2008, Havana.

8. Interview with author, September 17, 1968, Isle of Youth.

9. K. S. Carol, *Guerrillas in Power* (New York: Hill and Wang, 1970), 354.

10. Richard Gott, *Cuba: A New History* (New Haven: Yale University Press, 2004), 236.

11. Interview with author, September 5, 1968, Holguín.

12. Gott, *Cuba*, 243 (see n. 10).

13. Fernando Funes, "The Organic Farming Movement in Cuba," *Sustainable Agriculture and Resistance: Transforming Food Production in Cuba* (Oakland: Food First Books, 2002), 6.

14. Gott, *Cuba*, 244 (see n. 10).

15. Castro and Ramonet, *Fidel Castro*, 585 (see n. 1).

16. Ed Ewing, "Cuba's organic revolution," *Guardian* (London), April 5, 2008.

17. Gilda Zerquera, interview with author, December 12, 1992, Havana.

18. Archibald R. M. Ritter, "Cuba's Economic Performance and the Challenges Ahead," Canadian Foundation for the Americas, (FOCAL) Background Briefing, RFC-02-1, January 2002, 10.

19. Ibid., 5.

20. Gott, *Cuba*, 300 (see n. 10).

21. Carol J. Williams, "Cuba's two-currency system adds up to a social divide," *Los Angeles Times*, May 8, 2008. As of 2004, an estimated 10 percent of Cubans received hard currency remittances from relatives living abroad. U.S. residents sent an estimated $1.29 billion.

22. *CIA World Fact Book*, Cuba, Economy, updated May 1, 2008, www.cia
.gov/library/publications/the-world-factbook/geos/cu.html#Econ.

23. *Mercados Agropecuarios*, commonly called *agros*, refers to both larger
open-air farmers' markets and neighborhood stalls selling a limited number of
items. The stalls were operated by local farmer co-ops.

24. Reuters, "Cuba says nickel now top foreign exchange earner," January
15, 2008.

25. Many sources estimate Venezuela sends 100,000 barrels a day to Cuba,
but Cuba's ambassador to that country puts the figure at 90,000. See James
Painter, "Cuba set for small-scale change," BBC Online, February 25, 2008,
http://news.bbc.co.uk/2/hi/americas/7263541.stm.

26. All oil and gas figures from Marc Lacey, "Cuban refinery inaugurated,
with Chavez in spotlight," *New York Times*, December 22, 2007.

27. Castro and Ramonet, *Fidel Castro*, 598 (see n. 1).

28. The average Cuban salary in 2008 was about 400 pesos (US $17). Con-
vertible Pesos (CUCs) are a special currency usable only in Cuba. In 2008,
1 CUC equaled US $1.10.

29. Christina Martínez, interview with author, March 7, 2008, Havana.

30. Angela Weston, phone interview with author, May 15, 2008.

31. President Bush attacked Raúl Castro and called the reforms "empty
gestures." See Jennifer Loven, "Bush criticizes new Cuban leader," Associated
Press, May, 2008, www.time.com/time/nation/article/0,8599,1738316,00.html.

32. UN Human Development Reports, Cuba, 2007–8, http://hdrstats
.undp.org/countries/country_fact_sheets/cty_fs_CUB.html.

Chapter 8

1. Fernando Funes, interview with author, March 17, 2008, Havana.

2. Andrew Martin and Kim Severson, "Sticker shock in the organic aisles,"
New York Times, April 18, 2008.

3. In reporting about a sustainable logging operation in northern California, a lumber mill operator told me it actually costs less to produce trees using
sustainable and organic techniques, but he charges a 10 percent premium over
the price of his other wood. On the other hand, organic production at California wineries costs more than if they used chemicals. But wineries such as Fetzer
and Bonterra sell their wine for the same price as comparable nonorganic wines

and still make a healthy profit. That's because wine makers face fierce competition and worry that customers would not pay a premium for organic.

4. Fernando Funes, speech at agronomist meeting, March 17, 2008, Sancti Spíritus.

5. "Castro hits out at US biofuel use," *BBC News* online, March 29, 2007, http://news.bbc.co.uk/nolpda/ifs_news/hi/newsid_6505000/6505881.stm.

6. Jane Franklin, *Cuba and the United States: A Chronological History* (Melbourne and New York: Ocean Press, 1992), 93.

7. Paul Brown, "Kazakh dam condemns most of the shrunken Aral Sea to oblivion," *Guardian* (London), October 29, 2003.

8. Marcos Nieto and Ricardo Delgado, "Cuban Agriculture and Food Security," *Sustainable Agriculture and Resistance: Transforming Food Production in Cuba* (Oakland: Food First Books, 2002), 45.

9. Office of Global Analysis, *Cuba's Food and Agriculture Situation Report*, FAS, USDA, March 2008, 14–16.

10. Franklin, *Cuba and the United States*, 289 (see n. 6).

11. Nieto and Delgado, "Cuban Agriculture," 45 (see n. 8).

12. Fernando Funes, "The Organic Farming Movement in Cuba," *Sustainable Agriculture and Resistance: Transforming Food Production in Cuba* (Oakland: Food First Books, 2002), 8.

13. Office of Global Analysis, 16 (see n. 9).

14. José Casimiro, interview with author, March 18, 2008, near Sancti Spíritu.

15. Santiago Yáñez, interview with author, March 17, 2008, Sancti Spíritus. Yáñez is director of the Institute for Investigating Pastures and Forests, Cuban Ministry of Agriculture.

16. David Herszenhorn, "Tentative deal reached in Congress on farm bill," *New York Times*, April 26, 2008.

17. Yáñez, interview (see n. 15).

18. Raúl Ruiz, interview with author, March 17, 2008, Sancti Spiritus. Ruiz is deputy director, Institute for Investigating Pastures and Forests, Ministry of Agriculture.

19. Marta Núñez, interview with author, March 21, 2008, Havana.

20. Fernando Barrera, interview with author, March 16, 2008, San Cristóbal.

21. Ruiz, interview (see n. 18).

22. Marc Frank, "Cuba's agricultural decline sparks major reform," Reuters, April 3, 2008.

23. Sally Kohn, "Corporate agribusiness is behind our deadly food supply," *AlterNet,* December 18, 2006, www.alternet.org/environment/45530.

24. USDA press release, "Food security in the United States," November 14, 2007, www.ers.usda.gov/Briefing/FoodSecurity.

25. Dana Flavelle, "Ottawa funds 10% cull of pigs," *The Star* (Toronto), April 15, 2008.

26. Ruiz, interview (see n. 18).

27. The Helms-Burton Act bars foreign-owned subsidiaries of U.S. companies from investing in or trading with Cuba. A highly controversial section also seeks to penalize foreign companies that buy property once owned by Cuban Americans, even if they moved to the United States after 1959. For more details, see chapter 4.

28. Yáñez, interview (see note 15).

29. Marc Frank, "Cuba frets over import costs even as economy grows," Reuters, July 8, 2008.

Chapter 9

1. Desi Arnaz (1917–86) was born in Santiago, Cuba, and moved to the United States with his family when he was 16. Arnaz became the first famous Cuban American entertainer when he combined the music of his homeland with a contemporary sound appealing to American audiences. He's best remembered for portraying the character Ricky Ricardo on *I Love Lucy.*

2. Reese Erlich, "Cuba's growing tourism and music industries," *Common Ground* radio, Program 9738, September 23, 1997, www.commongroundradio.org/shows/97/9738.html.

3. Eliades Ochoa, interview with author, March 22, 2008, Havana.

4. Portions of this chapter first appeared in the *East Bay Monthly* magazine, November, 1999.

5. Santería is the Afro-Cuban religion that evolved during Spanish colonial times. Slaves pretended to pray to Catholic saints while in reality continuing to worship their traditional Yoruba gods.

6. Peter Watrous, "Film: Capturing a Cuban sound before it could die out," *New York Times,* June 6, 1999..

7. Rubén González, interview with author, July 19, 1999, Havana.

8. Eneida Lima, interview with author, July 19, 1999, Havana.

9. Mario Jorge Muñoz, interview with author, July 15, 1999, Havana.

10. Ibrahim Ferrer, interview with author, July 20, 1999, Havana.

11. *Reggaeton* emerged from Panama as a fusion of Jamaican and Latin musical styles. It includes rapping in Spanish. It is extremely popular in Cuba and many other Latin countries. *Timba* is a type of very danceable, upbeat Cuban music similar to salsa.

12. The CD *Cuba in Washington* features songs from Ochoa's group, Cuarteto Patria, as well as Grupo Changui de Guantánamo and Groupo Afro Cuba de Matanzas in a rip-roaring live performance. But they were considered "folkloric," and the CD wasn't even issued until 11 years after the performance, www.emusic.com/album/Various-Artists-Smithsonian-Folkways-Cuba-in-Washington-MP3-Download/10864592.html.

13. Lázaro Martínez, interview with author, July 17, 1999, Havana.

14. Giselle Garia, interview with author, October 8, 2003, Havana.

15. Violetta Pérez, interview with author, October 8, 2003, Havana.

16. Professor Marta Núñez, interview with author, March 21, 2008, Havana. When Professor Núñez lectures abroad, the University of Havana keeps 50 percent of her speaker's fee.

17. In a 1961 speech "Words to the Intellectuals" Fidel Castro said, "Within the revolution, everything. Against the revolution, nothing."

18. In the film *Lucía,* director Humberto Solás vividly portrays the lives of three different women named Lucía during various revolutionary Cuban upheavals, www.imdb.com/title/tt0064609. *Memories of Underdevelopment* won widespread acclaim in the United States, in part because of its willingness to criticize aspects of the revolution, as can be seen in this *New York Times* plot summary and review, www.movies.nytimes.com/movie/32147/Memories-of-Underdevelopment/overview.

19. Paulina Ugarte, interview with author, July 17, 1999, Havana.

20. Martínez, interview (see n. 13).

21. José Fuster, interview with author, March 19, 2008, Havana.

22. Dalia Acosta, "The times they are a-changin," Inter Press Service (IPS), April 7, 2008, http://ipsnews.net/news.asp?idnews=41895.

23. The film is badly overacted and features a soap-opera plot. For a laudatory summary of the film, see http://movies.yahoo.com/movie/1804462756/info.

24. David Adams, "Cuba troupe defects in Las Vegas," *St. Petersburg Times*, November 16, 2004.

25. Reuters, "Isaac Delgado defects to U.S.," January 26, 2007.

26. Bill Martínez, phone interview with author, April 22, 2008.

27. El Negro Hernández played at the 1999 "Cuban Bridge" concert in Havana. Gonzalo Rubalcaba performed at the 2002 Havana Jazz Festival, www .afrocubaweb.com/jazzfest2002.htm.

Chapter 10

1. Aracéliz Barrera, interview with author, December 10, 1992, near San Cristóbal, Cuba. Portions of this chapter are adapted from a 1993 NPR Horizon documentary about women in Cuba.

2. The attitude of male superiority known as machismo is prevalent throughout Latin America but is not qualitatively different from the male chauvinism of North America and Europe. A society's attitude toward women is a function of its political and economic system, as well as its cultural history.

3. Marisela Fleites-Lear, "Women, family, and the Cuban Revolution" (paper prepared for the Latin American Studies Association International Congress, September 1995), 4.

4. United Nations, "Cuba striving hard to eliminate persistent stereotypes, women's inequality," Department of Public Information, www.un.org/News/ Press/docs/2006/wom1570.doc.htm.

5. Ibid. Other statistics from Professor Marta Núñez, sociologist and consulting professor at the University of Havana, interview with author, March 21, 2008, Havana.

6. Fidel Castro and Ignacio Ramonet, *Fidel Castro: My Life* (New York: Scribner, 2006), 236.

7. José Luis Hernández, interview with author, March 16, 2008. San Cristóbal.

8. Panchita Cuni, interview with author, March 16, 2008. San Cristóbal.

9. Mariana Ramírez, interview with author, March 12, 2008. Havana.

10. Professor Marta Núñez, interview with author, December 13, 1992, Havana.

11. Professor Marta Núñez, interview with author, March 21, 2008, Havana.

12. Staff Writer, "Politburo member backs gay marriage in Cuba," PinkNews .co.uk, Feb. 11, 2008, www.pinknews.co.uk/news/articles/2005-6818.html.

13. Castro and Ramonet, *Fidel Castro*, 224 (see n. 6).

14. Ibid., 225.

15. Lee Lockwood, *Castro's Cuba, Cuba's Fidel: An American Journalist's Inside Look at Today's Cuba* (New York: Vintage, 1969), 107.

16. J. Edgar Hoover (1895–1972), the infamous head of the FBI, was himself a closeted homosexual, which didn't stop him from ruthlessly purging homosexuals from government service.

17. Fernando Ravsberg, "Controversial gay soap opera grips Cuba," BBC Mundo, May 3, 2006.

18. Esteban Israel, "Castro's niece fights for new revolution," Reuters, reprinted in Caribbean Net News, July 3, 2006.

19. Ramírez, interview (see n. 9).

20. Georgiana Bota, interview with author, December 15, 1992, Santiago, Cuba.

21. Cuban Supreme Court Justice Dr. Jorge Bodes, interview with author, July 20, 1999, Havana.

22. Interviews with Cuban students, Holguín, September 10, 1968. The *posadas* are rooms rented by the hour to couples, whether married or not.

23. Núñez, interview (see n. 11).

24. Margaret Randall, *Women in Cuba: Twenty Years Later*, p. 45, (New York: Smyrna Press, 1981)

25. UN Human Development Index, Cuba, 2007–8, http://hdrstats.undp .org/countries/country_fact_sheets/cty_fs_CUB.html.

26. CIA, "Chiefs of State and Cabinet Members of Foreign Governments," April 22, 2008, www.cia.gov/library/publications/world-leaders-1/world-leaders-c/cuba-nde.html. The Cuban cabinet had 27 filled positions as of this writing.

27. Fleites-Lear, "Women, family, and the Cuban Revolution," 12 (see n. 3).

Chapter 11

1. Francesco Belli, interview with author, March 13, 2008, Havana.

2. Luis Aragú, interview with author, March 15, 2008, Havana.

3. Cuban government census, "Characteristics of the Population," 2002,

www.cubagob.cu/otras_info/censo/poblacion.htm. Cuban anthropologists recognize 27 gradations of color in Cuba from very dark black skin to very light-skinned people of mixed race. In this book I use the term black Cuban to include everyone of African heritage, regardless of skin color.

4.   *Miami Herald*, "A barrier for Cuba's blacks; New attitudes on once-taboo race questions emerge with a fledgling black movement," June 20, 2007.

5.   Brazil, the last country to abolish slavery, did so in 1888, two years later than Cuba.

6.   Ms. Devyn Spence, interview with author February 27, 2008, Miami.

7.   PBS, "The Rise and Fall of Jim Crow," www.pbs.org/wnet/jimcrow/ stories_events_plessy.html.

8.   *Miami Herald*, "A barrier for Cuba's blacks" (see note 4).

9.   Professor Esteban Morales, Center for the Study of the U.S., University of Havana, interview with author, March 26, 2008.

10.   Ismael Barrera, interview with author, March 16, 2008, near San Cristóbal.

11.   Professor Marta Núñez, interview with author, March 21, 2008.

12.   Ángela Jiménez, interview with author, December 10, 1992, Havana. Part of Jiménez's story first aired in a 1993 NPR Horizons documentary about Cuban women.

13.   Ernestina Ford Jiménez, interview with author, March 21, 2008, Havana.

14.   Fidel Castro and Ignacio Ramonet, *Fidel Castro: My Life* (New York: Scribner, 2006), 229.

15.   Lee Lockwood, *Castro's Cuba, Cuba's Fidel* (New York: Vintage Books, 1967), 114.

16.   In Marxist terminology, an "idealist" is someone who promotes ideas not supported by material conditions. A "voluntarist" put his or her own voluntary wishes ahead of what the masses are ready to accept. In the context of Cuba in 2008, these are sharp criticisms of Fidel Castro.

17.   Mark Q. Sawyer, *Racial Politics in Post-Revolutionary Cuba* (New York: Cambridge University Press, 2006), 61.

18.   Ibid., 71.

19.   Ibid., 74.

20.   Ibid., 71.

21.   Ibid.

22. *Miami Herald*, "A barrier for Cuba's blacks" (see n. 4).

23. Conservative Cuban Americans and some media report numerous cases of police mistreatment of political dissidents both at the time of arrest and in prison. But physical brutality against common criminals or people stopped on the street is rare.

24. Castro and Ramonet, *Fidel Castro*, 230 (see n. 14).

25. Ibid., 230.

26. Sawyer, *Racial Politics*, 70 (see n. 17). In 1981, the life expectancy for white Cubans was 71.2 versus 70.2 for blacks. In the United States that year, it was 74.4 for whites and 68.1 for blacks. In 1982, over 98 percent of the Cuban population was literate, with only .2 percent difference between whites and non-whites.

27. Urbano Canizares, interview with author, January 27, 2008, Buffalo, New York.

Chapter 12

1. Associated Press, "Cuba: Bush chat with dissidents a 'show,'" May 12, 2008.

2. Martha Beatriz Roque, interview with author, March 29, 2008, Havana.

3. I was amazed that Roque could describe pre-1959 Cuba as democratic. In reality, Cuba has gone through a series of elections and coups, with the United States as the ultimate power broker, culminating in the Batista dictatorship (see chapter 2).

4. During numerous trips to Cuba, I encountered reporters from the *New York Times* and other major media. They had all met with officials from the U.S. Interests Section and been encouraged to interview dissidents.

5. Alfonso Chardy, "Aid to Cubans tracked to office of Posada pal," *Miami Herald,* May 21, 2008.

6. Ray Sanchez, "More details released on US Interests chief, Miami support to dissidents," *South Florida Sun-Sentinel*, May 20, 2008.

7. Prensa Latina, "New US subversion proof in Cuba," May 21, 2008.

8. EFE (Spain), "Prominent Cuban dissidents reject cash from U.S. government," June 16, 2008.

9. Thomas A. Shannon, Assistant Secretary for Western Hemisphere Affairs, State Department press briefing, May 20, 2008.

10. On April 11, 2002, right-wing military officers and businessmen overthrew the elected government of President Hugh Chávez in Venezuela. Within

47 hours, however, Chávez returned to power. The United States participated in planning the coup. See Ed Vulliamy, "Venezuela coup linked to Bush team," *The Observer* (London), April 21, 2002. Bush administration officials publicly backed the coup, withdrawing support only after it failed.

11. Eloy Gutiérrez Menoyo, interview with author, March, 28, 2008, Havana.

12. Madeline Baró Díaz, "Cuban exile risks U.S. prosecution," *South Florida Sun-Sentinel*, February 8, 2005.

13. Jay Taylor, interview with author, January 29, 2008, Arlington, Virginia.

14. ThinkForum, "The Gallup Organization's Cuba," Executive Summary, 2006, www.media.gallup.com/WorldPoll/PDF/TFCuba022207.pdf. Any poll in Cuba is problematic because people may or may not answer honestly given the lack of democracy. But numerous polls done over many years tend to show the same results, giving them greater credibility. This Gallup poll was conducted in September 2006.

15. The International Republican Institute, which is affiliated with the Republican Party, conducted a poll of 587 Cubans in March 2008. It showed about 50 percent of Cubans concerned with economic issues while less than 10 percent mentioned lack of political freedom. See Marc Lacey, "Rare poll finds that money woes are Cubans' top worry," *New York Times*, June 5, 2008.

16. Wayne Smith, interview with author, January 28, 2008, Washington DC.

17. Reese Erlich, "Where have all the dissidents gone?," *The Russia Project* radio documentary hosted by Walter Cronkite, http://russiaproject.org/part2/dissidents/essay.html.

18. DeWayne Wickham, "Varela Project offers false hope of change in Cuba," op-ed column, *USA Today*, May 24, 2002.

19. Nancy San Martin, "Wary exiles a challenge for dissident's Cuba project," *Miami Herald*, January 10, 2003.

20. Ibid.

21. Critics said that some people had been coerced into signing the pro-government petition and that the 99 percent "yes" vote didn't represent true popular opinion.

22. David Adams, "Crackdown on dissent a Cuban question mark," *St. Petersburg Times*, April 20, 2003.

23. "Cuba: One year after the crackdown," statement by Human Rights Watch and other groups, March 18, 2004.

24. Rosa Tania Valdes, "Cuba to free 7 dissidents at Spain's request," Reuters, February 15, 2008.

25. Jeane Kirkpatrick, "Dictatorships and double standards," *Commentary Magazine*, November 1979. Kirkpatrick (1926–2006) became a hero to anticommunist conservatives. Ironically, she called herself a Marxist, coming from the rightist sector of social democracy. She claimed to support socialism while denouncing communism. She was the ideological ancestor of contemporary neoconservatism.

26. Sánchez surveys the families of political dissidents, and Castro critics consider his compilation of political prisoners as the most accurate in Cuba. See Reuters, "Cuba rights abuses continue but fewer prisoners: Group," January 16, 2008.

27. Smith, interview (see n. 16).

28. CNN.com, "Videos hint at public discontent in Cuba," Feb. 7, 2008, www.cnn.com/2008/WORLD/americas/02/07/cuba.videos/.

29. Uncommon Sense, "Student inquisitor is arrested," February 8, 2008, http://marcmasferrer.typepad.com/uncommon_sense/2008/02/student-inquisi .html.

30. Rory Carroll, "Cuba censors cyber critic with block on island's popular blog," *Guardian* (London), March 26, 2008.

31. W. David Gardner, "Cuba to get high-speed Internet in 2010," *InformationWeek*, July 17, 2008.

32. Juan Fernández, interview with author, March 28, 2008, Havana.

33. Professor Marta Núñez, interview with author, March 21, 2008, Havana.

34. Margaret Randall, *To Change the World: My Years in Cuba* (Newark: Rutgers University Press, 2008), 111.

35. Ibid., 112.

36. Ibid.

Chapter 13

1. Yuri Andropov (1914–84) was general secretary of the Communist Party of the Soviet Union from 1982–84. He was severely ill for the last six months of

his life and unable to carry out normal activities. Soviet leaders never revealed his illness until after his death, nor did Andropov formally turn over his powers to anyone else.

2. Marc Lacey, "Castro 'serious': Report details many surgeries," *New York Times,* January 16, 2007.

3. Socialist countries have proven particularly inept at managing transitions from the founding father of the revolution to the next generation. When Stalin died of a stroke, his ministers engaged in purges and a major power struggle to succeed him. When Mao died, the new leaders purged his wife and top supporters, who came to be known as the Gang of Four. And, of course, North Korea's Kim Il Sung dealt with the issue by appointing his son, Kim Jong-Il, as leader for life.

4. Commission for Assistance to a Free Cuba, *Report to the President: Commission for Assistance to a Free Cuba, 2004,* www.state.gov/p/wha/rt/cuba/commission/2004/c12237.htm.

5. Senator Rolando Masferrer formed a private militia called "Los Tigres," which acted as armed thugs for Batista. Later Masferrer went on to form the terrorist group Alpha 66 in Miami.

6. In the early 1970s, CANF head Jorge Mas Canosa, with two notorious Miami drug dealers, set up a company that was suspected of being a money laundering operation. (See Ann Louise Bardach, *Cuba Confidential, Love and Vengeance in Miami and Havana* [New York: Vintage Books, 2003], 138.) In the 1980s, Cuban American CIA agent Felix Rodriguez and Luis Posada Carriles were involved in trading drugs for guns during the Iran-Contra scandal, according to former DEA agent Celerino Castillo III. (See Celerino Castillo III, DEA retired, written statement, Congressional testimony, House Permanent Select Committee on Intelligence, April 27, 1998. www.powderburns.org/ testimony .html. See also fromthewilderness.com/free/ww3/060705_cele_posada.shtml.) In the 1980s, Omega 7, a heavily armed anti-Cuba terrorist group, hired itself out to Miami drug lords, according to court records. (See Jim McGee, "Lawmen see firebrand turning to crime," *Miami Herald,* December 30, 1983.)

7. T. J. English, *Havana Nocturne: How the Mob Owned Cuba and Then Lost It to the Revolution* (New York: William Morrow, 2007), 209.

8. High-level officials in the pro-U.S. government of Hamid Karzai finance their political parties and militias with proceeds from the heroin trade. Reese Erlich, "Opium continues to sprout from number of Afghan fields," *Dallas*

Morning News, February 22, 2004; Reese Erlich, "Heroin smuggling on the rise in Afghanistan," Featurewell News Service, in *Berkeley Daily Planet*, March 9–11, 2004. See also the article by former U.S. counter-narcotics official Thomas Schweich, "Is Afghanistan a Narco-State?" *New York Times Magazine*, July 27, 2008.

9. Francisco "Pepe" Hernández, interview with author, February 25, 2008, Miami.

10. Life expectancy in the Russian Federation sank to 65 years, ranking Russia number 119 of 193 countries in the world. UN Development Reports, Russian Federation, 2007–8, http://hdrstats.undp.org/countries/country_fact_sheets/cty_fs_RUS.html.

11. Marc Frank, "Cuba's Raúl Castro charts own economic course," Reuters, printed in *Guardian* (London), June 17, 2008.

12. Associate Press, "Cuban Central Bank report advocates stronger peso, fewer subsidies," *International Herald Tribune*, May 10, 2008.

13. Larry Rohter, "Hillary Rodham Clinton—The Caucus—Politics," The Caucus Blog, *New York Times*, May 25, 2008, http://thecaucus.blogs.nytimes.com/2008/05/25/clinton-weighs-in-on-cuba.

14. *Miami Herald*, "Text of Obama's speech before CANF," May 23, 2008.

15. Jorge Ramos, "Entrevista con el candidato demócrata a la Presidencia de Estados Unidos," *El Mercurio* (Santiago, Chile), June 11, 2008. Obama was behind the curve on this issue. President Chávez had already called on FARC to lay down its arms and join the political process in Colombia.

16. Frank James, "Has Obama gotten to Texas conservative on Cuba?" The Swamp Blog, *Chicago Tribune*, February. 25, 2008, http://weblogs.baltimoresun.com/news/politics/blog/2008/02/has_obama_gotten_to_texas_cons.html.

17. Christopher Marquis, "Senate approves easing of curbs on Cuba travel," *New York Times*, October 24, 2003.

18. Phillip Peters, interview with author, January 31, 2008, Washington DC.

19. Wayne S. Smith, "House Democrats follow Republican lead on Cuba," Center for International Policy's Cuba Program, August 31, 2007.

20. Mary Clare Jalonick, "Rehberg switches position on Cuba embargo," Associated Press, July 23, 2008.

21. Dan Christensen, "Diaz-Balart back bill after donation," *Miami Herald*, June 2, 2008.

22. Prof. Andy Gomez, interview with author, February 27, 2008, Miami.

23. DeWayne Wickham, "Cuba's leaders have agenda ready for talks with next U.S. president," Gannett News Service, June 23, 2008.

24. Col. Lawrence Wilkerson, interview with author, January 29, 2008, Washington DC.

25. Ashton B. Carter and William J. Perry, "If necessary, strike and destroy: North Korea cannot be allowed to test this missile," Op-Ed column, *Washington Post*, June 22, 2006. Perry was secretary of defense under Bill Clinton, and Carter was assistant secretary of defense.

26. CIA veteran Art Brown wrote that under the U.S.-Korean agreement President "Kim Jong-il knows he still gets to keep his stockpile of plutonium and even hang on to his existing rack of nuclear weapons." See *New York Times*, "North Korea's stacked deck," July 15, 2008.

27. Condoleezza Rice, "Diplomacy is working on North Korea," commentary, *Wall Street Journal*, June 26, 2008.

28. Robert Muse, interview with author, January 28, 2008, Washington DC.

Acknowledgments

In researching this book, I traveled to Miami, Washington DC, Buffalo, and Cuba. I want to thank all the people I met who took the time to share their thoughts and analyses. Former government officials, leaders of the Cuban exile community in Miami, and officials in Havana all provided me with important information and background. I have kept all my notebooks and interviews dating back to 1968. I based much of this book on that real-time reporting.

I want to thank members of my family for their support during the writing of this book. My sister Jan Erlich-Moss, a professional photographer and university lecturer in Washington DC, shot the author's photo.

I especially want to thank Polipoint Press editor Peter Richardson, whose careful reading of the manuscript was invaluable. He read with a critical eye, and although not an expert on Cuba, helped immensely to improve the content and structure of the book.

A number of people read over the manuscript and offered helpful comments: Stephen Kinzer, Saul Landau, Margaret Randall, Portia Siegelbaum, Sierra Thai-Binh, and Karen Wald. Thanks to you all.

Index

About the Author

Best-selling author Reese Erlich has previously written *Target Iraq: What the News Media Didn't Tell You* (coauthored with Norman Solomon) and *The Iran Agenda: The Real Story of U.S. Policy and the Middle East Crisis*. Erlich is a freelance foreign correspondent who has won numerous journalism awards from a variety of organizations, including Project Censored and the Society of Professional Journalists. He won a Peabody Award (shared with others) in 2006.

Other Books from PoliPointPress

The Blue Pages: A Directory of Companies Rated by Their Politics and Practices
Helps consumers match their buying decisions with their political values by listing the political contributions and business practices of over 1,000 companies. $9.95, paperback.

Rose Aguilar, *Red Highways: A Liberal's Journey into the Heartland*
Challenges red state stereotypes to reveal new strategies for progressives. $15.95, paperback.

Jeff Cohen, *Cable News Confidential: My Misadventures in Corporate Media*
Offers a fast-paced romp through the three major cable news channels—Fox, CNN, and MSNBC—and delivers a serious message about their failure to cover the most urgent issues of the day. $14.95, paperback.

Marjorie Cohn, *Cowboy Republic: Six Ways the Bush Gang Has Defied the Law*
Shows how the executive branch under President Bush has systematically defied the law instead of enforcing it. $14.95, paperback.

Joe Conason, *The Raw Deal: How the Bush Republicans Plan to Destroy Social Security and the Legacy of the New Deal*
Reveals the well-financed and determined effort to undo the Social Security Act and other New Deal programs. $11.00, paperback.

Kevin Danaher, Shannon Biggs, and Jason Mark, *Building the Green Economy: Success Stories from the Grassroots*
Shows how community groups, families, and individual citizens have protected their food and water, cleaned up their neighborhoods, and strengthened their local economies. $16.00, paperback.

Kevin Danaher and Alisa Gravitz, *The Green Festival Reader: Fresh Ideas from Agents of Change*
Collects the best ideas and commentary from some of the most forward green thinkers of our time. $15.95, paperback.

Reese Erlich, *The Iran Agenda: The Real Story of U.S. Policy and the Middle East Crisis*
Explores the turbulent recent history between the two countries and how it has led to a showdown over nuclear technology. $14.95, paperback.

Steven Hill, *10 Steps to Repair American Democracy*
Identifies the key problems with American democracy, especially election practices, and proposes ten specific reforms to reinvigorate it. $11.00, paperback.

Markos Kounalakis and Peter Laufer, *Hope Is a Tattered Flag: Voices of Reason and Change for the Post-Bush Era*
Gathers together the most listened-to politicos and pundits, activists and thinkers, to answer the question: what happens after Bush leaves office? $29.95, hardcover; $16.95 paperback.

Yvonne Latty, *In Conflict: Iraq War Veterans Speak Out on Duty, Loss, and the Fight to Stay Alive*
Features the unheard voices, extraordinary experiences, and personal photographs of a broad mix of Iraq War veterans, including Congressman Patrick Murphy, Tammy Duckworth, Kelly Daugherty, and Camilo Mejia. $24.00, hardcover.

Phillip Longman, *Best Care Anywhere: Why VA Health Care Is Better Than Yours*
Shows how the turnaround at the long-maligned VA hospitals provides a blueprint for salvaging America's expensive but troubled health care system. $14.95, paperback.

Marcia and Thomas Mitchell, *The Spy Who Tried to Stop a War: Katharine Gun and the Secret Plot to Sanction the Iraq Invasion*
Describes a covert operation to secure UN authorization for the Iraq war and the furor that erupted when a young British spy leaked it. $23.95, hardcover.

Susan Mulcahy, ed., *Why I'm a Democrat*
Explores the values and passions that make a diverse group of Americans proud to be Democrats. $14.95, paperback.

Christine Pelosi, *Campaign Boot Camp: Basic Training for Future Leaders*
Offers a seven-step guide for successful campaigns and causes at all levels of government. $15.95, paperback.

William Rivers Pitt, *House of Ill Repute: Reflections on War, Lies, and America's Ravaged Reputation*
Skewers the Bush Administration for its reckless invasions, warrantless wiretaps, lethally incompetent response to Hurricane Katrina, and other scandals and blunders. $16.00, paperback.

Sarah Posner, *God's Profits: Faith, Fraud, and the Republican Crusade for Values Voters*
Examines corrupt televangelists' ties to the Republican Party and unprecedented access to the Bush White House. $19.95, hardcover.

Nomi Prins, *Jacked: How "Conservatives" Are Picking Your Pocket—Whether You Voted for Them or Not*
Describes how the "conservative" agenda has affected your wallet, skewed national priorities, and diminished America—but not the American spirit. $12.00, paperback.

Cliff Schecter, *The Real McCain: Why Conservatives Don't Trust Him—And Why Independents Shouldn't*
Explores the gap between the public persona of John McCain and the reality of this would-be president. $14.95, hardcover.

Norman Solomon, *Made Love, Got War: Close Encounters with America's Warfare State*
Traces five decades of American militarism and the media's all-too-frequent failure to challenge it. $24.95, hardcover.

John Sperling et al., *The Great Divide: Retro vs. Metro America*
Explains how and why our nation is so bitterly divided into what the authors call Retro and Metro America. $19.95, paperback.

Daniel Weintraub, *Party of One: Arnold Schwarzenegger and the Rise of the Independent Voter*
Explains how Schwarzenegger found favor with independent voters, whose support has been critical to his success, and suggests that his bipartisan approach represents the future of American politics. $19.95, hardcover.

Curtis White, *The Spirit of Disobedience: Resisting the Charms of Fake Politics, Mindless Consumption, and the Culture of Total Work*
Debunks the notion that liberalism has no need for spirituality and describes a "middle way" through our red state/blue state political impasse. Includes three powerful interviews with John DeGraaf, James Howard Kunstler, and Michael Ableman. $24.00, hardcover.

For more information, please visit www.p3books.com.

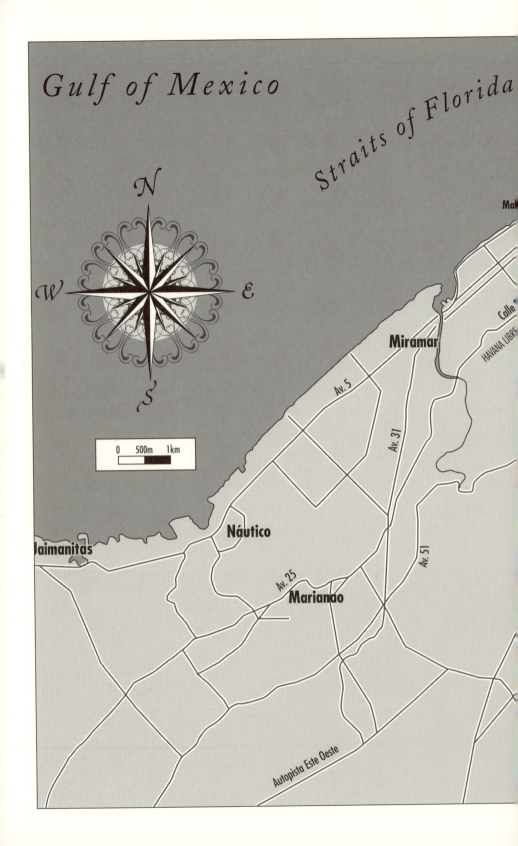

Gulf of Mexico

Straits of Florida

N

W ε

S

0   500m   1km

Miramar

Av. 5

Av. 31

Náutico

Jaimanitas

Av. 25

Marianao

Av. 51

Calle

HAVANA LIBRE

Ma

Autopista Este Oeste